MW01037612

# CRITICAL THINKING

*Critical Thinking* presents, defines and explains the intellectual skills and habits of mind that comprise critical thinking and its relationship to social justice. Each of the sequential chapters includes detailed examples and learning exercises that guide the reader step by step from intellectual competency, to critical thinking, to cultural cognition, and to the critical awareness necessary for social justice.

The book documents and explains the scope of multiple crises facing society today, including environmental destruction, income and wealth inequality, large-scale human migration, and the rise of autocratic governments. It shows how critical thinking, cultural cognition, and critical awareness lead to the possibility of solutions grounded in social justice.

All college students, especially those in the social sciences and humanities, will develop the intellectual skills necessary for critically engaging information in order to become active learners and effective agents in the world. This book complements information in introductory, interdisciplinary, or discipline-specific courses. Every chapter contains examples and exercises that can be assigned as homework, adopted as in-class activities, or both. The Conclusion also contains exercises for developing writing and basic mathematical competency skills.

**Joseph Zornado** is professor of English at Rhode Island College. He has published fiction, scholarly articles on literature and film, the books *Inventing the Child* (2007) and *Disney and the Dialectic of Desire* (2017) along with co-authored textbooks for social work and justice studies.

**Jill Harrison** is professor of Sociology at Rhode Island College, teaching justice studies courses at undergraduate and graduate levels. Scholarly publications include research on incarcerated men with a history of trauma and recidivism, and co-authoring *Professional Writing for the Criminal Justice System* (2017).

**Daniel Weisman** is professor emeritus of Social Work at Rhode Island College and has published on civil liberties, public policy, and pedagogy, notably *Professional Writing for Social Work Practice* (2018) and *Professional Writing for the Criminal Justice System* (2017). His practice includes policy advocacy and program evaluation.

# CRITICAL THINKING

## Developing the Intellectual Tools for Social Justice

*Joseph Zornado, Jill Harrison, and Daniel Weisman*

Routledge
Taylor & Francis Group

LONDON AND NEW YORK

First published 2020
by Routledge
2 Park Square, Milton Park, Abingdon, Oxon OX14 4RN

and by Routledge
52 Vanderbilt Avenue, New York, NY 10017

*Routledge is an imprint of the Taylor & Francis Group, an informa business*

© 2020 Joseph Zornado, Jill Harrison, and Dan Weisman

The right of Joseph Zornado, Jill Harrison, and Dan Weisman to be identified as authors of this work has been asserted by them in accordance with sections 77 and 78 of the Copyright, Designs and Patents Act 1988.

*British Library Cataloguing-in-Publication Data*
A catalogue record for this book is available from the British Library

*Library of Congress Cataloging-in-Publication Data*
Names: Zornado, Joseph L., author. | Harrison, Jill, 1963- author. | Weisman, Daniel, author.
Title: Critical thinking : developing the intellectual tools for social justice / Joseph Zornado, Jill Harrison and Daniel Weisman.
Description: First Edition. | New York : Routledge, 2019. | Includes bibliographical references and index.
Identifiers: LCCN 2019033753 (print) | LCCN 2019033754 (ebook)
Subjects: LCSH: Social justice. | Restorative justice. | Critical thinking.
Classification: LCC HM671 .Z67 2019 (print) | LCC HM671 (ebook) | DDC 303.3/72--dc23
LC record available at https://lccn.loc.gov/2019033753
LC ebook record available at https://lccn.loc.gov/2019033754

ISBN: 978-1-138-34284-2 (hbk)
ISBN: 978-0-429-43954-4 (pbk)
ISBN: 978-1-138-34289-7 (ebk)

Typeset in Bembo
by Taylor & Francis Books

To the United Nations Universal Declaration of Human Rights, adopted by the General Assembly of the United Nations on December 10th, 1948 as a result of the disasters brought upon the world by war.

# CONTENTS

# INTRODUCTION

## Why this book?

Welcome to an empowering journey that, we hope, will change the way you think about the world around you and your place in it. We wrote this book as a way to address the very social crises that have their roots in fear-based thinking often informed by nostalgia and superstition. Higher education is more than a way to pass on job training skills; we believe in lifelong learning. While higher education has always been about more than job training (though this is important), a college education means that we have learned to take responsibility for our own learning. We have become professional thinkers, as it were, curious, always learning, questioning, and seeking out evidence whenever possible to support important conclusions. What this means and how to go about doing it is the reason for this book. The higher mind, the critical mind, the enlightened mind, that mind that knows itself, the third-eye of wisdom, and many other traditions have named our innate capacity for *critical awareness*. This book breaks down critical awareness as an assemblage of practical thinking skills from which emerges the possibility for social justice as a restorative social practice.

Developing the critical thinking tools for social justice is a journey rather than a destination. Why? Because the one constant in life is change, and today change comes at a pace difficult to imagine even a generation ago. We are drowning in information, and our attempts to keep up with it have us locked into devices that shape how we think by offering to do our thinking for us.

More recently, the internet as a purveyor of information has come into question. It is all hackable, all trollable—capable of disruptive, provocative posts. The dilemma is difficult and many-layered. One person's truth is another person's "fake news." The information under consideration seems to hardly matter, but if it did, we might discover the information to be worthless and unreliable. Such is the danger of taking critical thinking seriously. Many truths crumble while new truths, provisional and subject to change, emerge.

We wrote this book because of the substantial personal and societal consequences at stake. The Information Age is quickly becoming an age of misinformation. Unfortunately, as we grow up how we learn to think usually falls short of what we define in this book as "critical thinking." And where critical thinking is lacking, social justice finds little traction. It is indeed a crisis of critical thinking that imperils us all. We believe that critical thinking, while an innate capacity of the human mind, must be learned and practiced.

We should note that critical thinking has no political agenda. One can use evidence-based reason and the scientific method to build bombs designed to wipe out populations. Social justice, on the other hand, simultaneously arises as an idea often with a political agenda. For social justice to occur, politics and policies usually must change. According to the United Nations "social justice is an underlying principle for peaceful and prosperous coexistence … and the promotion of human dignity."[1] Critical thinking serves as a way to promote social justice, particularly as we seek to understand the need for social change. Critical thinking is a tool while social justice is a goal. We present the habits of mind upon which "critical thinking" depend while at the same time build a case for social justice.

The evidence indicates that we are in the midst of historic social, political, economic, and environmental crises. What should we do about it? Is there anything to be done? Where should we begin? Our understanding of a topic, question, problem, or situation is only as good as the information we take in about it. So on the one hand, we have the problem of "information literacy" and the challenge of knowing whether we can trust what we read, hear, and think we know. And on the other hand, we must consider the question of *how* we think about the information we take in and accept.

Consider the situation that so many of us find ourselves in: we think ineffectively about misinformation and do not realize it. Psychologists call this the Dunning-Kruger effect, which we will discuss in more detail a little later. In short, we think we are intellectually competent because we have no idea how to assess whether we are—or not. The current crisis of critical thinking includes the Dunning-Kruger effect made worse by the ways in which digital technology provides a kind of legitimacy to shallow, partisan, often knee-jerk reactions to provocative questions: we find like-minded others and hold our positions in spite of the evidence. In cases like these the thinker can often confuse fear with passion. Or worse, we depend upon fatalism, or apathy, or we retreat to our safe silos, reassured by people who think like we do that "we" are right and "they" are wrong. From here, the opposite of social justice emerges: hate, hate-crimes, and an "us versus them" mentality based on race, class, gender identity, sexual orientation, and so on.

## The premise of this book

While we reject the idea of "conspiracy theory" as a way to understand what drives any given social crisis, that is, the idea that a conspiracy of secret, sinister figures lies behind any given social issue, we recognize economic inequality as a primary social crisis with clear "winners" and "losers." The winners in this case are large, international corporations and sometimes government officials—not individuals—and the community of businessmen and women who run these multinational corporations are the super-rich who represent a tiny fraction of the world's population, yet who lay claim to the earth's resources, support particular political candidates who will reaffirm their profit-seeking agenda, and either directly or indirectly impact our daily lives.[2] Meanwhile, this elite group can use an array of tools to protect and extend their wealth and financial interests: from offshore tax havens with anonymous owners to a bevy of lawyers and lobbyists who push a legislative agenda that keeps their industrial machine well-oiled.[3] These tools today include sophisticated campaigns across vast information networks that do not omit disinformation, and even conspiracy theories.[4]

The great project of modernity has left the world battered and bruised. Perhaps our fantasies have failed us. Or, one could argue, our fantasies have been fulfilled in the worst possible ways. As American ecologist Garrett Hardin wrote in his famous essay, *The Tragedy of the Commons*, "the damage that innocent actions by individuals can inflict on the environment" is profound.[5] He argued against Adam Smith's premise in *The Wealth of Nations* that in pursuit of individual gain the "invisible hand" of capitalism will guide us to success: instead, he argued, selfishness and greed will rule society and increase economic hardship for the many who do not have the means to so easily advance.[6] In today's terms, we have modified this laissez-faire approach to neoliberal capitalism: a platform that hands over the power of politics, economics, and the fate of the human condition, indeed, democracy itself, from the public sector, away from the Commons, to private markets and businesses.

Outflow from our civilization—from relentless capital pursuit—has put every major life system on the planet at risk; regardless of whether one accepts human causes for climate change, conflicts over allocation of scarce resources, food, water, and land are worldwide phenomena.[7] Garbage and the poisoning of air, water, and soil are criminal enough, and the evidence for these crimes is everywhere and in full view—yet the machine grinds on more furiously than ever.[8] Perhaps the most dangerous impact of unbridled corporate capitalism and the promotion and fantasy of consumerism is not the economic crises they have caused but the political crisis. As the domain of the state is reduced to protect the Commons, our ability to change the course of our lives through voting also contracts. For example, today we have global companies more powerful than nation states—they transcend borders, time and space.[9] Neoliberal theory asserts that people can exercise choice through spending, but certainly some have more to spend than others, including investing in powerful lobbying groups. In the great consumer or shareholder democracy, this means our democracy, the votes we cast are not equally distributed. The result is disempowerment of the poor and middle classes. As parties of the right and former left adopt similar neoliberal policies, disempowerment turns to disenfranchisement: many politicians and CEOs of transnational corporations support free-market capitalism while neglecting the social and economic crises of the Commons that simultaneously degrades the ecosystems and our communal health and well-being.[10]

Scientists around the world agree that our self-induced environmental crisis sourced by big business and their friendly politicians is actually a collection of multiple ongoing crises that include environmental destruction and is exacerbated by on-going social and economic inequalities. It is no longer a question of "if," but rather, "how bad will things get?" To what degree will we suffer the consequences of our actions? The onslaught of "fake news," the denial of science, and the rise of extremism go hand-in-hand and serve as avatars of ignorance, prejudice, and fear.

## Crises of the Commons and global political economy

Throughout this book we will refer to the activities of national and international organizations, political and economic, in relation to the crises of the Commons. We contend that these powers are not conspiratorial, although sometimes may work together when their immediate interests coalesce. Rather, the "political economy" refers to governmental and economic systems, individually pursuing their interests that interact to determine the parameters (purposes and limits) of public policy. Our interest is developing critical thinking skills to help one another identify political economies that are the most humane, or conducive of maximum social justice.

Prateek Agarwal, an economist and blogger, identifies four prototypes of economic systems: traditional (rural, agrarian, possibly feudal), command (dictated and controlled by the government), free market (ideally no government involvement in the economy; in practice, as little government as possible), and mixed (combination of the other three, but most commonly meaning government involvement in managing or tempering free market behaviors and consequences, typically by way of regulations, taxes and social welfare programs).[11]

Agarwal explains that traditional economies are widespread in poorer and relatively non-industrialized regions. In these cases, the economy tends to be localized and relatively unregulated. Command economies are typically found in countries ruled by dictators or juntas (e.g., communist, fascist). These systems are dominated by the government, which tightly controls economic activities, and may even own many of the economic resources. For example, in China, the government literally owns all the land. In pure free market systems, the government and economic systems are separate, with minimal political interference in the activities of industry, business (i.e., trade) or other commercial activities.

Yet we know of no pure free market countries, and just a few command economies (e.g., China, the world's second largest economy, somewhat fits this category); most countries have mixed economies, some combination of free market and command. Within these countries, the national debates focus on how much "command" the government should have and how much "free market" businesses should have. In many countries government, industry and consumer/citizens groups have established variations of regulated capitalism. Such a neoliberal policy combines politicians with large corporate executives and their lobbyists, along with the national interests of the people (although not always). As long as these local, national, and international discussions can guide decision-making and protect the

Commons, there is potential for promoting social justice. But even in mixed political economies, the Commons is falling under threat; the choices facing all political economies have become increasingly more restricted by the concentration of global wealth into very few corporate hands. As we report later in this chapter, one percent of the world's individuals controls over 50% of all global wealth, and their wealth is projected to increase by two-thirds before 2030.[12]

Individual wealth is just part of the picture. More important for the vulnerability of the Commons is the concentration of corporate wealth because we have entered "the age of meta-nationals," or stateless companies that choose locations for personnel, factories, executive suites, and their bank accounts based on where regulations are friendly, resources abundant, and connectivity seamless. Clever meta-nationals often have legal domicile in one country, corporate management in another, financial assets in a third, and administrative staff spread over several more. Some of the largest American-born firms—GE, IBM, Microsoft, to name a few—collectively keep trillions of dollars tax-free in offshore banks and holding companies incorporated in Switzerland, Luxembourg, the Cayman Islands, or Singapore.[13] These companies that transcend borders in order to maximize their profits and global power often avoid paying taxes because there is no world government or supra-national tax authority to demand it. Who is winning? Who is taking over the Commons?

Meta-nationals and their poorer relations, mere multinationals, can exploit weak business laws and take advantage of minimizing their taxes, among other corporate benefits. Among developing nations with fewer government standards in place, and/or few officials to check exploitation of resources, workplace safety, including few or no child labor laws, and no required minimum wage, allows private control to generate their end products and, ultimately, profits for their owners and shareholders. Because they can play localities and countries off each other, for meta-nationals have no home state, they can freely maximize their profits without accountability, or even input, from political entities that are responsible for maintaining the Commons.

History demonstrates clearly that multinational corporations are generally indifferent to the Commons, if not actively hostile; their priority is profit, not social justice, environmental sustainability or human dignity. Some corporations even appear to be generous and make public contributions to parks, hospitals, libraries, and other cultural and social institutions, but even so, predatory capitalism remains committed to profit before *all* other considerations. And a few countries, notably in Western Europe, North America, and elsewhere have managed to protect the Commons while servicing a form of capitalism that accepts a certain partnership with representatives of the Commons, because those governments have resisted economic and political pressure to adopt more extreme, unregulated financial market policies.

Countries that resist predatory capitalism are not socialist countries, contrary to what some might say. Sweden's economic systems remains centered on private ownership of the means of production. This also includes, occasionally, publicly owned entities. The Veterans Administration in the United States, or the national healthcare systems in Europe, Canada, Australia and New Zealand are all examples of a partnership between private business and the public trust. In such a system, the wealth-producing industry remains (mostly) privately owned and managed. Socialism requires the abolition of private property. While the notion of private property persists, capitalism remains firmly rooted.

Typically, countries that protect the Commons through political will, regulations, and law usually include a degree of environmental and workplace protections which include pollution, safety and anti-discrimination regulations, workers' rights that include maternity leave, as well as minimum wage law. What might a socially just economic system look like: redistributive progressive taxes, public health care, housing and transportation systems along with free guaranteed public education, retirement security, and sometimes more. It seems impossible to afford such a society, until we realize the inordinate, unsustainable economic inequality in western neoliberal capitalist countries and where, in the end, our wealth ends up. While citizens, employees and consumers in more socially just economies share in the cost structures, each of these social benefits comes at a cost to the profits corporations are allowed to enjoy.

The more managed mixed political economies also tend to enjoy a wide array of social rights, such as the freedoms of speech and the freedom of the press; the freedom to dissent and to assemble in order to challenge the government; religious freedom along with a secular political system. Simultaneously, these freedoms and the degree of balance between corporate interests and the fate of the Commons are today in jeopardy as they rarely have been before.

As we proceed to develop our analyses of major crises facing our planet in the pursuit of critical thinking and social justice, we must include in our analysis the political and economic context from which our current crises have emerged. To ignore this context in search of stop-gap solutions is at best disingenuous, and at worst, suicidal. This does not mean that we oppose private wealth, or advocate for any particular form of government or economy; rather, we oppose the unaccountable privatization of wealth into fewer and fewer hands at the expense of the masses, the environment, and future generations.

With or without the climate change, environmental studies have demonstrated that consumer culture has driven the environment to its knees. The Commons has been fenced long ago, and so lost to those who once shared a sense of ownership and care for it. Instead, we teach our children that to grow up means to seek "fun" and "pleasure" via "economic spending power." Our belief in the pursuit of things (packaged in plastic) is actually unhealthy for us—as well as the planet.[14]

Even our bodies have become privatized territories for corporate conquest and biogenetic expansion. Meanwhile, we subject ourselves to toxic environments in the misguided hope that our corporate masters have our human health and well-being as part of their portfolios. The evidence, however, argues otherwise.

Effective critical thinking means to reason well from reliable information. Every argument begins with a premise informed by basic facts we take to be true, from which we then make connections, draw out conclusions, and so on. For our argument in this book we begin with the following premises: we live in an economic system that embodies and rewards social injustice; capitalism is the driving social force behind climate change, environmental pollution, and the general destruction of the human-supporting global habitat. While human greed plays a part, we do not accept the notion that human nature is incapable of saving itself; at the same time, we believe that the current economic system will not be able to correct the many ills and harms it has inflicted on the air, sea, and land in the name of wealth acquisition.

And so this book is a call to the higher mind that aspires to realize itself in these challenging times. To wake up means that we must understand and be able to articulate the problems and challenges that face us, so that we might then be able to work effectively for socially just solutions.

In Chapter 2 we take up the question of *intellectual competence* as the foundational set of skills necessary for critical thinking. Intellectual competence depends upon the ability to identify and access *reliable* information in a world suddenly hostile to experts, facts, and science itself. We are awash in hacked data, and even our online footprint is part of that, but, fortunately, it is possible to reclaim and develop our intellectual acumen. Like anything else, it requires focus and attention. The reward is to establish a growing confidence with words and numbers and how they represent meaning: to take responsibility for the information that passes through our lives means to question it when possible, especially when it concerns an important issue, question, topic, or problem. A competent mind is an open mind, receptive and skeptical.

In Chapter 3 we explore *critical thinking* as a reasoning process that requires intellectual competence combined with the mind's higher function, *meta-cognition*. Meta-cognition refers to our ability to think about our thinking, that is, the ability in the mind to take a step back from the thoughts that fill it, and consider the questions, "How did things get to be this way?" "Why do I think that?" "What do I believe and why?" among other reflective questions. Our ability to assess our own reasoning according to accepted standards of rhetoric and evidence is a powerful way to break out of the Dunning-Kruger effect.

The current crisis of critical thinking has reached a scale hard to imagine even a generation ago. We have reached a point of "cognitive overload." We simply lack the skills, the time, or the space to think things through properly. We tend to gather information that already supports what we believe, or in other words, we "cherry pick" our information and evidence. Cherry picking is to learn only about specific bits of information that usually confirm our pre-conceived views and ignores inconvenient or nuanced material. Cherry picking confirms what we already believe, our opinion about a certain issue, question, or problem. Unless we know to check for ourselves, we may never realize that when we trust the analysis of others we may be engaged in a long series of "cherry picking" actually begun long before. This happened long before the internet and social networking, but social networking is the latest, most extreme example of how misinformation spreads as users share other users' information.

In Chapter 4 we focus on *cultural cognition* as the crucial link between *critical thinking* and *social justice*. Cultural cognition refers to the use of critical thinking to break down marginalized and disenfranchised classes and cultures and seek to understand another's perspective, culture, values, and beliefs. Entrenched social constructs serve to normalize systemic social injustice, and social injustice depends upon a view of the world largely divorced from inclusion or material evidence. Rather, social injustice rationalizes divisive, often violent beliefs and behaviors based on fear, superstition, anxiety, and nostalgia. While such habits of mind are on the rise, they are precisely at odds with social justice, and, as it turns out, the dignity and sustainability of human life. Cultural cognition provides us with the tools to reflect with humility and compassion.

In Chapter 5 we define *critical awareness* as the mind that is illuminated by critical thinking, compassion, and human dignity. To be critically aware is to be an intellectually competent critical thinker enlightened by empathy. Exercising critical thinking skills in an effective way represents an active struggle against the soporific solipsism (undisciplined simplicity) of mainstream media and its devotion to fantasy competitions of every kind. As such, effective critical thinking may align with political positions as required, but it is not a political position in and of itself. Rather, critical awareness represents a social and intellectual *way of being* in the world that serves as a kind of head waters for the social (and political) actions that might flow downstream from such a critical source.

In Chapter 6 we address the importance of restorative justice as the fullest fruit of social justice. Paulo Freire (1970) begins *Pedagogy of the Oppressed* on the premise that without critical consciousness, ordinary existence is a state of chronic dehumanization.[15] Social justice means environmental justice and economic justice and legal justice and intergenerational justice, justice between the oppressed and the oppressor. It also means socially just capitalism. Social justice operates from a place of empathetic compassion, collaboration rather than competition. Social justice assumes the right of everyone to expect and receive the material and social conditions that develop and maintain human dignity. Restorative justice, then, goes beyond doing good work at any point in time, to fulfilling a vision of a just society, and takes responsibility for injustices perpetrated in the past. It is a theory of justice that emphasizes repairing the social, political, and economic harm through extensive cooperative processes in order to reach a stable equilibrium among many complex, interdependent elements.

When we lose contact with our own innate human dignity, we will inevitably fail to see it in others. We are in danger of reducing others to whatever status we deem appropriate, especially if we are aligned with corresponding political ideologies of our society. At its worst, this phenomenon results in labeling someone the "other," who becomes nothing but a cockroach, or a scapegoat, in the eyes of the powerful. Such binary, either/or thinking, informs the logic of injustice.

Finally, in the Conclusion we present a brief guide to writing and the chapter offers a process by which students can learn to write clearly, effectively, and with purpose in different situations and for different audiences. We also consider several important mathematical and statistical terms, and introduce, or reintroduce, how to read graphs and tables. We review the logic behind deductive and inductive arguments so that we can better analyze scientific reports and decide whether we should believe them. The goal is to encourage the student to take responsibility for developing critical thinking skills: to question, remain curious, and seek out evidence to support important conclusions and to act on the injustices we see, connect with, and experience.

# Notes

1 "Social Justice in an Open World: The Role of the United Nations." *The International Forum for Social Development*. https://www.un.org/esa/socdev/documents/ifsd/SocialJustice.pdf. Accessed July 19, 2019.

2 "Richest People in the World." CBS News. https://www.cbsnews.com/pictures/richest-people-in-world-forbes/3/. Accessed July 19, 2019.

3 Citizens United v. Federal Election Commission. SCOTUS Blog. https://www.scotusblog.com/case-files/cases/citizens-united-v-federal-election-commission/. Accessed July 19, 2019.

4 Jan-William Van Prooijen and Karen M. Douglas. "Belief in Conspiracy Theories: Basic Principles of an Emerging Research Doman." *European Journal of Social Psychology*, Vol. 48, No. 7 (August 24, 2018): 897–908. https://www.ncbi.nlm.nih.gov/pubmed/30555188/. DOI 10.1002/ejsp.2530. Accessed July 19, 2019.

5 Garrett Hardin. "The Tragedy of the Commons," *Science*, Vol. 162 [3859] (December, 1968): 1243–8. Accessed July 19, 2019. DOI: 10.1126/science.162.3859.1243https://science.sciencemag.org/content/162/3859/1243.full/. Accessed July 12, 2019.

6 Adam Smith. *An Inquiry into the Nature and Causes of the Wealth of Nations* (London: W. Strahan and T. Cadell, 1776).

7 "We're Finally at the End of the UN Decade for Water 2005–2015—It Is Time to Say Good-bye." United Nations Department of Economic and Social Affairs International Decade for Action "Water for Life" 2005–2015. https://www.un.org/waterforlifedecade/scarcity.shtml. Accessed July 19, 2019.

8 For a list of the top 100 corporate polluters in the U.S. see https://www.peri.umass.edu/toxic-100-air-polluters-index-2018-report-based-on-2015-data

9 Mrinalini Krishna. "At $1 Trillion, Apple Is Bigger Than These Things." Investopedia. https://www.investopedia.com/news/apple-now-bigger-these-5-things/. Accessed July 19, 2019.

10 Garrett Hardin. "The Tragedy of the Commons." *Science*, Vol. 162 [3859] (December, 1968): 1243–8. https://science.sciencemag.org/content/162/3859/1243.full/ DOI: 10.1126/science.162.3859.1243. Accessed July 19, 2019.

11 Prateek Agarwal. "The Four Types of Economies." *Intelligent Economist*. https://www.intelligenteconomist.com/types-of-economies/. Accessed July 19, 2019.

12 Michael Savage. "Richest 1% on Target to Own Two-thirds of All Wealth by 2030." *Guardian*. https://www.theguardian.com/business/2018/apr/07/global-inequality-tipping-point-2030. Accessed July 19, 2019.

13 Parag Khana and David Francis. "These 25 Companies Are More Powerful Than Many Countries." *Foreign Policy News*. https://foreignpolicy.com/2016/03/15/these-25-companies-are-more-powerful-than-many-countries-multinational-corporate-wealth-power/. Accessed July 19, 2019.

14 Carie Golberg. "Materialism Is Bad for You, Studies Say." *New York Times*. February 8, 2006. https://www.nytimes.com/2006/02/08/health/materialism-is-badfor-you-studies-say.html.

15 Paulo Freire. *Pedagogy of the Oppressed* (London: Bloomsbury Press, 1968).

# 1

# GLOBAL CRISIS

## The sixth extinction

We live in an age burdened by an epidemic of anxiety and addiction placed on our path toward destruction. Reactionary political and social ideologies depend on fear and anger while channeling wrath as worship at the twin alters of violence and power. Our political discourse has become suddenly retrospective, and we look nostalgically backward in time for guidance. The great project of modernity has left the world aching and traumatized. What can disenfranchise a community more than having its most basic resources made toxic by the day-to-day manner in which those with wealth and power live, a way of living supported and caressed by political and corporate power?

The problems seem clear enough, but the solutions are slow in coming.[1] The cycle of poverty, lack of education, and limited access to employment, food, clean water, land and air perpetuate social and economic injustice. So what can we do about it?

Experts from the fields of political science, sociology, psychology, anthropology, history, and more warn us that a superficial, distracted population is a population at risk of demagoguery, authoritarianism, and violent impositions of power, all of which engender the conditions for social *injustice* to persist and expand. Experts have been warning us that the phenomenon of the social networking "bubble" serves as a reaffirmation of a user's fantasies and as a result by-passes brain centers that are the seat of meta-cognition. A recent study from the Pew Research Center on Internet and Technology, confirms that "people tend to seek information that aligns with their views," and this "makes them vulnerable to acting on mis-information."[2] And according to Kevin Kelly, the co-founder of *Wired* magazine, "truth is networked by peers. For every fact there is a counterfact and all these counterfacts and facts look identical online, which is confusing to most people."[3]

Constantly and everywhere, we are invited to enter, even retreat, into our bubbles. These patterns of entering and retreating may only grow worse over time. The biologist Rolston Homes observed that, "a general pattern of behavior among threatened human societies is to become more blinkered, rather than more focused on the crisis, as they fail."[4] The implications of Homes' observations are discouraging, for as social and economic crises mount, so too will be our need for distraction and fantasy, all as forms of disavowal and denial. But on other hand, if we have the ability to recognize the "general pattern of behavior" this suggests that the human mind is capable of making the sort of meta-cognitive leap required to save itself, if we can only act on what we discover.

Princeton University historian Cornel West maintains that we have been radically conditioned to look the other way when faced with the dehumanization of others, or, put another way, the degradation of the world.[5] Our world, he argues, is filled with "life-denying forces," bent on economic exploitation, scientific manipulation, state repression, bureaucratic domination, and racial, sexual, and heterosexual subjugation. According to West, these same life-denying forces represent the inevitable consequences of power unchecked by social justice, and this jeopardizes us all.

Environmental pollution represents incontrovertible evidence of these social and economic injustices that threaten life as we know it. The evidence shows that first-world market societies are having an inordinate amount of undesirable influence on the biosphere on the planet in which we inhabit and rely on. "No creatures have ever altered life on the planet in this way before," Elizabeth Kolbert writes in *The Sixth Extinction.* [6] The world has entered what is now known as the Anthropocene Era, precisely named to reflect the globalized impact of human civilization and the resulting global die-off of species.[7] Anywhere in the world biological systems of the planet are at risk, and not just from human pollution. Political and economic decisions and indecisions put millions of people in harm's way—it is political violence that incites wars and famine and species extinction.[8] The United Nations (2017) reports that more than 20 million people in Somalia, South Sudan, Yemen, and Nigeria teeter on the edge of famine, calling the situation "the worst humanitarian crisis since the end of World War II." The vital point is that the famines are not caused by drought but by the failure of political will to act.[9]

According to experts the Anthropocene Era is the commencement of negative, significant human impact on the planet. Born of the Industrial Revolution, perfected throughout the twentieth century, and accelerated during the first one-fifth of the current century, ecological scientists almost unanimously recognize that human activity has had a *geological* impact on the planet.

The vast gyres of plastic pollution in the world's oceans represent a terrifying symbol of an economic and political system run amok. Uninhibited private profit has placed itself above the public good, has appropriated the public commons as resources, extracts wealth, and poisons the resources we all need in the process—in the name of servicing economic markets. Meanwhile, consumerism requires an ideological justification, a fantasy imposed on the world to explain it, and the consumer's place within it, all of which obscures the true costs of the consumer lifestyle. How is it that corporate powers take virtually no interest in the generational costs to society of the toll industry takes, and has taken, on the air we breathe, the water we drink, and soil we need to grow our crops?

## Inequality in wealth and income

In 2017, the richest one percent of the world's population owned half the planet's wealth, an increase of 5 percent over 16 years.[10] And the concentration of wealth into fewer hands is only increasing. The Institute for Policy Study's inequality-tracking website reports:[11]

- "One-third of one percent of the world's population owns 11% of the planet's wealth."
- "Adults with less than $10,000 in wealth make up 64 percent of the world's population but hold less than two percent of global wealth."
- "The world's wealthiest individuals, those owning over $100,000 in assets, total less than 10 percent of the global population but own 84 percent of global wealth."
- "The 42 richest individuals (down from 380 ten years ago) own as much (wealth) as 50% of the world's population."

By every measure of wealth distribution, inequality is rising almost everywhere in the world, including the United States with 15,300,000 millionaires—the most in any country in the world—along with the so-called liberal democracies of Scandinavia and Western Europe. Since 1980, the global top one percent has "captured twice as much growth as the bottom half." The gap between the richest and poorest people is larger than ever, and it is growing.

Economic inequality is a symptom of an economic system that promotes and sustains the privatizing of the public Commons by transnational corporations. Environmental destruction, human migration, and autocratic regimes are only a few of the most extreme consequences. Those who are on the losing side of the economic inequality equation are disproportionately women, children, and people of color.

The Office of Economic Cooperation and Development (OECD) measures the level of economic inequality among its 36 member countries, primarily in Europe, North America, and Australia, New Zealand, South Korea, Japan, and Chile. OECD data do not include any African countries or most of Asia and South America, i.e., the world's poorer countries. For example, according to the World Bank, between 1995 and 2015, "(G)lobal wealth grew an estimated 66 percent (from $690 trillion to $1,143 trillion in constant 2014 U.S. dollars at market prices). But inequality was substantial, as wealth per capita in high-income OECD countries was 52 times greater than wealth in low-income countries."[12] Even among the richest countries, wealth inequality is persistent and growing.[13]

The OECD adds that "uncertainty and fears of social decline and exclusion have reached the middle classes in many societies. Arresting the trend of rising inequality has become a priority for policy makers in many countries. Even in countries that have enjoyed reliable economic growth, raising millions of families out of poverty, inequality has risen further. In terms of actual (rather than relative) wealth, OECD estimates that up to 25 percent of member countries' households have little in the way of economic resources and often are saddled with insurmountable debt.[14]

Economic inequality affects society by "undermining education opportunities for children from poor socioeconomic backgrounds." Poverty is a self-perpetuating cycle that impedes social mobility and makes economic advancement difficult, if not almost impossible. According to the OECD, children from the bottom 40 percent of households cannot afford education. "That makes them less productive employees, which means lower wages, which means lower overall participation in the economy."[15] It also means an uneducated electorate is prone to ideological manipulation, fear-mongering, scapegoating, and authoritarian *politicos* who appeal to emotion and reject reason and evidence. According to the evidence, economic inequality blocks people from accessing resources necessary for a well-lived life. Their interest may be in survival, let alone having the time and resources to campaign and vote for political, economic, or social change.

As the OECD examples indicate, richer countries are located in Europe, North America and Oceania; poorer countries are concentrated in Central and South America, mainland Asia, and Africa. Understanding the geography of economies helps explain world migration now and in the near future. Along with high poverty rates come local conflicts over scarce resources, such as arable land, potable water, and other natural resources necessary for life. Consequently, countries with poorer economies experience more civil wars, informal and illegal economies, human trafficking, various forms of political extremism, corruption, environmental destruction, and migration, both legal and illegal. While wealthier countries experience some of these same effects, these violent and nonviolent atrocities are more concentrated and widespread in poorer nations.

## Migration and the growth of dictatorships around the world

We believe that human migration across borders and the rise of authoritarian dictatorships are two sides of the same coin, and together are part of a larger crisis. While there is income inequality within nations, income inequality *between* individual nations promotes international migration. The income inequality world map identifies two geographic boundaries that separate rich and poor countries: the Mediterranean Sea in southern Europe, and the Rio Grande River at the border between the United States and Mexico. Countries north of these boundaries have experienced a rise in nationalism, hate groups, and autocratic political leadership, in part as a response to immigrants who, coming as economic, climate, or war refugees, have fled scarcity and violence in their homelands in the hope of finding safety, freedom, and economic opportunities for themselves and their families. Meanwhile the middle and working classes of the "richer" nations have experienced decades of economic stagnation along with growing income inequality and many see migrants as competitors for jobs they need.

Traditionally democratic countries have experienced mounting internal popular pressure to weaken democratic institutions in favor of autocratic ones. Such viewpoints encourage nationalism, and would-be dictators find easy scapegoats in migrants, who usually speak different languages, have different cultures and religions, and appear different, as in language, skin color, and other external features.

The European Union and the United States are two cases in point. The latter, in 2016, elected a self-defined "America First" populist who retained a strong base of public support after more than two years of overtly attacking democratic institutions, notably the free press, the courts, and the United States Congress. In Europe, nationalism is on the rise with numerous examples of whom the local press describes as narrow-minded political groups and politicians.[16] In Spain, for example, the BBC reports multiple far-right politicians from the Vox Party who were elected to parliament "to make Spain great again." [17]

In the midst of elections for leadership of the European Union, similar challenges to democracy were evident across the continent. In May 2019, the *New York Times* reported that

> (E)uropean politics have been fragmenting since the financial crisis of 2008, and populist anger deepened after an influx of migrants from Africa and the Middle East, reviving some of the continent's oldest and ugliest impulses toward discrimination and outright bigotry. Anti-Semitism is rising. Anti-elite and anti-immigrant sentiments remain acute. Nationalist and identitarian movements are gaining clout, while marginalized neo-fascist parties have become more vocal and gaining membership.[18]

What explains the rise of hate campaigns in Europe and the United States? Why have despotic appeals to historic ethnic, racial, religious, and sexual orientation prejudices become so well-received by so many?

## The crisis of critical thinking

Research shows college graduates in the United States rank 17th out of 18 comparable countries for "problem solving abilities in a technology rich environment" (OECD 2016). According to the Educational Testing Service, only *four percent* out of 100,000 students tested demonstrated proficiency in their capacity for critical thinking. The Stanford History Education Group in 2016 found that the outlook is "bleak" for young people who deal with information-overload every day. While some knowledge has been transmitted to and acquired by college graduates, there is still a fundamental disconnect. "In short," John Baldoni writes in *Forbes*, "young people may possess the quantitative skills without the qualitative abilities to make informed decisions about what the data tell them. Not only is this a challenge for the workplace, but it's also a challenge for making life decisions."[19]

When polled, faculty respond in favor of critical thinking but routinely are unable to demonstrate what it means or how they specifically teach it. According to Pearlman and Carillo,

most faculty reported that, for variety of institutional, discipline, or pedagogi-
cal reasons, they did not explicitly assess critical thinking in their classrooms.
Without explicitly connecting the teaching and assessing of critical thinking,
faculty could only *hope* that students are really developing as critical thinkers.[20]

Hope, in this case, is simply not enough in the pursuit of a more socially just world.

Yale University historian Timothy Snyder, analyzing the popularly-supported
fall of European democracies during the twentieth century, identifies five key criteria that taken together demonstrate the crucial role intellectual competency plays
in preserving democracy in the face of forces promoting dictatorships.[21] Prominent
on Snyder's list is the need to "defend institutions" by choosing an institution we
care about—the legal system, journalism, a labor union—and studying it.

As we learn about the history, roles, activities, and contributions of the institution(s)
we care about, we should become aware—and beware—of superficial memes, falsified
and oversimplified headlines, and other misinformation that appeals to our fear, and
not our empathy. Along the way, we should also be open to criticizing institutions'
behaviors, from the viewpoint of improving, not destroying. All human systems need
constructive accountability, so in other words, we need to continually ask *why, how,
when, where*, and *to whom*. To study institutions is a way to study ourselves, for they
provide for so much of our social identities. And, as Snyder tells us, it is essential for the
preservation of our democracy. "To abandon facts is to abandon freedom," Snyder
writes. "If nothing is true, then all is spectacle."

Along with the proliferation of anti-science among politicians and corporate
leaders, we are witnessing the cynical use of "alternative facts" as a parody and
mockery of the fruits of critical thinking. Indeed, critical thinking often leads one
to the conclusion that the "truth" is difficult to determine amid a host of competing claims to what it is, what it means, and how it impacts people, groups, and
whole societies. Consider the ongoing popularity of Margaret Atwood's *The
Handmaid's Tale* as an example. If the "truth" can be imposed at the end of an AR-
15 rifle, it is certainly possible that a society might oppress some individuals and
groups in support of others. Perhaps we already live in such a world.

"We inhabit a world of niche interests and platforms and distractions," writes Peter
Hamby, an American political journalist. He describes our interconnected world as the
scene of bizarre juxtapositions: everyone is supposed to be paying attention to their own
thing while participating together—yet isolated and miles apart—in the greatest social
engineering experiment ever undertaken. Experts who study the problem agree: our
attention spans are shrinking.[22] Hamby's point, along with others like Nicholas Carr, an
American author on technology, business, and culture, that we have reached, even cres-
ted, a transitional moment in the history of the human mind. Book-reading once helped
the mind to develop focus and concentration—because by reading books we practiced
and developed these very skills every time we opened one to read. The current decline in
long-form reading in favor of the shallow skimming required today by our digital devices—and the fact that fewer people read books today than they did even thirty years
ago—coincides with the rise of the internet. While convenience and access have come to

define our relationship to information, our uptake of that information has shortened our attention spans and left fallow the fields of deeper, more focused thought.

We often have multiple screens displaying information of different sorts at the same time while monitoring multiple networking sites. In 2018, *Axios* reported that "over 70 percent of the American population regularly uses a digital device while watching TV."[23] We skim surfaces and flit from input to input on our devices. The habits of mind and body that accommodate our ability to remain deeply focused atrophy under our current cultural conditions. Our narrowing attention span is one of many challenges we face when deciding to take responsibility for our own intellectual growth and development.

Many of us spend more and more of our time in digital bubbles that are corrupted by confirmation bias and the Dunning-Kruger effect. (Recall that the Dunning-Kruger effect refers to the conditions that underlie intellectual incompetence and lack of critical thinking.) Kruger and Dunning observed that, "people tend to hold overly favorable views of their abilities in many social and intellectual domains." The cognitive dilemma is that "people who are unskilled … suffer a dual burden." This now famous study noted how people make "erroneous conclusions" and "unfortunate choices," but their incompetence robs them of the meta-cognitive ability to realize what is wrong, or not well thought out, about their choices and conclusions. Somewhere along the way we lose our "capacity to distinguish accuracy from error," and as a result, we no longer think effectively. "Paradoxically, improving the skills of participants, and thus increasing their metacognitive competence, helped them recognize the limitations of their abilities."[24] In other words, developing skills on the one hand, and meta-cognitive awareness on the other, is the road to intellectual competence, critical thinking, and social justice.

The Dunning-Kruger effect is another way of describing what others have called "confirmation bias," the habits of mind that routinely reaffirm our already-held beliefs. "Confirmation bias," writes one expert "suggests that we don't perceive circumstances objectively. We pick out those bits of data that make us feel good because they confirm our prejudices. Thus, we … become prisoners of our assumptions." Our social network bubbles engender habits of mind that lead us away from skeptical awareness, critical thinking, and personal agency precisely because it offers an illusion of recognition that we all seek. The problem is, that "once we have formed a view, we embrace information that confirms that view while ignoring, or rejecting, information that casts doubt on it."[25]

We assemble our information "bubble" almost without realizing it. We like this and mute that, and within our digital communities we circulate there, sliding into other groups that comprise a group of groups, all of which reaffirms our fears, confirms our shared animosities, and offers a shared language that articulates what we think and what we feel, and what we think we know.

## Climate change, food production, and the environment

As we alluded to earlier, growing migration from south to north is influenced in large and small ways by climate change. As populations continue to experience extreme weather conditions that include rising sea levels and negative environmental effects, such as loss of land and access to potable water, these adverse consequences provoke human mobility, which often instigates a conservative political backlash.[26]

Since 1980, according to the United Nations and many other scientific reports, greenhouse gas emissions have doubled.[27] These reports show that carbon dioxide in the atmosphere has risen and measures well-above 415 parts per million, up from 270 parts per million since the beginning of the industrial revolution. Human causes—the burning of fossil fuels like coal, oil, and natural gas—are the primary sources of carbon dioxide released into the atmosphere in the form of pollution. Other heat-trapping gases like methane combine with $CO_2$ to create the greenhouse effect, a warming of the planet, a shifting climate, and a general melting of the world's glaciers and polar ice caps. We may already be living with an irreversible feedback loop where climate change begets more climate change; warming begets more warming, more thawing, and more extreme weather conditions.

Because of these climate changes and loss of habitat, about one million of the world's species are threatened with extinction due to human activity, according to a United Nations report issued in May 2019.[28]

> "Nature is declining globally at rates unprecedented in human history—and the rate of species extinctions is accelerating, with grave impacts on people around the world now likely," warned the United Nations Intergovernmental Science-Policy Platform on Biodiversity and Ecosystem Services (IPBES) 2019 report. "The health of ecosystems on which we and all other species depend is deteriorating more rapidly than ever. We are eroding the very foundations of our economies, livelihoods, food security, health, and quality of life worldwide."

Specifically, according to the U.N. report, the environmental losses and threats include:

- "The average abundance of native species in most major land-based habitats has fallen by at least 20%, mostly since 1900."
- "More than 40% of amphibian species, almost 33% of reef-forming corals and more than a third of all marine mammals are threatened."
- An estimated 10 percent of insect species are threatened.
- "At least 680 vertebrate species (became extinct) since the 16th century and more than 9% of all domesticated breeds of mammals used for food and agriculture (became) extinct by 2016, with at least 1,000 more breeds still threatened."
- Destruction of environments—about 75 percent of the world's land and 66 percent of the oceans "have been significantly altered by human actions."
- Timber harvesting is up 45 percent since 1980; agricultural food production is up 300 percent since 1970.
- "More than a third of the world's land surface and nearly 75% of freshwater resources are now devoted to crop or livestock production."
- Reduction in the census of the world's agricultural pollinators (bees, other insects and birds) "threatens up to US$577 billion in agricultural production."

- At least one million people worldwide "are at increased risk of floods and hurricanes because of loss of coastal habitats and protection."
- Approximately 33 percent of fish stocks are harvested at unsustainable levels.
- "Plastic pollution has increased tenfold since 1980, 300–400 million tons of heavy metals, solvents, toxic sludge and other wastes from industrial facilities are dumped annually into the world's waters, and fertilizers entering coastal ecosystems have produced more than 400 ocean 'dead zones,' totaling ... a combined area greater than that of the United Kingdom."
- "The land area occupied by cities has doubled since 1992."

While some have claimed that the climate change is a "natural" event that happens periodically, the evidence for human activity as the primary cause is undeniable, and all around the world governments are recognizing that climate change is, in fact, a climate crisis that affects us all.[29]

We are in the grip of a global economic order that has long privileged private wealth over the public Commons. This has meant the privatizing of the world's natural resources, transferring them to capitalist owners who remain intent on accruing wealth without limit, even when it means polluting the air, soil, groundwater, or oceans. We are, according to experts, in the midst of a "sixth extinction," a disaster great enough to permanently interrupt the current global economic and environmental systems.[30]

As the UN warns, species are disappearing at an accelerating rate, along with the undeveloped habitats that sustain them. For example, the number of Indian states hit by heatwaves grew to 19 in 2018 from 9 in 2015, and this year 23 states are expected to experience similar dire results. In the spring of 2019, The *New York Times* reported that at least 36 people died in India as temperatures soared to 123 degrees Fahrenheit.[31]

By 2050, experts claim that due to climate change and rising temperatures there will be more plastic than fish in the sea. Already plastic has been found in the deepest places in the ocean. Scenes of vast swaths of plastic washing up on beaches in the Pacific are common.

Coral reefs around the world are in danger, or are dead or dying, often faster than scientists can measure. Rising ocean temperatures and the acidification of the oceans threaten all marine life, and coral reefs are one of the most diverse ecosystems on the planet that are in peril. The reefs assist in carbon and nitrogen sequestration, help sustain marine life and protect coastlines from violent storms.[32]

Meanwhile, scientists have observed marine species disappearing even as commercial fisheries struggle from years of overfishing. In the north, Arctic sea ice continues to shrink each summer while in the south, Antarctica's glaciers are melting at a vastly accelerated rate from estimates of just a few years ago. Sea levels will flood coastal cities and drive tens of millions (or more) to higher ground over the coming decades.

Unfortunately, meta-national and multinational corporations that profit from polluting the earth have more resources and resolve at their disposal than advocates for environmental protection and intervention. Can the economic system that gave rise to the climate crisis solve the climate crisis? The answer is no. The economic system that privileges the accumulation of wealth over and above the public good has brought us all to the brink of a sixth extinction, along with the rhetoric of climate change denial and anti-science.

Environmental justice and social justice go hand in hand. David Pellow, professor of Environmental Studies and Director of the Global Environmental Justice Project at the University of California–Santa Barbara, argues, "We've got to find a way to see all of us—both humans and nonhumans—as having shared fates." Relying on governments to solve environmental justice problems may not always be the best option, Pellow maintains. After all, he says, "governments are in some ways the primary engines of climate change and certain environmental harms." [33] Ecological sustainability and social justice are symbiotic issues, and only by empowering and democratizing communities can we then take the direct action we need to solve ongoing crises of justice.

---

### EXERCISE

Choose any of the environmental threats discussed in this chapter. First, note your reaction(s): detached, concerned, annoyed, scared, angry, other. Why? Are you tired of hearing about environmental destruction? Second, do an internet search for information about the topic. See how much "information" is available. How much misinformation can you find? What are your criteria for believing and dismissing others' assertions from these websites?

---

Up to this point, we have identified some of the many dangers of environmental degradation and the economic and political landscapes that foster them. Now let us bring into the discussion what is happening with our food chain. From a western perspective, this is part of the environmental crisis that we may not even know exists. Overproduction of staple crops like corn, wheat, and soybeans has neutered the land and impacted plant, animal, and human health. Such massive overproduction by large agricultural businesses creates poor quality soil, in large measure due to carbon sequestration with almost no crop rotation. In turn, this has negatively impacted our food supply, our environment, and our health.

In 2006 Michael Pollan wrote *Omnivore's Dilemma* to address the history and consequences of massive industrial food production in the United States.[34] Our food is made in large part by corn subsidies and similar products that we might argue do not qualify as food at all. Getting beef, chicken, and pork to market means fattening them as quickly as possible with corn and soy, and a host of antibiotics, including timlicosin, a drug, according to the American Veterinary Medical Association, that has killed 25 people and caused adverse health effects in thousands more.[35] Because cows and sheep eat beans and vegetables that the animals would otherwise not choose to eat themselves, essentially to fatten them up quickly, strong antimicrobials are fed to them to prevent respiratory and liver diseases before slaughter. Even our farm-raised fish eat crop-based corn, soy, and wheat. For example, salmon are given "pink-ifying pellets" to give their meat the color consumers expect, but farm-raised salmon is actually grey in color due to the food source. Wild salmon, by contrast, have more nutritional content because they earn their pink meat by eating foods like free-floating crustaceans and tiny shrimp. The color of their flesh is natural and not fabricated by chemicals and unnatural food sources.

Because of the animals' food sources, meats are also easily contaminated with E. coli bacteria that cause a whole host of problems for the animals, including destroying their livers. The trick is to slaughter a cow within 14 months before they become so sick that the meat cannot be used for human consumption. In fact, this first happened with Mad Cow (Bovine spongiform encephalopathy) disease, diagnosed in the United Kingdom in 1986.[36] While experts have not been able to pinpoint the exact cause of Mad Cow disease, it is thought to originate with infectious proteins the animals eat that target their brain, spinal cord, and small intestine. The disease destroys the animal's nervous system and toward the end of its short life, it is unable to stand. Its impact on humans is also significant: A human form of Mad Cow is called Creutzfeldt-Jakob disease, which is also a degenerative and fatal brain disorder, contracted by eating contaminated meat. In the US, 350 people die from the disease every year.[37] Like human deaths associated with timlicosin exposure, Creutzfeldt-Jakob has no cure, and like cows, death comes quickly, usually within one year.

While there is no cure for diseases such as this, the ranchers' goal is to keep the animals healthy long enough to slaughter for human consumption. Paradoxically, though, the sheer number of antibiotics, fungicides and insecticides used to make the meat safe to eat can also render it unsafe to eat! In fact, fermenting grain, common to the industrial livestock industry, can do severe damage to a cow's stomach where the acid gets trapped in the bloodstream, multiplies, and makes the animal sick, which in turn, makes us sick. Additionally, farm workers who experience long term exposure to these pesticides are at a much greater risk for contracting debilitating diseases like Parkinson's, asthma, leukemia, and non-Hodgkin's lymphoma, among other health risks.[38]

Put aside for the moment worker and consumer health, and consider how the antibiotics, pesticides, and pharmaceutical herbicides make their way into and destroy clean water and soil.[39] Pesticide drift is the airborne movement of these chemicals during and after the application process. Spray droplets and vapors move with the wind and via air currents that travel into school playgrounds, homes, well water, and many other unintended locations. Herbicide drift can also damage other crops, making them unsellable for human and animal consumption. While industrial food production is efficient, it is certainly not without its hazards.

What prompted such unnatural and ostensibly harmful food production? From the economic side, traditional supply and demand is full of danger for farmers, growers, and ranchers, so the only way to make money is to get their products to market as efficiently as possible. Their economic security depends on it. To support this endeavor, feed the nation and avoid economic hardship, President Franklin D. Roosevelt created the Farm Bill, or the Agricultural Adjustment Act, in 1933 during the Great Depression. This act ensures farming subsidies and crop insurance, which is renewed with bipartisan congressional support every few years. Because these government subsidies support large agribusinesses to produce commodity crops, abundant supplies of corn, soy, and wheat, the biggest government payout for crop insurance and subsidies under the Farm Bill goes to big agribusinesses: payment is based on production, even when times are good.[40] The more you bring to market, the more subsidy monies you receive from the government. While it is important to have crop insurance to protect farmers against unforeseeable disasters like drought or violent storms, the subsidies artificially drive down the price of crops, namely crops of corn, wheat, and soybeans. It is what some may call a "Catch-22," an impasse from which there is no escape. The more you plant and bring to harvest, the lower the price is due to abundant supply. In fact, the government pays farmers not to plant sometimes, depending on the supply and demand for certain crops.[41]

Small-scale farmers, growers and ranchers also receive support from the Farm Bill, although their subsidies and insurance are much smaller. Small farms do not have protections against price fluctuations the way the big agribusinesses do, such as what might happen if a drought or violent storm damages a crop, or an illness disqualifies animals for human consumption. While the Farm Bill is designed to provide some support by guaranteeing a minimum price for a crop, the very structure of our industrial food system protects and returns profit to big agribusinesses, not to the traditional family farmers and ranchers. The producers of herbicides, pesticides, antibiotics, and other chemicals, and even the seeds the farmers must buy, bring the profits largely to these complex systems of big agro-businesses.[42] What farmers and cattle ranchers once returned to the soil in the form of rotating the crops and tilling the land by hard, manual labor for crops to grow, or to allow freely wandering animals to graze their pastures and thus returning nutrients to the soil with natural fertilizer, just does not exist for large scale production today. Livestock are confined for maximum fattening with the goal of getting their meat to consumers as quickly as possible.

Today agriculture production is not as much about farming as it is about deploying smart biotechnology: farmers and growers purchase agrochemicals and fertilizer that help mitigate disease agents in the soil, deploy irrigation and computer systems that calculate the proper dose of water or food for specific crops or animals, and purchase genetically manipulated seeds to withstand drought and disease. There is nothing rustic or simple, and perhaps we should include healthy, about high-tech farming and growing today; yet our government funds and supports this process and these agribusinesses in the interest of assuring us that we will always have food available.

One particular Supreme Court case serves to illustrate the impact large agribusinesses have on small farmers. In the 2013 case of *Bowman v. Monsanto Company, No. 11–796,* Indiana farmer Vernon Hugh Bowman was found guilty of violating Monsanto's genetically patented soybean seeds.[43] All farmers who use their seeds must sign a contract whereby they must promise not to use the seeds from a resulting crop to start a new crop. You must buy seeds every time. Bowman signed the Monsanto contract, but then decided to plant a second crop that year from seeds he obtained from a communal grain elevator. He did not pay for the genetically modified seeds that were mixed in among other seeds he purchased from the grain elevator. He did admit in court that he had hoped to get Monsanto's genetically modified and patented seeds but there was no way to know for sure. In the Bowman case, he had signed only one contract but claimed that there was no prohibition on using seeds for a second crop later in the same season, a loophole in the contract, he claimed, and Monsanto seeds just happened to be mixed in with others at the elevator. He had a successful second harvest, and used the seeds from this harvest for additional soybean crops without paying Monsanto for their use. Monsanto sued for patent violation and the case went all the way to the US Supreme Court which upheld an earlier federal judge's decision and ordered Bowman to pay Monsanto $84,000 for using their patented seeds.

Replanting soy, wheat, and corn and other subsidized crops is on-going and quick, making them relatively cheap to grow, especially genetically modified seeds that withstand plagues, drought, and a whole host of other dangers, and without the need for crop rotation—a time-intensive endeavor that wastes land and money.[44] The patented pesticides and herbicides used on these crops also help prevent problems with insects, parasitic infestation, weeds, or diseases caused by plant pathogens, but there is a catch. The catch is that growing corn crop after corn crop depletes the nutrients in the soil, soil diseases increase, and crop yields are less efficient. For many scientists the conclusion is that our modern agrochemical system has created the food supplies we demand but at the same time greatly diminishes the biological diversity necessary for rich, nutritive soil that can grow nutrient-dense foods. The oppressive consolidation of just a few crops hurts farmers, growers, and ranchers as their land ends up producing less and less high quality food for humans and animals. No matter how high-tech agribusiness gets, they cannot consolidate soil. It is a complex organism and always responds positively and productively to diversity, especially crop rotation, to keep producing healthy, nutritious food. In fact, an added bonus to crop rotation is the reduction of nitrous oxide, a greenhouse gas that traps 200–300 times more heat in the air than $CO_2$. [45]

Agribusiness does have a dramatic and unwelcome effect on climate change. Since the 1970s soil degradation has increased due to large-scale farming. It can be argued that big business is not necessarily concerned with an environmentally friendly approach that costs extra time and money and eats away their profits. Less varied, large farms with industrialized crops, cows, hogs, sheep, chickens, etc., have contributed to speeding up the climate change process because of the economics behind this kind of corporate farm-to-table production. Mega-sized farming and ranching encourages practices that degrade the soil, waste fertilizer, mishandle manure, and flood chemicals into our soil and air, all of which increases emissions of greenhouse gases. With pesticide use and abundant chemicals, crop rotation is something of the past, large scale production discourages "no till" farming and crop rotation that would otherwise grab carbon dioxide and nitrous oxide from the air, store it in the soil, and not only improve soil health but assist with tribulations of climate change. While subsidies allegedly support farmers, ranchers, and growers, government support discourages innovation and diversification of land use, and these actions are needed to make a sustainable, living wage that produces healthy, nutritious food in a global, competitive economy.

The efficiency of the industrial agricultural machine means that we have surplus to spare. With the help of farm subsidies, corn is abundant, and it is mixed into everything from the American diet, petroleum (ethanol), other biofuels and bio-based plastics, animal feed, high-fructose corn syrup, toothpaste, and even diapers, to name just a few products that use corn. In fact, 93 million acres of corn are grown every year.[46]

The reality is that growing corn, wheat, and soy crops year after year creates yields that are less efficient; soil diseases increase; and sustainable agriculture, where once crop diversification was not only important but common among family farms, is traded for protection against price fluctuations, less year-round income, and a modicum of financial stability for our farmers, ranchers, and growers with government insurance and subsidies. The conclusion that can be drawn from these examples is that modern agricultural production does not follow traditional supply and demand models and unquestionably promotes diminishing biological diversity, relentless consolidation, and poor health of our soil, our crops, our animals, and at the end of the chain, has undesirable impact on our health and wellbeing.

It is certainly hard to argue that diversification of crops along with the careful nurturing of soil, air, and water for sustainable agricultural exists in industrial farming and ranching. What is clear is that not everyone has access to healthy food, despite agricultural policies that are intended to maintain abundant production—no food scarcity – and support our nation's nutritional goals. The cynics among us do question why we continue to have outdated USDA guidelines on nutritional requirements that overemphasize carbohydrates like bread, cereal, pasta, and rice.[47] If we truly were a free market economy engaged in a philosophy of socially just capitalism, profitability of large agribusinesses through subsidies and other government supports would not control the lives of farmers, ranchers, growers or consumers the way they control us now. It is our health, the animals' health, and the stewardship of our crops and the environment that are on the losing end of such profit-seeking motives. No doubt farmers, growers, and ranchers have extremely tight profit margins, and many often succumb to and participate in agribusiness methods to sustain their economic security. For example, the meta-national company Bayer-Monsanto controls 25 percent of the world's seeds and is on its way to becoming the 'one-stop shop' for all agrochemicals, pesticides, and computer-aided services for farmers and ranchers.[48]

Consider an example of the most common, go-to products on the market today: chicken nuggets. In 2017 The *Washington Post* called it "the year of chicken nuggets," a processed food more akin to science than a food item, made with a mixture of additives of names that cannot easily roll off the tongue, such as Dimethylpolysiloxane, an antifoaming agent, and TBHQ, a petroleum derivative used to stabilize varnishes, perfumes, resins, oils, and also a key ingredient in Silly Putty, caulks, and sealants.[49] Other ingredients include 50 percent meat, corn starch, yellow corn flour, fat, ground bone, blood vessels, connective tissue, chemical pesticides, and genetically modified food like hydrogenated oils, and autolyzed yeast extract. These factory-farmed chickens are treated with hormones, medicated with pharmaceuticals, and the food they eat laced with pesticides. The goal is to slaughter them before significant diseases render them unfit for human consumption. Factory-farmed chickens, which are 99 percent of all American chickens, are typically fed genetically engineered corn and soy beans and often have serious health problems that include chronic respiratory illnesses and bacterial infections. Although a chicken's life outside of a factory might span between 10 and 15 years, factory-raised chickens are artificially hatched, fattened, and slaughtered as early as six to seven weeks old.[50] According to the *Guardian*, if consumers knew how farmed chickens were raised, "they might never eat their meat again."[51] And, by comparison, chances are if you ate a hamburger today it would come from an animal that was kept alive with similar antibiotics during the last few months of its life to delay the destruction of liver abscesses and bovine respiratory distress. In your hamburger, you will likely consume herbicides, pesticides, and insecticides—along with a micro-dose of plastic.

---

### RESEARCH EXERCISE

Take a look at your favorite chocolate bar and read the ingredients list. What is in chocolate? Define each of the ingredients as your first task. Find out which of the ingredients are naturally occurring and which are added during production. Scientists have discovered some chocolate contains dangerous levels of lead, and sometimes cadmium. Children are especially vulnerable to heavy metal poisoning. Why does chocolate have heavy metals in it? As you research your chocolate bar, find out where the cocoa beans (also spelled cacao beans) grow. Once the beans are harvested, how many different countries contribute to the making of your chocolate bar? Who owns the cocoa bean farms that grow your candy bar? Dig deeper and see if you can find out how much cocoa farms pay their workers. How much chocolate do the owners produce and sell each year? How much is the company worth? How many countries and companies are involved in production and distribution of your chocolate bar?[52]

---

While remarkable changes have occurred in our ability to feed ourselves, the reformulation of processed food can and does make us sick and overweight. Fortunately, many educated consumers have become aware of these issues, and organic food sales and farmers' markets have doubled. Those individuals who can afford to pay the higher prices for higher quality food are perhaps somewhat healthier for it, but it is not a remedy for the vast majority of consumers of the world. For example, using a traditional economic supply and demand model, if we used grass-fed hens or allowed the cows to graze in fields of green pastures, the process of getting them to market would take a lot longer, and it would certainly cost a lot more due to a less industrialized, inefficient system. Cows raised in feedlots are usually slaughtered within 14 months while cows allowed to roam a pasture eating grass are slaughtered between 18 and 24 months. The pasture-fed cows typically do not need antibiotics or hormones, which as many small farmers say is as it should be, from pasture to plate.

Hopefully by now we have begun to understand that the modern era of raising beef and growing food crops has tremendous environmental impact, and yet this is actually not new information. In 1971, Francis Moore Lappe, in her bestselling book *Diet for a Small Planet*, showed how we could sustainably grow more food, a wider variety of food, and have a more diverse and nutritious diet if we altered the frenzy of growing corn and soybeans, particularly for meat production.[53] It was the first book of its kind to note the harmful environmental impact of mega-farming on the planet, and how it contributed to food scarcity worldwide. Lappe argued that world food hunger is not caused by the lack of food, but rather the industrial complex that ignores the environment and the human needs that go with it.

Despite many government reports and academic research showing the critical need for change, particularly to stabilize the climate by using crop rotation and improve the quality of the food we eat, big agribusinesses continue to expand and become even more powerful. In 2018 the U.S. Department of Agriculture's Economic Research Service confirmed that the practices of large scale farming have a negative impact on the planet by damaging the viability of rural communities, reducing diversity of production, and creating environmental risk.[54] Our agricultural technology clearly emphasizes over production with the support of farm subsidies that in turn favor only certain commodity crops and meta-national agribusinesses. Farmers and ranchers are locked into a system in which small family-run ranches and farms cannot compete with supersized industrial food production.[55] These smaller farms risk going out of business; the climate continues to decline; and what we eat becomes more precarious to our health than ever before.

## A case example

We take root, grow, and flower in our social environment as surely as plants convert soil and sunlight to leaves, flowers, and food to eat. While our genetic nature plays a fundamental role in who we are, science has begun to document how our genetic make-up is the biological equivalent of pure potential. We may or may not actualize our genetic potential depending on our environment, which nurtures our growth and development from birth to maturity, and beyond. The air we breathe determines the health and condition of our lungs. The light we see helps our eyes to develop, and so, too, our brains, as does the water we drink help our body to do all kinds of things. We are, after all, 60 percent water. But what if the water we drink, the air we breathe, the food we eat, and even the media we consume are full of toxic elements, but in amounts often difficult to detect without instruments keener than our own senses?

There was a time when leaders consulted with experts and read their books. In fact, the Environmental Protection Agency owes its very existence to a book: *Silent Spring* by Rachel Carson (1962). She was the first to sound the alarm that the people, and the environment that sustains them, exist in a porous relationship to one another. The pesticides we had been introducing into the air, water, and soil had begun to take an egregious toll on the food chain—birds, Carson warned, may not be born because of the persistence of DDT (dichlorodiphenyltrichloroethane). DDT was responsible for killing off birds and other creatures while failing to solve the problems it was deployed to mitigate, such as the bubonic plague, malaria, body lice, and pest control on farms. The consequence of over spraying would lead to an environmental catastrophe, she warned, including epidemics of cancer in humans. We are porous, Carson proved, by using scientific reasoning and available evidence to show how toxins persist in the environment, and go where we never intended them to go across the food chain. Even then she believed the evidence indicated that the pesticide threat to life on the planet was as great as the threat of the Cold War. The "silent spring" she warned of referred to the death of birds from DDT poisoning, but it also suggested a wider die-off if the mass spraying of pesticides continued. John F. Kennedy was so moved by the book that he defended Carson's controversial work and promoted the existence of a federal agency to regulate and control toxins in the environment. The Environmental Protection Agency was signed into law by President Richard Nixon in 1970 with a mandate to rescue the environment from environmental degradation. So, how well is the EPA doing?

Consider the fact that nearly all of our personal knowledge about the environment, the impact of greenhouse gases, the rates of inner city crime, poverty, and so on, all come to us from second-hand sources: we learn from others, unless we are one of the few who go out to collect and analyze information first hand. The rest of us gather information from articles written by scientists, or sometimes journalists interpreting scientific information, or sometimes aficionados, and sometimes bots, trolls, and critics paid by the very industries purportedly under study. Written almost 60 years ago, Rachel Carson's observations about our relationship to our environment remain as true as ever: people are permeable and absorptive—or to put it another way: "we are what we eat" and we need to be mindful about the short term and long term consequences of our actions as individuals and as a nation. We must protect the Commons.

Needless to say, the Environmental Protection Agency and similar institutions are constantly under threat due to lobbying by large industries that profit from bringing food and other consumer items to market quickly, and without much regard for our health and well-being. Their focus certainly does not appear to be about socially just capitalism or the stewardship of the planet. Instead, their arsenal includes corporate capitalism rather than a thoughtful, measured approach to profit-seeking objectives and that can include outright science denial and the spread of misinformation. Our challenge is this: we need to sharpen our critical thinking skills so that we can distinguish fact from fiction. We must use rigorous questioning: What do know and how do we know it? Where does our "information" come from and how seriously should we take it? What are our standards for accepting or disagreeing with authorities' assertions?

The next chapter takes up questions like these and introduces the skills and habits of mind necessary to achieve intellectual competence, the first and most important step to critical thinking and the pursuit of social justice.

## Notes

1 In *The Shock Doctrine* Naomi Klein argues that the solutions are slow in coming precisely because the problems themselves have been caused by the current economic system in service of market forces. She argues that there has been "orchestrated raids on the public sphere in the wake of catastrophic events, combined with the treatment of disasters as exciting market opportunities. She calls it "disaster capitalism" (6). It was in operation in Chile, Iraq, Sri Lanka (after the tsunami)—and was "the preferred method of advancing

corporate goals: using moments of collective trauma to engage in radical social and economic engineering" (8). Klein, Naomi. *The Shock Doctrine: The Rise of Disaster Capitalism* (New York: Henry Holt, 2007). Print.

2 Janna Anderson and Lee Rainie. "The Future of Truth and Misinformation Online." *Pew Research Center Internet & Technology.* www.pewinternet.org/2017/10/19/the-future-of-truth-and-misinformation-online/. Accessed July 19, 2019.

3 Pew Research Center. "The Future of Truth and Misinformation on Line." October 19, 2017, https://www.pewinternet.org/2017/10/19/the-future-of-truth-and-misinformation-online/. Retrieved May 8, 2019.

4 Holmes Rolston III. "Four Spikes, Last Chance." *Conservation Biology*, Vol. 14, No. 2 (2001): 585. https://doi.org/10.1046/j.1523-1739.2000.00053.x. Accessed July 19, 2019.

5 Cornel West. *Race Matters, 25th Anniversary.* (New York: Penguin-Random House, 2017).

6 Elizabeth Kolbert. *The Sixth Extinction: An Unnatural History* (New York: Holt, 2014).

7 As an example these animals, among many other animals and plants, have become extinct in the last decade: Western Black Rhinoceros, Caribbean Monk Seal, Pinta Tortoise, Formosan Clouded Leopard, Tasmanian Tiger, Madagascar Hippopotamus, and Passenger Pigeon. To learn more about the sixth extinction of plants and animals see https://www.biologicaldiversity.org/programs/biodiversity/elements_of_biodiversity/extinction_crisis/

8 Carol Jean Gallo. "A Famine Is Never Just a Famine—It's Political Violence by Starvation." *United Nation News and Commentary Global Forum.* https://www.undispatch.com/famine-never-just-famine-political-violence-starvation/. Accessed July 19, 2019.

9 Sophie Chou. "Drought Doesn't Cause Famine: People Do." *Public Radio International (PRI).* https://www.pri.org/stories/2017-03-27/drought-doesnt-cause-famine-people-do. Accessed July 19, 2019.

10 Robert Frank. "Richest 1% Now Owns Half the World's Wealth." *CNBC.* https://www.cnbc.com/2017/11/14/richest-1-percent-now-own-half-the-worlds-wealth.html. Accessed July 19, 2019.

11 "Global Wealth Inequality: The Richest 1% Own 45% of the World's Wealth." *Global Inequality.* https://inequality.org/facts/global-inequality/#us-wealth-concentration. Accessed July 19, 2019.

12 "The World Bank Working for a World Free of Poverty." *The World Bank.* https://www.worldbank.org/en/news/press-release/2018/01/30/world-bank-report-finds-rise-in-global-wealth-but-inequality-persists. Accessed July 19, 2019.

13 "GINI index (World Bank estimate)—Country Ranking." *Index Mundi.* https://www.indexmundi.com/facts/indicators/SI.POV.GINI/rankings. Accessed July 19, 2019.

14 Carlotta Balestra and Richard Tonkin. "Inequalities in Household Wealth Across OECD Countries: Evidence from the OECD Wealth Distribution Database." *OECD Statistics Working Papers.* https://read.oecd-ilibrary.org/economics/inequalities-in-household-wealth-across-oecd-countries_7e1bf673-en#page1. Accessed July 19, 2019.

15 Christopher Ingraham. "How Rising Inequality Hurts Everyone, Even the Rich." Economic Policy. *Washington Post.* February 6, 2018. https://www.washingtonpost.com/news/wonk/wp/2018/02/06/how-rising-inequality-hurts-everyone-even-the-rich/?utm_term=.8b4136ce71e4.

16 "Europe and Right-Wing Nationalism: A Country by Country Guide." *BBC News.* https://www.bbc.com/news/world-europe-36130006. Accessed July 19, 2019.

17 Guy Hedgecoe. "Spanish Vox Party: Nationalists Vow to 'Make Spain Great Again.'" *BBC News.* https://www.bbc.com/news/world-europe-46043427. Accessed July 19, 2019.

18 Steven Erlanger. 2019. "European Elections Will Gauge the Power of Populism." Europe. *New York Times.* May 19.

19 John Baldoni. "Wanted: Millennials Who Can Think Critically." *Forbes.* https://www.forbes.com/sites/johnbaldoni/2018/05/16/wanted-millennials-who-can-think-critically/#597eeb085238. Accessed July 19, 2019.

20 "Faculty Unanimous in Frustrations about Critical Thinking." *The Critical Thinking Initiative.* https://www.thecriticalthinkinginitiative.org/the-critical-thinking-initiative-blog. Accessed July 19, 2019.

21 Timothy Snyder. *On Tyranny: Twenty Lessons from the Twentieth Century* (New York: Tim Duggan Books, 2017).

22 Nicholas G. Carr. *The Shallows: What the Internet Is Doing to Our Brains* (New York: W. W. Norton, 2010).

23 Hamby, Peter. 2018. "That Is What Power Looks Like: As Trump Prepares for 2020, Democrats are Losing the Only Fight That Matters." *Vanity Fair.* May 26. https://www.vanityfair.com/news/2018/05/democrats-are-losing-the-only-fight-that-matters

24 Justin Kruger and David Dunning. "Unskilled and Unaware of It: How Difficulties in Recognizing One's Own Incompetence Lead to Inflated Self-Assessments." *Journal of Personality and Social Psychology*, Vol. 77, No. 6 (1999): 121–34. Accessed July 19, 2019, https://pdfs.semanticscholar.org/e320/9ca64cbed9a441e55568797cbd3683cf7f8c.pdf.

25 Shahram Heshmat. "What Is Confirmation Bias? People Are Prone to Believe What They Want To Believe. *Psychology Today.* Accessed July 19, 2019. https://www.psychologytoday.com/us/blog/science-choice/201504/what-is-confirmation-bias.

26 "Migration and Climate Change." *UN Migration.* https://www.iom.int/migration-and-climate-change-0. Accessed July 20, 2019.

27 Hannah Ritchie and Max Roser. "$CO_2$ and Other Greenhouse Gas Emissions." *Our World in Data.*https://ourworldindata.org/co2-and-other-greenhouse-gas-emissions. Accessed July 20, 2019.

28 "UN Report: Nature's Dangerous Decline 'Unprecedented'; Species Extinction Rates 'Accelerating.'" *Sustainable Development.*https://www.un.org/sustainabledevelopment/blog/2019/05/nature-decline-unprecedented-report/. Accessed July 20, 2019.

29 Ibid.

30 Elizabeth Kolbert. *The Sixth Extinction: An Unnatural History* (New York: Picador, 2015).

31 Mujib Mashal. 2019. "India Heat Wave, Soaring Up to 123 Degrees, Has Killed at Least 36." Asia Pacific. *New York Times.* June 14. https://www.nytimes.com/2019/06/13/world/asia/india-heat-wave-deaths.html.

32 "Human Impact on the Reef." *Biodiversity and the Great Barrier Reef.*https://www.qm.qld.gov.au/microsites/biodiscovery/05human-impact/importance-of-coral-reefs.html. Accessed July 20, 2019.

33 David Naguib Pellow. *What Is Critical Environmental Justice?* (Cambridge, UK: Polity Press, 2017).

34 Michael Pollan. *Omnivore's Dilemma* (New York: Penguin Press, 2006).

35 Greg Cima. "FDA warns Micotil 300 is Dangerous." *JAVMA News.*https://www.avma.org/News/JAVMANews/Pages/171115j.aspx. Accessed July 20, 2019.

36 "Mad Cow Disease." *HealthLinkBC.*https://www.healthlinkbc.ca/health-topics/tu6533. Accessed July 20, 2019.

37 "Creutzfeldt-Jakob Disease Fact Sheet." *Patient and Caregiver Education.* https://www.ninds.nih.gov/Disorders/Patient-Caregiver-Education/Fact-Sheets/Creutzfeldt-Jakob-Disease-Fact-Sheet. Accessed July 20, 2019.

38 "Impacts of Pesticides on Our Health." *Pesticide Action Network.* www.pan-uk.org/health-effects-of-pesticides/. Accessed July 20, 2019.

39 Mae Wu, Dylan Atchley, Linda Greer, Sarah Janssen, Daniel Rosenberg and Jennifer Sass. "Dosed Without Prescription: Preventing Pharmaceutical Contamination of our Nation's Drinking Water." *NRDC.*https://www.nrdc.org/sites/default/files/hea_10012001a.pdf. Accessed July 20, 2019.

40 Diana R. H. Winters. "Everything You Need To Know about the Upcoming Farm Bill Debate." *Health Affairs.* https://www.healthaffairs.org/do/10.1377/hblog20180215.383921/full/. Accessed July 20, 2019.

41 Amy Mayer. "Paying Farmers Not To Farm? Not Exactly." *Harvest Public Media.* https://www.harvestpublicmedia.org/post/paying-farmers-not-farm-not-exactly. Accessed July 20, 2019.

42 Verlin Klinkenborg. 2012. "Did Farmers of the Past Know More Than We Do?" Sunday Review. *New York Times*. November 3. https://www.nytimes.com/2012/11/04/opinion/sunday/crop-rotation-and-the-future-of-farming.html

43 Adam Liptak. 2013. "Supreme Court Supports Monsanto in Seed Replication Case." Business. *New York Times*. May 13. https://www.nytimes.com/2013/05/14/business/monsanto-victorious-in-genetic-seed-case.html

44 "Corn and Other Feedgrains." *United States Department of Agriculture. Economic Research Service.* https://www.ers.usda.gov/topics/crops/corn-and-other-feedgrains/. Accessed July 20, 2019.

45 Gevan Behnke, Stacy Zuber, Cameron Pittelkow, Emerson Nafziger and Maria Villamil. "Long Term Study Shows Crop Rotation Decreases Greenhouse Gas Emissions." *Illinois Aces.* https://aces.illinois.edu/news/long-term-study-shows-crop-rotation-decreases-greenhouse-gas-emissions. Accessed July 20, 2019.

46 "Corn Planted Acreage Up 3 Percent from 2018; Corn Stocks Down 2 Percent from June Last Year." National Agricultural Statistics. *United States Department of Agriculture National Agricultural Statistics Service.* https://www.nass.usda.gov/Newsroom/2019/06-28-2019.phpates. Accessed July 20, 2019.

47 *Huffington Post.* "What the Government Got Wrong about Nutrition." https://www.huffpost.com/entry/usda-dietary-guidelines-diabetes_n_5635554. Accessed July 14, 2019.

48 "Bayer to Buy Monsanto, Creating a Massive Seeds and Pesticides Company; The Megamerger Is Likely to Face Intense Regulatory Scrutiny." *Scientific American.* https://www.scientificamerican.com/section/reuters/bayer-to-buy-monsanto-creating-a-massive-seeds-and-pesticides-company/. Accessed July 20, 2019.

49 Michael Pollan. *Omnivore's Dilemma* (New York: Penguin Press, 2006).

50 "Chickens Used for Food." *PETA Issues: Animals Are Not Ours.* https://www.peta.org/issues/animals-used-for-food/factory-farming/chickens/. Accessed July 20, 2019.

51 Felicity Lawrence. "If Consumers Knew How Farmed Chickens Were Raised, They Might Never Eat Their Meat Again." *Guardian.*https://www.theguardian.com/environment/2016/apr/24/real-cost-of-roast-chicken-animal-welfare-farms. Accessed July 20, 2019.

52 Peter Whoriskey and Rachel Siegal. "Cocoa's Child Laborers." *Washington Post*, https://www.washingtonpost.com/graphics/2019/business/hershey-nestle-mars-chocolate-child-labor-west-africa/?fbclid=IwAR3DNMgyqS2xxcLCPdntClvUfsChXX2QVmOaYHOge8yOdfKCfXfqcwjA8OE&noredirect=on&utm_term=.c83cfa6f094e. Accessed July 23, 2019.

53 Frances Moore Lappe. *Diet for a Small Planet* (New York: Ballantine Books, 1971).

54 James M. MacDonald, Robert A. Hoppe and Doris Newton. "Three Decades of Consolidation in U.S. Agriculture." *U.S. Department of Agriculture, Economic Research Service.* https://www.ers.usda.gov/webdocs/publications/88057/eib-189.pdf?v=0. Accessed July 20, 2019.

55 Jesse Colombo. "Here's Why More American Farms Are Going Bankrupt." *Forbes.*https://www.forbes.com/sites/jessecolombo/2018/11/29/heres-why-more-american-farms-are-going-bankrupt/#32aa63ac65a7. Accessed July 20, 2019.

# 2

# INTELLECTUAL COMPETENCE

## What is intellectual competence?

Intellectual competence requires that we take responsibility for educating ourselves. While many people seek information online, this does not automatically lead to intellectually competent ways of engaging information. It takes work and practice to gather reliable information, sort through what it means, determine why it is important—or why it is, perhaps, less important—in order to develop our understanding of an issue, a problem, or a question. Our understanding is no better than the information we have at our disposal, which is why intellectual competence requires that we learn how to determine the reliability of what we read. With reliable information in hand, we build our knowledge base in order to express with clarity what we know, how we know it, and why it matters. From here, our depth and breadth of understanding develops because, as we will see, when combined with critical thinking, intellectual competence is the first, most important step to higher order thinking that we call *critical awareness*.

Everything we have discussed so far involves the problem of thinking, and that we are inclined to think narrowly and in familiar ways. Generally speaking, we like to stick to what we know. We seek out those who speak our language and confirm our sense of the world. Our "discourse communities" help to normalize our beliefs. The larger a group becomes, the more "normal" it seems. How do we break out of the circular, or "solipsistic," thinking of our digital bubbles? Intellectual competence requires that we assume agency and responsibility over ourselves and what we think, and *how* we think. The first step is to take a bold step back and risk questioning everything.

Philosophers like Emmanuel Kant, David Hume, and Rene Descartes share an understanding about the nature of human knowledge and how we "know" things in the first place. They believe knowledge is founded on human intuition, that is, the "feel" for some idea that "rings true." Descartes referred to intuition as *pre-existing knowledge* gained through contemplation and rational thought. We knew things, somehow, by osmosis perhaps, and if we thought long and hard, we might "discover" what we always somehow knew deep down.

Similarly, Hume believed that it is the nature of the human mind to combine thoughts and ideas together and form explanatory thought maps that make sense of the world, although he cautioned that linking ideas together does not make them into "truth." There may in fact be a sizeable gap between the "map" of the world we create in our minds and the actual material conditions of reality. The associations our minds make, Hume warns, may be important, but unlike Descartes, our natural proclivity to link ideas does not necessarily lead to real knowledge.

During the late eighteenth century, Immanuel Kant proposed a moral theory similar to the New Testament's "Golden Rule," but based on reason: it made rational, practical, and moral sense to treat others the way we want to be treated. As a way of being with others in the world, Kant anticipated a kind of early form of "game theory." In "game theory," the best solution to social conflicts is the one in which both sides come away with a "win" rather than pursuing a competition based on scarcity, where there is a winner and loser. To see the world in this way, Kant explained, represents a key moment of intellectual growth, for it marks the moment of the human being's emergence from selfish isolation into a world of interdependence and connectedness.

To awaken intellectually requires that we first recognize that most people practice a form of thinking that tends towards solipsism, meaning that we trust only what we know, and listen to others only if they agree with what we believe. We do not question how we think, or what we think about, or why we think and behave in the ways that we do. Rather, we simply press on with our self-centered thinking. Solipsism in its most basic form is like living in a hall of mirrors. We can see only ourselves no matter which direction we look, and we use what we see in the mirror as evidence for what we already believe. The illusion is enough to persuade us that what we think is pretty much what *everybody* thinks: solipsistic thinking results in a seemingly reliable baseline sense of reality that does not need to be questioned—rather, it affirms itself. It is obvious. It is true.

The tendency towards solipsistic thinking combined with intensely misinformed digital bubbles is a recipe for extremism to proliferate, which correlates with the rise of digital culture and digital social practices. Solipsistic thinking relies on clichés and generalities, is prone to conspiracy theories, and is most likely informed by a relatively uniform social network ecosystem. We love memes because they say everything and they say nothing. They are a digital manifestation of our solipsistic tendencies. At its worst, solipsistic thinking leads to angry confidence and self-righteous narcissism. The solipsistic mind functions largely in an unreflective state, and when anxious our mind is often unable to slow the train of its thoughts, let alone discover a way to change tracks.

## Civic ignorance and the challenge of intellectual competence

According to available data for the United States, ignorance of basic knowledge in the general population is widespread. According to a 2017 University of Pennsylvania poll:[1]

- More than one in three Americans (37 percent) could not name a single right protected by the United States' Constitution's First Amendment.
- Only one in four Americans (26 percent) can name all three branches of their government. One in three (33 percent) cannot name any branch of government.
- A majority (53 percent) mistakenly believe the Constitution affords undocumented immigrants no rights.

In 2014 a study found that "42 percent of Americans think the Constitution explicitly states that 'the first language of the United States is English'; and 25 percent believe Christianity was established in the Constitution as the official government religion."[2] Neither is true. The study notes that, "only 40 percent of adults know that there are 100 senators in the U.S. Congress, while a great majority of Americans have no idea of when or by whom the Constitution was written. A 2010 Pew Research Center survey of American's knowledge of public affairs and politics revealed similar findings, namely that political literacy has been in rapid and continual descent since its high water mark of the 1950s.[3] Several factors have contributed to the decline in political literacy, including "collapses" of both the educational system and the journalism profession. We are losing our literacy along with our history.[4]

## Information literacy

Intellectual competence refers to our ability to engage with and make sense of the information circulating around us all the time. As we discussed in the first chapter, the sheer volume of information makes it difficult to focus while the rapid pace that information now comes at us is so fast and in such high volume that it requires us—if we want to try and keep up — to flit quickly and repeatedly from one thing to the next. We are training our minds to move laterally and shallowly across surfaces. Such habits of mind undermine intellectual competence and the potential for meta-cognition and critical thinking.

The challenge then is to develop the mind's latent abilities by practicing with the most ordinary of skills—like reading, writing, and arithmetic. Without some mastery of the most basic languages of the mind—like words and numbers—we cannot do intellectually competent work. What better place to practice than on the information we receive each day. But is it even possible to assess the quality and accuracy of what we see and take in each day? The very question strongly implies that the answer is yes. But in order to become self-consciously deliberate about information, its quality, its accuracy, its motive, and so on, means that we have to slow down and work the problem.

The difficulty in overcoming the Dunning-Kruger effect lies in the fact that while we are trying to overcome it we are also being conditioned *by* it. How can we find a way out of the Dunning-Kruger hall of mirrors? First, to become intellectually competent means to take responsibility for the information we consume and the choices we make.

The American Library Association defines information literacy as "a set of abilities requiring individuals to 'recognize when information is needed and have the ability to locate, evaluate, and use effectively the needed information,'" adding that, "Information literacy forms the basis for lifelong learning. It is common to all disciplines, to all learning environments, and to all levels of education. It enables learners to master content and extend their investigations, become more self-directed, and assume greater control over their own learning."[5]

Information literacy is essential for achieving intellectual competency. Information literacy can be organized around five basic sets of skills and practices identified by the American Library Association.[6]

1.  Selecting the problem or question: this first item requires that we become consciously aware thinkers—*aware* of how much time we spend thinking and focusing on a particular problem or inquiry. Beyond that, figuring out what the problem or question is, for us in a particular moment in time, will largely determine the types of information sources we must seek out in order to work the problem or answer the question.

2.  Locating and accessing the information related to the question or problem: gathering materials involves active engagement of our senses to capture the full range of information about a specific thing, or idea, including evidence that challenges our own views. Learning effective research methods is essential. Knowing how to identify the more obvious differences between reliable and unreliable sources of information goes a long way in establishing a reliable overview of what others have thought about the problem or question we are researching. We may also have to gather our own data first hand, which means we follow scientific research methods to evaluate the validity and reliability of new facts or find support for old ones.

3.  Evaluating the information's content and reliability: evaluation may mean a quantitative analysis, that is, our information is in the form of numbers and statistics that must be translated effectively into accessible information. Evaluation may also mean qualitative analysis, that is, interpretation of data that includes ethnographic research and case studies, to name a few. Developing knowledge of how both numbers and words work lies at the heart of intellectual competence, which requires both a quantitative and qualitative skill set. Scientific data, material facts, statistical tests, and all the rest that quantitative and qualitative data can provide mean nothing without rigorous analysis and the ability to interpret the results. Without language, facts would have no voice. With words and numbers working together, however, we have the skills necessary to make sense of, and then act in and on the world.

4.  Engaging with selected information appropriately as part of our own work: engagement means researching the topic in question, examining, developing understanding, talking about, writing about, and questioning assumptions and facts. This may be for self-satisfaction (the individual pursuit of clarity just because we are interested in knowing) or, often with others, problem-solving

or pursing social justice online, in print, verbally or otherwise. Engaging with information means to consult with and perhaps to join a larger conversation.

5.  Prescribing proper credit to information sources: while identifying our sources helps us to avoid problems with plagiarism, committing to citing our sources helps to hold ourselves accountable to intellectual integrity and how best to achieve it in our own work.

To take responsibility for the information we consume each day means to be able to determine relevant information compared to less relevant information, and this helps us to be able to discern the difference between reliable information and information that is unfounded, sloppy, incomplete, or worse, deliberately misleading. Intellectual competence is both a habit of mind and a set of skills that lead to the ability to "recognize when information is needed," access it, assess it, and use it appropriately.[7]

We should note too that to do work effectively with information—to ask the questions information literacy asks—is to make an important leap into meta-cognition. We are in effect thinking about our thinking. Meta-cognition comes in to play whenever we try and step outside of our situation in order to see it from an alternate perspective. Information literacy means, quite literally, that one must become literate in the languages of different "discourse communities." A discourse community is a group of people who share similar views and a similar way of expressing their views. Different communities engage in different discourses, and to join one of them we might need to learn the language, for some are highly technical, while others more casual and accessible, and still others may be defiantly extreme. All of this may sound like another way of labeling the digital "silos" we tend to live in, but some discourse communities are more meta-cognitively aware than others, and so they seek to correct themselves for error and inaccuracy.

While some of us may seek information first hand—like the scientist who decides to study the air she breathes in order to find out what it is—most of us will not have the ability, the time, or the resources to do first-hand observations, data collection, and analysis. Does this make us intellectually incompetent? Of course not. But to decide on important issues related to the actual material conditions of our lives we have to rely on what *others* have seen and measured first hand, *and trust their authority*. We should remember that intellectual competence requires that we trust in others—in their expertise, and in the evidence they have gathered, and in the scientific method by which their thinking is checked and confirmed—or denied—by others in their scientific discourse community. Few of us can re-confirm what scientists for centuries have proven about the material world—that it is round, for example. This is why information literacy is so important. If we do not know the difference between accuracy and error, we do not really know anything.

Despots, tyrants, and would-be authoritarians around the world have an aversion to an independent press, which can offer counterpoints to officially-sanctioned and self-serving information. Today, the notion of an independent press has given over to the rise of "fake news." Constitutional protections for the press can be helpful but not a guarantee of an independent and free press. Unfortunately the concentration of media ownership in fewer corporate hands has transformed the press into a minefield of ideological camps, committed more to their partisan ideals rather than the common benefit and wealth of all. The incessant attacks on the veracity of the press convince many citizens that the media system is rigged against certain political leaders, certain social movements, certain public crises, and sometimes the public at large.

In Europe and the Americas, these trends are particularly noticeable. Powerful elites seek to ensure their positions directly or through surrogates by creating or acquiring television and radio stations along with traditional newspapers, all in order to dominate the information industries in their respective countries. In the United States, a self-styled bastion of free speech and a free press, six corporations control 90 percent of all news and entertainment media, including publishing houses, internet utilities, and video game developers. Even and especially the software platforms that underlie social networks are imagined, constructed, and deployed by a small, elite group of computer and internet giants.[8]

In a world dominated by corporate media, interests that are often working hand in glove with those in political power, the danger in not engaging in critical thinking cannot be overstated. In countries all over the world societies are forced to embrace political authoritarianism that threatens to block, up-end, and overturn fundamental principles and practices of social justice.

One example of the threat to an independent press is the case of Sinclair Media Group and TV stations across the United States. In 2018 the Sinclair Broadcast Group, valued at about $600 million (a tiny percentage of any of the Big Six), controlled 193 television stations across the US and was seeking to purchase more, to become the largest broadcaster in the country. Sinclair sent all of its television stations a script that required the news anchors to read it verbatim during television news broadcasts:

Text of Sinclair script, read by local stations' newscasters:

UNIDENTIFIED REPORTER #1: The sharing of bias and false news has become all too common on social media.

UNIDENTIFIED REPORTER #2: On social media. And more alarming, some media outlets publish these same fake …

UNIDENTIFIED REPORTER #3: Publish these same fake stories without checking facts first.

UNIDENTIFIED REPORTER #4: Unfortunately, some members of the media use their …

UNIDENTIFIED REPORTER #5: Use their platforms to push their own personal bias and agenda to control …

UNIDENTIFIED REPORTER #5 AND UNIDENTIFIED REPORTER #6: To control exactly what people think.

UNIDENTIFIED REPORTER #7: And this is extremely dangerous to our democracy.

UNIDENTIFIED REPORTER #5: This is extremely dangerous to our democracy.

**TABLE 2.1** The Big Six media corporations (2018)

| | Total assets (rounded, in billions) | Electronic media owned (examples) | Print media owned (examples) |
|---|---|---|---|
| Comcast | 148 | NBC, Syfy, Hulu, Comcast Network and Xfinity (Internet), Weather Channel, Telemundo, Universal, DreamWorks Classics, SNY | (Investments but no completely owned publishers) |
| Disney | 88 | A&E, ABC, ESPN, History, Lifeline, Lucas, Pixar, Disney, Marvel Studios, GameStar, Twenty-First Century Fox | Disney Press, ESPN Books, Hyperion, Marvel Comics, Ultimate Comics |
| TimeWarner | 61 | CNN, Hulu★, Cinemax, HBO, Turner, Warner | Time, Life |
| News Corp | 56 | Fox, National Geographic, Voyage, YES, SUN | Wall Street Journal, Barron's, HarperCollins, Modern Publishing, SmartMoney |
| National Amusements | 43 | BET, CBS, MTV, Nickelodeon, Paramount, Showcase, Showtime, Spike, VIACOM, CNet | Pocket Books, Simon & Schuster |
| SONY | 34 | SONY, STARZ, TRUE, TriStar | SONY |
| Total | 430† | 90% | |

Note:
†Wealthier than 168 of 194 international economies in 2018 (countries and territories), according to the International Monetary Fund: https://www.webpagefx.com/data/the-6-companies-that-own-almost-all-media/; http://statisticstimes.com/economy/countries-by-projected-gdp.php

UNIDENTIFIED REPORTER #4: This is extremely dangerous to our democracy.[9]What is the issue? According to industry standards, Sinclair violated the journalistic integrity of its newscasters by forcing them to read a statement as "news" that was, in fact, promotional, by hiding the information about the source of the statement. The Federal Communications Commission had earlier fined Sinclair $13.3 million in 2017 for running over 1,700 commercials disguised as news stories in news broadcasts. They all failed to reveal that material they promoted as news was actually editorial commentary designed to portray Sinclair as honest, and other news outlets as "fake news" peddlers. Sinclair embedded its political commercials within its own news broadcasts across all of its television stations over a six-month period.

The point here is to offer one well-documented example of the ways in which wealth and power often come to play a supersized role in the information we consume each day. The path to becoming a fully competent adult begins with taking responsibility for our growth as intellectual beings. It is key to an individual's development of the life cycle, especially if we are to live to our fullest potentials.[10] To achieve intellectual competence requires practice and mental rigor. Intellectual competence represents that foundation for successfully negotiating the stages of human growth and development identified by experts like Maslow and Chickering. Consider the possibility that complacency is a symptom of intellectual incompetence.

Social networking platforms have launched global campaigns to combat "fake news" and the influence of "troll farms," even as they have been subjected to public and political scrutiny for publicizing a wide-range of social, cultural, and political misinformation and disinformation. In newspapers around the US in May 2018, Facebook listed ten steps people can take to protect themselves from misinformation across all platforms, analog and digital. When reading or consuming information, Facebook asks us to:

- Be skeptical of headlines: headlines are often misleading, and online users often respond only to headlines without reading the entire article.
- Look closely at the link (url). Who is the web source of this information?
- Investigate the source if you have any doubts about it.
- Watch for bad grammar: it helps to know grammatically correct English, whether you choose to use it or not. Misspellings and awkward wordings are correlated with scams.
- Consider the photo: is it too good to be true? It may be.
- Inspect the dates and be sure you understand the timeline in question.
- Check the evidence: who are the experts? Are they named?
- Compare the story to other stories that address the same issue.
- To ask: is it a joke? Is it satire? Is it irony?
- To be willing to accept that what we thought was true was really an outright lie.[11]

Facebook's ten points ask us to question everything. Some news is fake, or propaganda, or simply "click bait." Some news is accurate, but others have labeled it fake for political purposes. It is crucial that we learn the difference.[12] In short, Facebook teaches us to test everything and to trust nothing when it comes to the information we consume on all sorts of social networks.

In 2017, the Pew Research Center and the Imagining the Internet Center at Elon University surveyed a sample of professionals involved in the information industry, with a question about "fake news":[13]

In the next ten years, will trusted methods emerge to block false narratives and allow the most accurate information to prevail in the overall information ecosystem? Or will the quality and veracity of information online deteriorate due to the spread of unreliable, sometimes even dangerous, socially destabilizing ideas?

According to Pew's report, of the 1,116 respondents, just over half believed that our information ecosystem *will not* improve, while 49 percent said the information environment *will* improve. The 51 percent who voted that the information ecosystem will not improve cited two reasons: first, because the fake news ecosystem preys on our darkest instincts and has a parasitic relationship to our "primal quest for success and power." These pessimists "predicted that manipulative actors will use new digital tools to take advantage of our inbred preference for comfort and convenience and our craving for the answers we find in reinforcing echo chambers." Second, "our brains are not wired to contend with the pace of technological change: the rising speed, reach, and efficiencies of the internet and emerging online applications will magnify these human tendencies and that technology-based solutions will not be able to overcome them."

Almost half, on the other hand, remain optimistic about our ability to manage the information ecosystem, generally for two reasons: first, they articulated confidence in engineers to develop technology that solves the problems that earlier technology created. To them, "the rising speed, reach, and efficiencies of the internet, apps, and platforms can be harnessed to rein in fake news and misinformation campaigns." Second, they believe in human nature, maintaining that in the end we always "come together and fix problems." The examples they used are these: In the end, people have adapted to change and survived; we will find a way to enhance the information environment for the public good; and "better information literacy among citizens will enable people to judge the veracity of material content and eventually raise the tone of discourse."[14]

What does it mean that the experts were almost evenly split on their predictions? Will it all work out because: new software, new algorithms, and new technology will protect us from ourselves? Or on the other hand, does the internet represent the most powerful tool ever invented to manipulate and control whole populations? Where is the information juggernaut taking us?

Information literacy helps us to understand that to comprehend, analyze, and synthesize information effectively and competently, we must deliberately test what we think we know. By actively seeking out alternate perspectives we identify our blind spots. Meanwhile we must be mindful that any and all information we depend upon to inform us and our beliefs must be as accurate and reliable as possible.

Most of us have mastered the skills required to access internet search engines. In fact, access is all too easy, which means that the information we find is often of unequal validity. How do we determine whether or not to believe what we read, or see, or hear? The simple fact is that some sources of information are more accurate than others; some recycle incomplete or inaccurate information as established fact, while other purveyors promote deliberately misleading stories designed to mislead for different reasons, from satire and entertainment to political propaganda, and even a kind of "psy ops," that is, psychological operations meant to weaken an enemy's resolve. In this case, everyone is the enemy, anyone is a potential target, and should someone take an interest in our presence in the social network ecosystem, trolls, bot farms, and frustrated users may all decide to make us their next target.

Information has never been more available—and never more dangerous. More users read more information today than we ever have before. It is a remarkable explosion of literacy, language, and writing, albeit always determined by the internet platform providers, by its governing software, by its primary algorithms. In fact, according to the World Economic Forum, no one and everyone owns the internet and the content on it: it is a vast "network of networks" owned by individuals and corporations and linked together by servers in countries with varying laws and regulations.[15] The same article warns of the dangers ahead: Joseph Nye, professor at the Harvard Kennedy School of Government, states that a worst-case scenario is possible, and that is the abundance of "malicious actions of criminals and the political controls imposed by governments would cause people to lose trust in the Internet ..."

Keep in mind that almost everything on the internet is in some way or another compromised. While once information was free, today we pay for it by submitting ourselves to advertising, and by accepting a certain amount of surveillance while online, which for most of us is a steady constant. One must search library data bases from colleges and universities and some .org sites in order to avoid the kinds of advertising that targets us while we use a .com search engine.

As we experience the internet today, advertising is a complex and crucial part of it. Its growth was based on learning how to advertise online that made the fortunes of some of today's billionaire class. Advertising had to become smarter—it did and continues to do so. It had to follow us, track our online habits, and react accordingly. In the end, internet advertising anticipates our needs by interpreting our behavior online, so that the internet would, first and foremost, exist to service consumer capitalism.

Targeted advertising is facilitated by sophisticated data mining of our daily activities. While some cell phone transmissions can be turned off, smart cars cannot. According to a 2019 *New York Times* report, "(T)oday's cars are equipped with telematics, in the form of an always-on wireless transmitter that constantly sends vehicle performance and maintenance data to the manufacturer. Modern cars collect as much as 25 gigabytes of data per hour." The data represent a $750 billion industry predicted by 2030, in which car manufacturers plan to "monetize" by selling to vendors, such as insurance companies and advertising businesses. The result will be highly personalized messaging that will appear creditable and compelling, and may include political information and misinformation. Disconcertingly, these not-too-futuristic opportunities to make money and even to manipulate elections are not far down the road, making it much more lethal to sustain democratic societies.

Beyond advertising and the toll it takes on credibility and reliability of information, other factors may compromise the reliability and validity of what we read and hear. Pharmaceutical companies routinely test (or pay for selected others to test) the drugs they develop for efficacy and safety. Such a practice is a kind of solipsistic, self-confirming feedback loop. Pharmaceutical corporations are ever eager to bring new medications to market. They invested hundreds of millions, or in the case of Viagra, billions of dollars, to find a way to get a pill designed to treat hypertension and angina on the market for an entirely different use—erectile dysfunction.[16] As both manufacturers and scientific testers of their own products, they have a dangerous conflict of interest in the field of medical technology, including pharmaceuticals. They make money only as long as we are ill, believe ourselves to be ill, and are convinced that their remedies will make us better. According to Kaiser Health News (2019) and reported by NBC, spending on health care marketing doubled between 1997 and 2016 to $30 billion per year, and all the while critics contend that viewers and "patients are often misled by ads that advocate high priced drugs."[17]

Even university-based research can be tainted by connections to big money. For example, in 2018 the US National Institutes of Health withdrew funding from a Harvard University study of alcohol's effects on human health because the research was mostly funded by breweries and distilleries. According to the study's data, there were positive health consequences associated with the moderate consumption of alcohol.[18]

Fact checking is important, and one common site that is routinely used for definitions and brief histories of information is Wikipedia. However, because it is not rigorously peer reviewed by other experts tasked with verifying the validity of its content, most scholars view Wikipedia with skepticism. Even so, other experts report that Wikipedia has now become more reliable than the Encyclopedia Britannica. Such a scenario underscores the challenge of developing our information literacy and intellectual competence in today's crowd-sourced world of information.

Internet sites with addresses that end in .edu or .gov rather than .com or .net suggest that the information presented is "not for profit" and as such is inherently more reliable. But even peer-reviewed information that we find from authoritative sources should be confirmed by visiting more than one respected source. Always check the time-stamp of what you read online. And take note of the experts they quote and the sources they cite for their data.

The internet's information ecosystem is well-populated by professional-appearing but partisan sites operated as "think-tanks," like the Heritage Foundation or the Brookings Institution. Some are highly respected by experts in the field, while others less so.[19] A quick search on any organization's "about us" link will provide information about who funds the organization. Digging a little deeper has never been easier or more necessary. We should take a few minutes to cross reference the citations we find and the authors who are the "main experts" cited by doing another internet search. If we find on an internet source's main page a branded advertisement, or if it identifies its financial sponsor, that means we are in the world of "for profit" information. Our curiosity about the subject in question is for sale, and advertisers are paying web sites to put their ads in front of us.

Meanwhile, traditional print journalism continues to collapse. Fewer and fewer newspapers exist, and the ones that do are thinner, with fewer locally-sourced stories and more reprints from national services like Associated Press. The print media has become more subject to ownership by large conglomerates, such as Sinclair and the Big Six, as discussed above, and they have been put under increasing financial pressure to keep their costs low because people expect their news to be "free" and always updated. The daily independent local newspaper is from a bygone era when we had to pay daily for the news. Fewer subscriptions mean fewer advertisers. All of this results in costing too much to print the news these days. Top-drawer city, regional, and national newspapers must compete with cable, electronic, and conglomerate-owned news outlets.

The information ecosystem as it is now poses serious challenges to intellectually competent thinking: if anyone can post anything, or pose as a doctor, or falsify studies, or it is a bot, or a troll, just whom or what can we trust? We have to remain skeptical. Are we being manipulated? Is the information part of a confirmation-bias bubble that we have inadvertently entered? How do we weigh one message against another and decide what to believe? Without intellectual competence, we can be easily stymied and misled.

Ultimately, intellectual competence strives for an understanding of an issue, a problem, or a question that leads to *clarity* in language, *reliability* of information, *depth* and *breadth* of understanding and a clear sense of the *significance* of what is at stake.[20]

The intellectually competent person:

- knows how the government works, how decisions are made, how laws are passed, and how citizens can participate in their society.
- knows how to read a map and can locate major land groups, global hemispheres, north and south poles, major oceans, major countries, and major cities.
- knows how to read, write, and communicate effectively.
- knows how to use basic mathematics, read charts and graphs, understand fractions and percentages, and can articulate the difference between basic statistical terms.
- knows how to discern reliable from unreliable sources of information on the internet.
- knows how to reason to a conclusion based upon evidence.
- knows how to learn and takes responsibility for continued (i.e., lifelong) learning.

## Beginning research

- Establish an "information basecamp," that is, a reliable place from which to begin your climb. But how do you know the difference between reliable and unreliable information at the beginning? See what the internet recommends for general introductions to the topic, question, problem, or issue in question.
- Once you find reliable introductory information, read diligently. Keep a file of your research in the form of notes, websites, quotes from experts, and bibliographic information.
- Read as much as possible. Reading helps us develop a deeper vocabulary, a wider and more detailed understanding of history, and the more specialized language of the topic we are researching.
- Read what the experts are reading.
- Once you have a bit more knowledge about your topic, question, issue, or problem, refine your search with more precise search terms gained from your beginning research and dig a little deeper.
- Keep reading.

## The need for evidence

The first challenge of intellectual competency lies in understanding the enormity of the task. Consider that if the popular news media dutifully reports what corporate billionaires want people to hear about day-to-day, then we have been put at risk of losing our ability to work and think on behalf of our own best interest. We unknowingly serve corporate masters who seek only the maintenance of the status quo. What if the status quo is socially unjust? Or what if it puts the environment—and the human species itself—at risk?

It is not uncommon to hear people say something like "the system is rigged." With software engineers and algorithms determining so much of our communication and contact with others (and ourselves) it is not hard to understand how most people feel that somehow the system is rigged, precisely as populist politicians have often claimed in their stump speeches. In this condition, we let others think, interpret, and articulate the world for us because we feel powerless and frustrated in the face of a system that is pre-arranged to favor select social and economic groups.[21]

The popularity of conspiracy theories suggests people are, on some level, hungry for knowledge and understanding but lack the intellectual discipline to distinguish information from propaganda, truth from lies. Conspiracy theories rely on the belief that nothing in the world happens by accident, that nothing appears on the surface as it really is, and that every phenomenon is somehow connected. The end result is that, in an effort to explain what we do not understand, we concoct elaborate explanations based on reasoning and evidence that do not stand up to the standards of intellectual competence. The problem is that we do not realize this important point. In fact, conspiracy theories often reject any evidence that exists against them by calling it part of the conspiracy. Such an argument renders it impossible to prove a conspiracy theory as either true *or* false because the standard of reason and evidence has been abandoned. As a result, the truth of any conspiracy theory is really a matter of faith rather than of evidence.

Paranoia correlates closely with conspiratorial thinking, both of which are features of the narcissistic personality. The prevalence of conspiracy theories today points to what may easily be understood as a reasonable and legitimate distrust of authority along with a need to question the nature of things. Surely the difference between a scientific fact and a conspiracy theory hinges upon the issue of evidence. Conspiracy theories claim powerful forces are at work to achieve their aims while simultaneously engaged in cover-ups of their activities, and because the evidence is always incomplete, they cannot ever meet a deductive or even an inductive level of validity. If we grasp after an explanation—no matter how unsupported by evidence it is—we indulge our desperation and leave our reason to the wayside. In the end we become caricatures of ourselves, indulging in ideas and behaviors that are, at root, anti-intellectual, anti-science, and anti-life.

The enthusiasm with which many conspiracy theories are embraced is evidence of how desperately people want to understand the world around them, yet handicapped as they are, become duped by incompetent thinking with unreliable information.

What is the difference between these popular beliefs? Which qualify as conspiracy theories, which may be true?

- The government collaborates with Extraterrestrials, who secretly run the world.
- Electricity rates are rigged by corporate fat cats.
- Apollo 11 never landed on the moon.
- Health care in the United States is rigged by greedy, conspiring corporations.
- Chemtrails from airplanes control the weather.
- There are Extraterrestrials living with Nazis in the South Pole.
- The water we drink carries mind-control chemicals.
- The CIA killed John F. Kennedy.
- The Earth is flat.

How can we tell the difference between "conspiracy theory" events and legitimate explanations? Consider that over a third of U.S. citizens believe that global warming is a hoax while fully half of Americans believe in some sort of conspiracy theory.[22]

Just as complacency is a symptom of intellectual incompetence, so too is a mind prone to conspiracy theory. A belief in a conspiracy theory is often supported by an enthusiastic engagement with the "research" that "proves" the conspiracy theory while simultaneously dismissing all other evidence to the contrary. The belief in conspiracy theory as a symptom suggests that behind it lies an intellectual hunger, a desire to get to the bottom of an issue, and all inquiry begins here. Along with this hunger, we might feel a shared sense that the system is somehow rigged or manipulated, and that traditional discourse communities are deceived, or compromised, and so dispense misinformation in order to mislead. Along with this hunger and skepticism, however, goes a significant degree of intellectual *in*competence so that the mind willing to engage will also be easily mislead.

While we might explore how we *feel* in relation to a conspiracy theory we subscribe to, we might also use a belief as an opportunity to explore how we know what we know, and whether or not we should reconsider our beliefs and redirect our cognitive efforts to something more intellectually competent. Conspiracy theories depend on a fundamental misunderstanding of the difference between two related, but different ideas that are often routinely confused for one another. For example, it is important to know the difference between *correlation* and *causation*.

A causal relationship exists between two events when, as the result of an action, a second action or event is directly effected; the effects observed in the second event depend upon the action of the first event and so were "caused" by it. The first effect, referred to as the independent variable, can predict the outcome, referred to as the dependent variable: this is a *causal* relationship. On the other hand, when two events that appear to occur in sequence, near one another, perhaps influencing one another, but cannot be determined if the independent variable caused the dependent variable, or simply arose simultaneously, then we consider the two events "correlated."

*Correlation* means a relationship between two or more phenomena, but not a causal, determining influence of one over another. Some pairs of correlated events are actually caused by a third event that precedes both, or a mediating event that links the first event to the variable it is correlated with. At other times the apparent correlation is spurious, that is, an example of a random occurrence that has no significance whatsoever. There are three criteria for establishing cause and effect: an association or correlation; time ordering, i.e. the independent variable must come before the dependent variable; and non-spuriousness, that is, no other extraneous variable can better explain the causal connection between the independent and dependent variables.

A causal relationship between two events is an example of "cause and effect." Think of a billiard ball striking another ball and sending it across the pool table. The first ball was a cause, the second ball's motion the effect. But note also how almost every cause is also an effect. In other words, how did the first billiard ball come to be in motion? A pool cue stick struck it and set it in motion. In this sense then the pool cue was the cause, and the first ball's motion an effect.

Correlation leaves open the question of whether there was a definitive "cause and effect" relationship between two events. Some funny correlational examples found in basic statistics classes are: Margarine appears to cause divorce; US spending on science, space and technology is linked to suicide by hanging and strangulation; ice cream sales are associated with violent murder; and per capita cheese consumption is correlated with the number of civil engineering doctorates awarded. With such considerations in mind, scientists must work very hard to prove that another variable may be the missing link to get to cause and effect. In the example of ice cream sales and violent murder, the missing link is the time of year. The data show that the strong connection between ice cream sales and violent murder can both be explained by summer time, but the problem remains to find other explanations that explain the apparent causal relationship.[23]

Needless to say, scientists must design their research very carefully to discover hidden variables, weeding out bias, circular reasoning, and self-fulfilling prophecies. They also must be very careful not to overstate their results and conclusions.

Illusions of causality occur when we develop the belief that there is a causal connection between two events that are actually unrelated, likely the case with ice cream sales and violent murders. Such deceptions have been proposed to lie beneath pseudoscience, conspiracy theories, magic, and superstitious thinking, which in turn can lead to grievous consequences to our health, finances, and overall well-being.[24] On the other hand, scientific thinking can destroy our cognitive biases and is the best possible safeguard against such illusions of causality, but it does not come intuitively and must be vigorously studied.

According to Douglas, Sutton, and Cichocka in their article, "The Psychology of Conspiracy Theories," the less curious we are about how cause and effect works, the more likely we are to believe in conspiracy theories.[25] An understanding of cause and effect, along with the limits of correlation, can help us break through the habits of mind prone to narcissism and wishful thinking. Understanding cause and effect means that we understand the nature of the relationship between two (or more) phenomena or observations, and whether they are causal, correlational, or neither. Correlations are often the first stepping stones toward proving or supporting a position, but more rigorous testing is required. Remember that sometimes the difference between correlation and causation is simply a matter of evidence. In other words, we may suspect causation between two events, but have no evidence, so at best we can claim a correlational relationship and then engage in more sophisticated testing. But once an observer discovers evidence, and others corroborate it, we can give support to such rigorous scientific investigation and its impact on its target of study.

The reverse of such rigorous testing is that, on the other hand, we are more likely to accept the postulates of pseudoscience, propaganda, and superstition wherever there is fear combined with ignorance, a lack of evidence, and poor-quality engagement with information that circulates in our digital bubble. We need outside perspectives in order to challenge our beliefs and submit them to critical scrutiny.

An important challenge to intellectual competence and becoming more fully functioning as cognitive beings is that conspiracy theory is a form of fantasy, offering a way to cope with uncertainties that might otherwise contradict our preferred beliefs and challenge our comfort zones. On the one hand we believe and claim to want to know how and why things happen, yet on the other hand, we seek safety in dismissive (and false) explanations. Consequently, we are easy pickings for peddlers of conspiracy theories, who provide convenient alternatives to the rigors of intellectual discipline. We know something is happening, and we want to know what it is, sometimes quite desperately, and so we latch on to unsupportable explanations that simultaneously dismiss scientific evidence as "fake" or merely someone's "opinion." The way out of this intellectual cul-de-sac is education.

## When the dream becomes a nightmare

Politicians and potentates playing upon people's fear and ignorance is not a new phenomenon; it is, rather, a familiar tactic of social power that informs relations between rulers and their subjects. We use media, entertainment, and fantasy to normalize power relations, even when they work against our self-interest and the pursuit of basic human rights. Rarely, if ever, does such power show humility, or the possibility that they could be wrong, with their knowledge and beliefs about the world.

Fantasy represents a world in which an individual's choices are clear, challenges have meaning, and our human story is linked to some higher power that shapes our ends. To be reassured of such things, however, comes at a price: mass-market fantasy exists in the name of mass consumer markets with big money, and is designed to indoctrinate the young into a mass consumer society. We learn, via fantasy, how to live in the world. Our shared cultural fantasies—including our religions—try to make sense of the chaos and uncertainty of our human existence, including a shared belief that the world is meant to be organized around an endless list of "us versus them" binary conflicts that inform and structure every scale of our lives, from the family, to the community, to the global environment. While religion might teach its adherents to service their religion of choice—along with the culture that supports it—mass market fantasy's only job is in servicing a company's profit margin.

The danger of mistaking fantasy for reality is that it simultaneously serves as a justification for the ideological status quo even as it normalizes ever more new and intrusive degradations of human dignity. Fantasy simplifies. It serves as a screen so that the privileged no longer have to contemplate—let alone be aware of—the effects of power and the consequences of their privilege. In this state of mind the privileged may pursue their desires and maintain their identities unhindered by material or philosophical concerns.

## The greatest fantasy of all: us versus them

Evolutionary science tells us that genetically we are all one family. Our superficial differences are just that—superficial, and only apparent when misrecognizing our inherent interconnectedness as a species. In fact, there is no "race" according to many scientists. People have adapted to live all over the world, but we remain one species, differentiated by culture, but not by biology.[26]

Now consider the horrific genocide in Rwanda that happened between April and June of 1994. In 100 days, 800,000 mostly Tutsis were slaughtered by the hands of their fellow Rwandans, the Hutus. The genocide has its history in the country's colonization by Belgium, which finally relinquished power in 1962. All during this time and prior to the Belgian colonialization, the two ethnic groups intermarried, spoke the same language, shared the same traditions, and inhabited the same communities. However, in 1916 the Belgian colonists believed that the minority Tutsis were superior to the Hutus and started favoring them with trade deals, loans, and political favoritism. While the Tutsis enjoyed better jobs, educational and business opportunities with the colonists, resentment grew among the Hutu.

The original German colonizers of central Africa brought with them ideas about race and racial superiority long before they came to Rwanda. In Rwanda, however, the colonizers brought with them their ideology about "race" and used their observations of the people to confirm their own biases, a sense of superiority found in the German cultural tradition, especially in their Protestant understandings about race as they read in the Bible's Old Testament.

The conflict first began with European colonization of Africa—itself an extended act of domination and hegemony. When the Belgians were given the newly created country of Rwanda, they divided the population into three distinct groups. The Tutsi were the elite and amounted to 15 percent of the population. The Hutu and the Twa were the common masses, 85 percent of the population, and they were not allowed to own land, denied higher education, and could not work in government jobs. How did the Belgians originally determine who was who based on race in their new country? If you can believe it, they determined race by the size of an individual's nose, the color of their eyes, and their height and weight. To the Europeans the Tutsis had the desired characteristics and features, so they were labeled as the "superior" Rwandan. In this way the Tutsi were identified and made different from all the others, which with all of these artificial characteristics led to what many call Africa's Great War.

The Belgians gave the Hutu, Twa, and Tutsis identity cards to differentiate their race. The identity cards could have simply labeled everyone "Rwandan," but instead differentiation was determined by ethnicity and how they appeared "on face value." If you were tall, had a longer, thin nose, a certain eye color, and weighed "less," then you were officially classified a "Tutsi," and if you were shorter than some arbitrary average, then you became officially "Hutu." Despite inter-marrying and living and working alongside each other harmoniously for decades, it probably is not too difficult to determine why the Hutus came to deeply resent the status the Belgians had conferred upon the minority Tutsi population.

The build-up to the genocide was rationalized on the assumptions that somehow the Tutsis were superior to their Hutu countrymen and women. To the Belgians, they looked and acted "civilized" and "intelligent," all based on European standards. With the Belgians' help politically and economically, the Tutsis enjoyed prosperous business relationships with their European counterparts, in large part due to their new-found status.

So when the Belgians finally left Rwanda in 1962, the majority Hutu population challenged the status quo and regained control of the Rwandan government, blaming every political or economic crisis on the Tutsi regime. Their hold was fleeting, and as the economy worsened, Hutu President Juvenal Habyarimana began losing popularity and scapegoated the Tutsis. The Tutsi were the "other" that had infiltrated the Rwandan house and were no longer welcome. They were "cockroaches" that needed to be exterminated.

When the President Habyarimana's plane was shot down in April 1994, the scapegoating turned to genocide. Believing that the Tutsis were behind the plane crash that killed the president, the presidential guard immediately began a campaign of retribution and demanded that the Hutus kill their Tutsi neighbors, family members, and any Tutsi sympathizers. They believed that the only way to get the country back on track would be to completely exterminate the Tutsi population. Organized gangs of militias literally hacked their way through the countryside with machetes, or blew up people in churches, where they sought refuge from the slaughter. People accepted incentives such as food, money, and Tutsi land if they helped the Hutu militia to kill off the Tutsi population. Those who refused to help, on the other hand, were labelled Tutsi sympathizers and slaughtered.

Over 800,000 people died in the first 100 days. At one point, Tutsi rebels were able to regain power with the help of a well-disciplined army of exiled Tutsis who returned to Rwanda from Uganda to provide military support. This army drove the Hutu into the Democratic Republic of the Congo (then called Zaire) where many live today. The tables now turned, but this time it would be the new Tutsi-dominated government that would kill the Hutu. They even called themselves the *genocidaires*. Because the Tutsi government feared that the Hutus would regroup and return from the Democratic Republic of the Congo to finish what they had started, they engaged in border skirmishes to force them to immigrate and stay in the DRC.

Although the killing spree in Rwanda officially ended in 1994, the presence of Hutu militias in Democratic Republic of the Congo has led to years of conflict since the initial genocide. There have been an additional 5 million lives lost between 1994 and 2003, and many areas along the border between the two countries continue to be plagued by violence.[27]

In spite of these tragic outcomes, and many like it around the globe, the idea that some of us are similar and some of us different is central to the way we achieve a sense of identity; we define who we are as we acquire social belonging, first through family and family relationships, and later by our own efforts as we interact with others beyond our immediate family. When we join a church, a temple, a club, or some other social group, membership in that group is often based on group-created criteria. Some of those criteria serve to help distinguish club members from non-members. The need to belong creates *exclusivity* and *privilege*. We come to accept the idea that some belong while others do not as a basic part of the fabric of our cultural reality.

Often the price of our own community membership may demand that we "take sides" and see the world as a binary conflict between "us" and "them." The conflict of "otherness" has been exploited countless times, and today those who exploit the concept of "otherness" do so in order to foment exclusionary ideologies that normalize social practices that violate the human rights of others.

The alternative to close-minded, fear-based hatred is open-hearted engagement. Non-violence allows us to take on a difficult topic that invites discussion without the threat of fear. When we become less defensive, we can work with others with compassion and empathy. From here we have the chance to acknowledge the reasons for our steadfast opinions and beliefs.

Has a non-violent response to power ever worked? Has compassion ever stopped genocide? Research and find out. The approach invites reflection because it engages each person to step back, relax a little, and *think*. To do this effectively and mindfully, reflection requires a discipline of both mind and body. Our day-to-day values and feelings cause certain steadfast thought patterns to arise, and we can often get stuck in our habits of mind without realizing the long term impact that our "permanent" beliefs and values can have on our personal growth and development, our relationships with friends and family, and our community. We risk becoming lost in the closed maze of solipsistic thought. Trapped, we go around and around with little or no positive outcome when we get stuck like this, and our beliefs against "the other" remain polarized.

If we reach a conclusion *without evidence* or with evidence that is *unreliable* and based in feeling and not fact, we fail the demands of intellectual competency. Unfortunately emotion overwhelms reason and we carry on with the illusion of *knowing* in the form of angry words and policies meant to defend against or destroy our perceived enemy. Sorting our reliable information from superstition, fantasy, and wishful thinking does not come easily, and the consequences of enacting a delusion can be devastating.

In order to build reliable knowledge, that is patterns of events from which we can accurately predict recurrence under specified circumstances, such as time of year or with particular populations, we first repeatedly record apparent associations and then we try to construct theory that explains why these occurrences would be related, and in which direction (does A possibly cause B or maybe it is the other way around?).

Once we have a theory that can be rigorously tested, we set out to do just that: measure the patterns that would support or refute the theory. Meanwhile, we comb the literature about A and B, to see what others have found in their research, perhaps finding modifications of the theory. For example, maybe there needs to be a specific condition for A and B to have a causal connection, like only for middle income college educated women over 40 living in urban areas. The scientific method is demanding and often frustrating, but anything else falls short of knowledge-building, and allows for solipsistic thinking to go unrecognized.

## Ways of reasoning

What follows is a primer on the most basic elements of formal reasoning. It would be misleading in a discussion about intellectual competence to ignore deductive and inductive logic, for they inform some of our most basic thinking operations; recognizing them in our own thinking process allows for more precise and effective problem-solving.

Deductive reasoning, or a deductive argument, begins with a premise that is assumed to be true and the reasons to a conclusion using examples that are also offered as true. If the premise is true, and the examples that extend the premise are true, then the conclusion must be true. If, however, anyone of these stages of reason is in doubt, then the conclusion has not been proved and the argument is not valid.

The most famous example of deductive reasoning:

1.    All men are mortal.
2.    Socrates is a man.
3.    Socrates is mortal.

Note that deductive reasoning requires evidence that supports a foundation statement and second proposition. Both statements must be accurate, reliable, and true. Statement One is a global truism; Statement Two describes a member of the universe described in Statement One. Then Statement Three is irrefutable because it is based on both truisms, and presents no additional conditions. If this logical construct is interrupted, the third statement cannot be accepted as true.

Consider this example:

1.    All humans are mortal.
2.    My neighbor Mike, who voted for Brexit, is human.
3.    All humans voted for Brexit.

What is wrong with this "logical" reasoning? The answer is Statement Two specified one person, Mike, and left out everyone else. Then Statement Three made a global statement that included those excluded people. A correct Statement

Three would be: My neighbor Mike is human; voting for or against Brexit is irrelevant. Mike is mortal because he is human, and all humans are mortal.

Another way to summarize deductive reasoning is to build from the general to the specific: establish a truism about a large (general) population, then propose the existence of that realism for each (specific) member of the population. In contrast, inductive logic begins with specific case observations, and tries to extend those behaviors or properties to larger, more general, groups to which the observed person belongs.

It is not uncommon to confuse deductive reasoning with inductive reasoning. In inductive reasoning we reach a conclusion by extrapolating from specific phenomena some sort of general rule or explanation. Philosophers maintain that induction is a less certain form of reasoning because an inductive argument's conclusion can never be definitively proven. For example, the argument that left-handed people are inherently more religious, based on the observation that all my left-handed friends and relatives are more religious than the right-handed people I know, is a case of inductive reasoning. It is a broad generalization from specific observations. Inductive reasoning lacks definitive proof but sometimes offers a way to understand the relationship between discrete phenomenon and a general proposition. Inductive reasoning works hand in hand with arguments that seek to demonstrate correlation, but have difficulty establishing causation. In general, conspiracy theory relies on inductive reasoning.

While less certain than deductive reasoning, inductive reasoning can be very useful for developing insights and raising questions for inquiry although conclusions reached via inductive reasoning are always provisional and subject to revision as new evidence emerges. Even so, everyday thinking is marked by inductive reasoning. There is information, or data, which are analyzed, with conclusions drawn. But the data may change, new information emerge, and our conclusions must also change. Consider, for example, how almost all of us knows someone whose behavior we find inappropriate. Perhaps one of our neighbors is a single mom. She lives two streets over. She smokes cigarettes around her kids. Another neighbor, also two streets over, smokes cigarettes around her kids. It seems that the neighbors two streets over all smoke around their kids. The evidence seems to represent an entire group of people who act the same way. We decide that we do not like her, or that "type" of people who live two streets over. At its worst—and all too commonly—inductive reasoning justifies bias and prejudice based on "the evidence." In this way, prejudice often masquerades in the guise of reason.

Deductive reasoning refers to the process of building new understandings on the basis of empirically testable universal observations, moving from general truths to specific ones. For example, if all dogs begin life as puppies (universal truth), my adult dog was first a puppy (specific conclusion reached by the universal truth). A strong deductive statement is true by virtue of the universality of the premise (no exceptions) and the connection between the premise and the conclusion. We can also conclude that all adult dogs were once puppies, another universal truth that flows from the original premise.

A weaker deductive conclusion occurs when terms are poorly defined or the premise is not universally true. For example, "Canadians are really nice people; my Canadian colleague must be really nice." While the logic progresses from the general to the specific, the term "nice" is unclear and the premise does not explicitly include all Canadians.

Inductive reasoning applies logic from the specific to the general. For example, every dog I've ever seen has spots and short tails, therefore all dogs must have spots and short tails. Inductive logic comes in six varieties:

- Generalized inductive reasoning (the puppy-and-dog example, above) draws a conclusion from personal experience. "Every electric car I have seen is blue; all electric cars are probably blue."
- Statistical inductive reasoning draws a generalized conclusion based on specific situational statistics. For example, "80 percent of people reading this book believe in a Higher Power (specific situational data), therefore eight out of ten people in society probably believe in God" (general conclusion).
- Sample induction means that we draw a conclusion about one group based on a different group. As in the above example: "There are ten electric cars in this neighborhood and all are blue; therefore, the electric cars in all other neighborhoods are also blue."
- Analogous inductive reasoning draws a conclusion based on the shared qualities of two different groups. "My whole family likes chocolate. My cousin's family members probably all like chocolate, too."
- Predictive induction means to draw a conclusion based on a prediction made using a past example. "We visited this town last summer and all hot dog stands were shut down. When we visit again, there will probably be no hot dog stands open."
- Causal inference induction draws a conclusion based on the belief in a causal connection. "All the kittens in the pet store are black. I just caught a glimpse of a small black baby animal in the back of the store. It was probably a kitten."

Based on these observations, we would reasonably have more confidence in conclusions reached through deductive than inductive logical methods. But not all deductive processes result in reliable conclusions, as the example about "nice Canadians" illustrates. Yet, both methods have useful knowledge-building purposes because they direct our attention to possible correlational relationships which we can further test.

When thinking inductively, "a conclusion is either strong or weak, not right or wrong." We tend to use this type of reasoning everyday as we draw conclusions from experiences and then update our beliefs as required by new information. Inductive reasoning allows for insight and intuition to propose a possible conclusion. Superstition and inductive reasoning go hand-in-hand. Why? Because two unrelated things may be linked and thought to be causal, not by evidence but by wishful thinking. "Our world is not always as predictable as inductive reasoning suggests."[28]

If we employ inductive reasoning deliberately and with mindfulness, inductive reasoning helps us speculate about the larger community and society based upon anecdotal evidence and experience. It may be true that a specific situation actually does indicate a problem in the larger community. What might an addiction to nicotine and tobacco have to do with the bigger social picture? Are the neighbors who live two streets over and smoke in front of their children perpetrators or victims? Or both? Or neither?

Key to both deductive and inductive reasoning is the quality of the evidence upon which we build an argument. Without reliable premises (based on information and evidence), deductive reasoning fails to offer sound conclusions. On the other hand, without reliable, accurate information, inductive reasoning leads to conclusions that are virtually useless—and may not be based on evidence at all, but on our prejudices and biases.

## A few words about numbers

A discussion of information literacy and intellectual competence would not be complete without acknowledging that intellectual competence requires knowledge of both words and numbers. Even more than words, when numbers in the form of percentages, graphs, and charts appear online, or in the news, they are so frequently inaccurate and misleading that it would be easier for us to assume that they are all suspect and should not be taken at face value, and we would not be far from wrong. Mathematical literacy is at an all-time low for the majority of the consuming public.

Mathematical literacy is so important and represents our capacity to formulate, employ, and interpret information in a variety of contexts. It includes our ability to effectively manage and respond to information in diverse situations. Understanding numeracy is a significant part of intellectual competence, for when we are mathematically literate we are able to recognize the role that the language and skills associated with basic mathematics play in the world. Basic skill areas include addition, subtraction, multiplication and division of numbers. Understanding how basic mathematical functions operate helps us to develop our sense of reasonableness when encountering results. If something seems off, wrong, or wildly outside our sense of estimation and approximation, we should find out how the results were obtained and seek a second opinion, or perhaps do the math ourselves. This would include appropriate computational skills, perhaps some basic statistics, fundamentals of geometry, the ability to measure, to use a ruler, and to read and interpret tables, charts, and graphs.

Higher-order cognitive activities include logical reasoning and information processing. While a complete quantitative manual is far beyond the scope of this book, intellectual competence requires that we work to understand graphs, percentages, the significance of the terms "mean" versus "median," and what an "outlier" signifies in terms of statistical analysis. These are a few of the crucial building blocks for understanding quantitative information, and for raising pertinent questions when committing to sorting it all out.

## A quantitative problem

If we averaged the annual incomes of all the people sitting in a doctor's office waiting room, we would likely get something close to middle class, more or less.

Then suppose the richest person in town walks in. When you average in that person's income, the total group average will likely jump by several tens of thousands of dollars. Similarly, if a few people with no income walk in, they will lower the group average substantially. Thus, averages are often misrepresentations of a group's characteristics. Otherwise stated, a group's average score on any rating (like income, age, education and shoe size) will likely coincide with very few members of the group. Most people will be somewhat near the average but not on or adjacent to it, depending on how much variation there is in the group. Consider this when we try to determine the "average" person. According to math, the average person probably does not exist.

Two particular factors promote inaccuracy of averages: small sample size and outliers. Small samples are amenable to large instability of average scores. Our doctor's waiting room group's average income will jump much more if there are three or four patients in the room rather than fifteen or more. Understanding the data further, the super wealthy individuals in the doctor's waiting room may be outliers. Outliers are those sample members who are least like the rest of the group. Sometimes misrepresentation takes the form of a report's basing its results on outliers, not the main group. Sensationalizing a single individual's experience— perhaps misrepresenting it as typical, or at least illustrative—is quite common, but no less misleading. We always ask whether a highlighted case study (or example) is representative of the full population in question.

A third factor is the problem of including and accurately measuring members of minority groups. Often, outliers will include members of a minority that tend to be under-sampled. As consumers of numerical reports, we should be sensitive to the sample's accurate representation of the full population it claims to portray, especially how minority group members were included in a study and the degree to which they are similar or different from reported numbers.

Statisticians use "measures of dispersion" (i.e., "standard deviation") along with averages, to show how much or little the full sample comes close to its average. But often these statistics are too difficult to report in the news. As a result, dispersion often goes misreported or ignored in order to simplify the mathematics for the target audience.

Another way to summarize our waiting room group's income is to analyze the numbers in terms of the group median instead of group mean or average. To determine a median income, for example, we must order the group members' incomes from least to greatest. The income that falls in the exact middle of the rank-ordered list represents the median income. In this method, a very wealthy or a very poor member of the waiting room group does not change the median salary by much, if at all. While this may seem a good way to avoid outliers, medians are only a measure of a central tendency and do not tell us much about the precise value of what we need to understand and analyze. Neither can medians help us do some other mathematical calculations or statistical tests.

Reports that include numerical data frequently appear as graphs, charts, or other representations of the data. While data routinely demonstrate correlations, rarely do they prove causation in one easy graph. We would do well to approach any such claim with skepticism and questions. There are statistical tests for causation, but they require elaborate and precise methods. For this discussion of intellectual competency, it is sufficient to realize that correlation is a requirement for, but not equal to, causation.

---

**RESEARCH EXERCISE**

Access mainstream news outlets like the *New York Times*, the *Washington Post*, Fox News, CNN, among others, and find articles that depend upon graphs, numbers, or a simplified representations of numerical data. Does the article help you understand the numerical data? Does the report of numerical data make sense? Can you determine whether or not the numbers are reliable, and reliably presented?

---

## Resistance to change

Perhaps the most difficult challenge we face when pursuing intellectual competency is the anxiety we face when confronted with the prospect of change. Most people seem to prefer the way things are, rather than any great change, for fear of the unknown. According to experts, "our brains use the same algorithm and neural architecture to evaluate the opportunity to gain information, as it does to evaluate rewards like food or money."[29] Our biology, it seems, roots us in a survival mode in which we instinctually choose ignorance as a way of protecting ourselves from truly unwelcome news. According to Dr. Tali Sharot, professor of cognitive neuroscience in the Department of Experimental Psychology at University College London, "the pursuit of knowledge is a basic feature of human nature, however, in issues ranging from health to finance, people sometimes choose to remain ignorant." We tend to avoid the kind of knowledge that might change our minds, at least at first. We make our worlds from the stuff we think about, and so it makes a certain kind of sense. "People are motivated to seek information that can create positive beliefs and avoid information that can create negative beliefs, which can explain why people avoid medical screenings even in cases when those tests can save them."[30] Our fear distorts our reason. And as Shri Nisagadatta Maharaj, author, philosopher, and Indian spiritual teacher, once said, "To know that you are a prisoner of your mind, that you live in an imaginary world of your own creation, is the dawn of wisdom."[31]

This is as true for individuals as it is groups. Abdel-Ghany researched organizational behavior and listed sources of individual resistance to change in professional organizations:[32]

> Resentment of others, frustration in their day to day work, fear of others, feelings of failure, low motivation to the point of depression, a loss of curiosity and the desire to learn. In this frame of mind we prefer stability, steady habit and persistence. In order to pursue our path, we engage in selective perception, denying our own eyes

at times as we navigate uncertainty. Everyone is worried about getting fired, getting old and so we doubt ourselves and live in chronic insecurity.

The misery of the job is preferable to the uncertainty of the unknown. And from what amounts to a depressed point of view, we find it difficult to imagine anything different, or how such change could be possible.

First, we must know ourselves. It is possible to develop an understanding of ourselves by taking up a position outside of our own solipsistic bubbles—by testing our cognition. This process requires that we work to understand how cause and effect functions in our lives, similarly and differently from others, so that we might change for the better as a result of critical reflection. We must realize that we have the power to choose, based upon honest assessment of the evidence.

## Notes

1  "Americans Are Poorly Informed about Basic Constitutional Provisions." Annenberg Public Policy Center at the University of Pennsylvania. https://www.annenbergpublicp olicycenter.org/americans-are-poorly-informed-about-basic-constitutional-provisions/. Accessed May 1, 2019.
2  "America's Changing Religious Landscape." Pew Center Report. https://www.pew forum.org/2015/05/12/americas-changing-religious-landscape/. Accessed July 23, 2019
3  C. J. Werleman. "The Shocking Numbers: Americans Are Dangerously Ignorant on Politics. *Salon.* https://www.salon.com/2014/06/18/the_shocking_numbers_america ns_are_dangerously_ignorant_on_politics_partner/. Accessed July 23, 2019.
4  C. J.Werleman. "The Shocking Numbers: Americans Are Dangerously Ignorant On Politics." *Salon.* https://www.salon.com/2014/06/18/the_shocking_numbers_america ns_are_dangerously_ignorant_on_politics_partner/. Accessed May 12, 2019.
5  "Information Literacy Competency Standards for Higher Education." *American Library Association.* www.ala.org/Template.cfm?Section=Home&template=/ContentManagem ent/ContentDisplay.cfm&ContentID=33553. Accessed July 12, 2019.
6  Ibid.
7  Ibid.
8  "Media Conglomerates: The Big 6." *WebFX.* https://www.webpagefx.com/data/ the-6-companies-that-own-almost-all-media/.
9  David Folkenflik. "Sinclair Broadcast Group Forces Nearly 200 Station Anchors to Read Same Script." *National Public Radio.* https://www.npr.org/2018/04/02/598916366/ sinclair-broadcast-group-forces-nearly-200-station-anchors-to-read-same-scriptce. Accessed July 12, 2019.
10  The respected biologist and educational researcher Arthur Chickering theorized that we develop over a series of seven steps, which he called vectors. The first vector included three key areas: intellectual, manual and interpersonal. Taken together, his seven vectors are: intellectual development; learning to manage emotions; developing interdependence; pro- gressing toward mature relationships; establishing identity; developing purpose; and estab- lishing integrity. Taken from "Student Development Theory." *Weebly.com.* https:// studentdevelopmenttheory.weebly.com/chickering.html. Accessed July 12, 2019.
11  "Information Literacy Competency Standards for Higher Education." *American Library Association.* http://www.ala.org/Template.cfm?Section=Home&template=/ContentMa nagement/ContentDisplay.cfm&ContentID=33553. Accessed July 12, 2019.
12  Abrar Al-Heeti. "Facebook Will Fight Fake News with Real Newspaper Ads (and More)." *C/NET.* https://www.cnet.com/news/facebook-is-fighting-misinformation- with-news-literacy-campaign-help-from-researchers/. Accessed July 12, 2019.

13 "Elon's Imagining the Internet Center and Pew Research Center Examine On Line Trust." Elon University. https://www.elon.edu/e-net/Article/151247. Accessed July 23, 2019.

14 Janna Anderson and Lee Rainie. "The Future of Truth Online." *Pew Research Center.* www.pewinternet.org/2017/10/19/the-future-of-truth-and-misinformation-online/. Accessed July 12, 2019.

15 Nye, Joseph S. "Who Owns the Internet and Who Should Control It?" *World Economic Forum*, August 11, 2016. https://www.weforum.org/agenda/2016/08/who-owns-the-internet-and-who-should-control-it. Accessed July 23, 2019.

16 David Kushner. "How Viagra Went from a Medical Mistake to a $3 Billion Dollar a Year Industry." *Esquire.* https://www.esquire.com/lifestyle/health/a22627822/viagra-erectile-dysfunction-pills-history/. Accessed July 23, 2019.

17 Liz Szabo. "Health Care Industry Spends $30 Billion a Year on Marketing." *NBCNews.* www.nbcnews.com/health/health-news/health-care-industry-spends-30-billion-yea r-marketing-n956251. Accessed July 12, 2019.

18 Roni Caryn Rabin. "An 'Unbiased' Study Is Found to be Industry-Friendly." *New York Times.* June 19, 2018.

19 "The 50 Most Influential Think Tanks in the United States." *TheBestSchools.* https://thebestschools.org/features/most-influential-think-tanks/. Accessed July 12, 2019.

20 The Foundation for Critical Thinking. www.criticalthinking.org. Accessed July 12, 2019.

21 Heather Long. "71% of Americans Believe Economy Is Rigged." *CNN.* http://money.cnn.com/2016/06/28/news/economy/americans-believe-economy-is-rigged/index.html. Accessed July 12, 2019. Joseph E. Stiglitz. "The American Economy Is Rigged." *ScientificAmerican.* https://www.scientificamerican.com/article/the-american-economy-is-rigged/. Accessed July 12, 2019.

22 John Sides. "Fifty Percent of Americans Believe in Conspiracy Theory. Here's Why." *Washington Post.* https://www.washingtonpost.com/news/monkey-cage/wp/2015/02/19/fifty-percent-of-americans-believe-in-some-conspiracy-theory-heres-why/?noredir ect=on&utm_term=.952177169727. Accessed July 12, 2019.

23 Helena Matute, Fernando Blanco, Ion Yarritu, Marcos Díaz-Lago, Miguel A. Vadillo, and Itxaso Barberia. "Illusions of Causality: How They Bias Our Everyday Thinking and How They Could Be Reduced." *Frontiers in Psychology.* https://www.ncbi.nlm.nih.gov/pmc/articles/PMC4488611/. Accessed July 12, 2019.

24 Ibid.

25 Karen M. Doublas, Robbie M. Sutton, and Aledsandra Cichocka. "The Psychology of Conspiracy Theories." *Directions in Psychological Science.* https://journals.sagepub.com/doi/full/10.1177/0963721417718261. Accessed July 12, 2019.

26 Megan Gannon. "Race Is a Social Construct, Scientists Argue." *LiveScience.* www.scientificamerican.com/article/race-is-a-social-construct-scientists-argue. Accessed July 12, 2019.

27 "Congo Says Soldiers Killed in Border Skirmish with Rwanda." *Reuters.* https://www.reuters.com/article/us-congo-rwanda-violence/congo-says-soldiers-kille d-in-border-skirmish-with-rwanda-idUSKCN1FZ26H. Accessed July 13, 2019.

28 "Deductive vs Inductive Reasoning: Make Smarter Arguments, Better Decisions, and Stronger Conclusions." *Farnum Street.* https://fs.blog/2018/05/deductive-inductive-rea soning/. Accessed July 13, 2019.

29 University College London. "How Your Brain Decides Between Knowledge and Ignorance." *MedicalXpress.* https://medicalxpress.com/news/2018-06-brain-knowledge. html. Accessed July 13, 2018.

30 Ibid.

31 Josie Glausiusz. "Living in a Dream World." *Scientific American.* https://www.scientificamerican.com/article/living-in-an-imaginary-world/. Accessed July 1, 2019.

32 Mohamed Abdel-Ghany. "Readiness for Change, Change Beliefs and Resistance to Change of Extension Personnel in the New Valley Governorate about Mobile Extension." *Annals of Agricultural Sciences*, Vol. 59, No. 2, December 2014, 297–303.

# 3

# CRITICAL THINKING

## A note about critical thinking and faith

As we prepared this book, we often returned to the question of whether religious faith and critical thinking were compatible. Was it consistent for someone to be a critical thinker as well as a person of religious faith? Or are critical thinking and religious faith mutually exclusive? Statisticians tell us that nearly 80 percent of the world's population believes in a higher power,[1] so it is important to understand how faith and critical thinking can—and must—work together. Recall that religion offers a way of thinking about our lives in the form of truth that comes from beyond the material world, and that does not require evidence. The truth is discovered by revelation, not reason. As a result, the ideas in which we have faith cannot be empirically tested or proven. The nature of faith is to believe in things "not seen." Critical thinking, on the other hand, requires evidence-based reasoning that necessitates wide-eyed skepticism. Further, critical thinking requires that we test our reasoning process, our interpretations, our analysis, and our conclusions of what it all means, even by sharing it with researchers involved in similar investigations. From Chapter 2 remember that we are going for more than correlations—we are meticulously looking for logic and causality.

The problem with scientific truth, critics say, is that it is always an incomplete approximation of the truth, incomplete and full of gaps, which is why to believe in the scientific method and the truths it reveals requires a kind of "faith," perhaps not unlike theism. The problem with any religious belief is that the truth born from this dedication requires followers to accept the absolute, complete, and unchanging nature of its religious principles. The confidence that one's faith is the "only" legitimate faith has provided countless justifications for wars the world over, much suffering, and crimes against humanity, all in the name of a religious allegiance.

The twentieth-century American philosopher Brand Blanshard (1892–1987), whose father was a Congregational minister, offered this advice about scientific truth:

"Reality is a system and truth is the approximation of thought to reality."[2] He was critical of reductionist accounts of mind, for example, conspiracy theories, and argued that thought, the activity of the mind, must be aimed at truth. Blanchard spent his life vigorously testing and rejecting various psychological and philosophical theories and wrote extensively about the nature of logic, truth, and reason.[3] A lifelong explorer and writer on logical positivism, he attacked free thinking not grounded in science and philosophies of old. Although he was skeptical of religion, he was also sympathetic and adopted Quakerism for his spiritual path to a higher power.

Religious faith offers a way of seeing the world in immutable and ever-lasting terms. For critical thinking, on the other hand, the truth is a moving target dependent on cultural and historical frames of reference. It should be noted that some scientific truths remain fixed over time—the laws of aero-dynamics for example—but our understanding of them increases as we study the phenomenon, so in that way even fixed truths evolve and grow as our understanding evolves and grows. Social truths function similarly, but are often based not on evidence, but on tradition, nostalgia, or superstition. How else can we explain, for example, that in the past slavery was a popular prac-tice, and for others, human sacrifice was perfectly normal? At other times people accepted the need to burn so-called heretics at the stake. All of these practices were part of the normal functioning of what surely felt like stable and sustainable societies, particularly for the well-to-do members. Never-theless, there have been many deeply religious leaders who have proclaimed their religious faith while practicing critical thinking as part of their higher calling: Mahatma Gandhi, Martin Luther King, Jr., Mother Theresa, and the Dalai Lama, to name only a few.

While social justice implies a certain political sensibility, critical thinking (like faith) is not necessarily in need of any political or social agenda. Critical thinking skills can be used to feed the hungry and care for this sick just as well as they can be used to build advanced weapons systems. For critical thinking to take an ethical direction, the critical thinker must choose the way of *human dignity* for self and others *as a fundamental birthright,* [4] more of which we will discuss in later chapters. For now, intellectual competence informed by empathy for others points the way to cultural competency, critical awareness, and social justice. It should be noted here that ethics of social justice are latent potentialities within critical thinking *and* religious faith. We accept that the two constellations can coexist. In spite of their differences, perhaps critical thinking and religious faith have more in common than we might first imagine.

## QUESTIONS FOR REFLECTION

- Do you practice a religion? Do your religious beliefs inform your social beliefs, your social practices, or your attitudes about race, gender, sex, or social class? Have you inherited any beliefs or practices that you have mixed feelings about?

## What do we know and how do we know it?

Many people in seats of social and cultural power have actively made up "alternative facts" in order to advance their agendas; for them, the truth in a "post-truth" world is whatever they say it is. Curiously, this is not far from the way the Catholic Church functioned in the Middle Ages. The pope decreed a truth, and so it became true. Our capacity for critical thinking has been at odds with the powers that be for a long time. Logical, independent and free-thinking skeptics ask too many questions and often resist demands for blind obedience. When we think critically, rigid superstitions begin to dissipate as sobering realities sink in.

Ordinary definitions of critical thinking usually describe it as a combination of abilities: understand information, synthesize it, and use discipline-based skills like reading, writing, and math to make sense of it. While it is true that critical thinking cannot proceed without these skills—the skills we call intellectual competence—critical thinking goes one step beyond intellectual competence. The one step beyond critical thinking is crucial: *meta-cognition*. Meta-cognition is the awareness of higher order thinking skills.

Without meta-cognition, we may believe that we understand what we analyze, or that we have synthesized what we know into a basic understanding of a social problem, but if we fail to step back from our reasoning and subject it to skeptical scrutiny, we may never realize that we are trapped in a solipsistic bubble of social injustice even while we congratulate ourselves for the efficiency of our slave trade, our human crematoriums of Nazi Germany, or our coal burning factories that pollute the air we breathe. The point is that injustice and suffering are made possible by understanding, analysis, and synthesis, yet such skills are not enough for critical thinking to emerge as critical awareness and in rigorous support of social justice.

Meta-cognition is the practice of analyzing how we think *after the fact* by way of reflection and, when necessary, self-correction. The question remains: according to what grading scale do we assess our thinking, our conclusions, and our actions? While meta-cognition offers a way to take a step back to reflect, do we necessarily "step-back" into an ethical dimension from which we then discover the errors of our ways? Or might meta-cognition—our capacity to think about our thinking—already be corrupted? If the goal is to improve our ability to recognize the ways in which we often repeat the same critical mistakes in different scenarios, we need to have a shared moral and ethical frame of reference. In this chapter, we focus on defining the kind of critical thinking demanded by the social sciences, the humanities, and beyond. In the following chapters we will take up how critical thinking, informed by reason and evidence, arrives at a moral and ethical frame of reference from which social justice can emerge.

Like all effective educational processes, critical thinking may introduce us for the first time to how little we actually know about what we thought we knew. The more we learn the more we realize how little we truly know. This process may stir up feelings of defensiveness as some of our cherished beliefs come into question. Our identifications with our communities, on line and in "real life" make us who we are, in large measure, so they can be difficult to question our involvement with them. Like clothing, we wear our identifications out for the world to see.

One cannot be in a constant state of questioning like this, but a critical inventory of the wardrobe of our minds is part of the way in which we develop our meta-cognitive capacities. Our goal is to see more clearly into the questions of who we are and how things came to be that way, and how things are evolving now. A critical thinking inventory develops meta-cognition by asking questions like:

- Of what am I absolutely certain?
- What are core beliefs I have about myself? Where and when did I learn them?
- What drives my personality?
- How do I feel? What do I *believe* about how I feel?
- Who is my community? What do I believe about others who are outside my community?
- What do I know about history? How does the present day fit in the larger historical continuum?
- Do I know how to think? Am I intellectually competent?
- Is the evidence conclusive? Are there other ways to analyze the evidence?
- What would someone from a different culture think about me?

According to Jeremey Donovan, author of several books on business leadership and marketing strategies, to think critically often means to participate in evidenced-based reasoning that sometimes falls short of the logical structures that make up competent thinking.[5] To grow, we need to both learn the "underlying grammar" of rational thought while working to open up the space within our own minds for meta-cognition to emerge. Working through our own personal inventory is one way by which we come to discover the degree to which we are the products of our environment, and that few, if any, of our thoughts are original or belong only to us.

It should be noted, too, that the habits of mind that are habitually routinized with internet use are diametrically opposed to the habits of mind essential to critical thinking. Misleading inductive reasoning is widespread. Arguments based on correlations are passed off as examples of rock-solid cause and effect logic. The relationship between an event as a cause, and the apparent consequences that result are overstated if not utterly fictionalized. So-called experts cite "alternative facts" to prove deductive conclusions, but the premises are demonstrably false. Indeed, the problem may be greater than we realize. The future, according to Aviv Ovadya, founder of the Thoughtful Technology Project, and who predicted the fake news crisis in the 2016 US presidential election, will arrive with a slew of slick, easy-to-use, and eventually seamless technological tools for manipulating perception and falsifying reality.[6] And this false reality already has a few terms coined — "reality apathy," "automated laser phishing," and "human puppets." Artificial intelligence may someday be able to help us discern correlations from causations, fact from fiction, but experts think such computing intelligence is decades away. If, or perhaps when, it arrives, this technology will bring with it its own set of social challenges related to social *in*justice. And so we are left to our own devices, that is, to our own cognitive capacities as the means to liberate our day-to-day thinking from delusion, fallacious reasoning, and the many social injustices that ignorance and fear perpetuate.

## Know thyself

Plato tells the story of the death of Socrates. He was condemned to die for leading young Greeks away from the religion of their fathers and into the light of critical inquiry, which for Socrates resulted in radical doubt and profound humility. He found that nobody really understood anything of what they believed, though they blithely went on as if they did. Rather than certainty, Socrates claimed that the only true wisdom was in knowing that we know nothing. All thinking, especially critical thinking, requires humility. Critical thinking may often lead to the conclusion that there are no absolutes, no fixed points or predetermined *forms* in the universe, and that no thing or form or idea exists outside and separate from human perception. Our thinking at best captures an approximation of reality, but not reality itself.

Rather than speculate on the unknowable, Socrates admonished his students to understand themselves. But what does it mean to "know thyself?" For this discussion it means to call into our conscious awareness our deepest memories. To explore the ways in which we came to be the person we are, speak the language we speak, believe the beliefs we hold, and live, work, eat, and play the way we do. By studying ourselves we come to liberate ourselves from ordinary, incompetent thinking. Topics for self-study include:

- How the mind and body produce awareness.
- How culture reinforces habitual behaviors.
- How feelings inform beliefs and behavior.
- How personal identity emerges from culture *as* culture.

If we fail to know ourselves we remain, in a word, asleep; in such a state we inevitably fail to recognize when leaders manipulate social discourse with fallacious reasoning, misrepresented information, and opinions offered as fact. We must reclaim our focus and make every effort to develop our capacity to concentrate.

In *Hyper-focus: How to Be More Productive in a World of Distraction*, Chris Bailey, a business-oriented productivity consultant, writes that there is no shortage of reasons our minds wander and we find focusing on cognitive tasks more and more difficult.[7] Unfortunately, our digital culture depends upon a mind that flits from task to task as it skims across surfaces. According to experts like Bailey, as ordinary and routine as our internet habits are today, not less than everything is at stake if we pursue them without recourse to deep focus activities. "If somebody were to exploit our attention economy and use the platforms that undergird it to distort the truth," warns Aviv Ovadya, "there are no real checks and balances to stop it."[8] Recent events have proven this to be a prescient warning: social network sites have been infiltrated by foreign actors seeking to destabilize western societies by passing themselves off as members of the very communities they seek to undermine.

Yet, rather than engaging in critical thinking to beat back this attack on our hearts and minds, we can be duped and ill-prepared by the digital platforms we use to help us confront the very real challenges we face to move forward. Critical thinking demands our full attention; we must develop our ability to focus by attending to the present moment. To attend to the present moment means that we confront those things that interrupt our attention—that have made focusing difficult, if not impossible, to think critically. Once identified, we may put these distractions in their place and can become masters of our own minds.

The psychologist and professor Mihaly Cszikszentmihalyi argues that the solution is to willfully immerse ourselves in the "total experience" of critical thinking.[9] To practice this requires us to choose a task that is roughly equal to our ability to complete it. Taking such a first step requires that we seek an understanding of our cognitive ability in general, and a measure of our knowledge in terms of a specific issue, problem, or question. The Dunning-Kruger effect tells us that we will probably overestimate our ability and our knowledge, meaning that we may have to admit that we are largely incompetent, at least at first. Critical thinking requires that we take the first steps toward meta-cognition from the first moment.

If we successfully pair our abilities with a task *we feel some stake in*, then we will likely engage more fully in our work. If, however, we feel put upon or coerced to do such work, our work will be less successful and far less enjoyable. When we commit to a task with what Cszikszentmihalyi calls "hyper-focus," we are more likely to succeed, and we will be more likely to surrender to "hyper-focus" if we feel some agency, or the capacity we have to act independently and mindfully, in choosing our work. While this may seem obvious, it bears repeating: we are more engaged and more productive when we fully and deeply focus on our work. The challenge is creating an environment conducive to work that allows us to avoid distraction. We need, as twentieth-century writer Virginia Woolf once wrote, "a room of one's own."

Cszikszentmihalyi maintains that we must self-consciously commit ourselves to a particular task—focus is not something that happens *to* us. Intentionality is the key. In productivity circles, intentionally committing to a task with hyper-focus is known as Parkinson's Law: with too much time on our hands, our work expands to fit into the time available to complete it. That is, small tasks that should take a couple of hours to complete may fill an entire workday if we have the time available.

Parkinson's Law works hand-in-hand with our tendency to procrastinate when we believe that we have plenty of time available to us with no firm timetable, except perhaps a final deadline looming in the distance. Procrastination thrives on distraction and in fact is another version of it. Note how the tools we use to distract ourselves enable us to procrastinate, and as we procrastinate we dig ever deeper into the tools that allow us to do it, sometimes avoiding the task for hours, days, weeks, even years. What gets in the way of focus and instead emerges as distraction and procrastination? When we feel anxiety and fear, perhaps frustration and a sense of inadequacy, we are more likely to let ourselves fall into a "time trap" that encourages mindlessness and delay.

What we lack is a learning process that serves as a kind of ladder that lifts us out of the hole we have dug for ourselves. Each rung is a self-conscious intention towards the task that always includes at the outset the intention to face our fears, befriend our anxiety, and accept the fact that everyone can feel inadequate and unequal to a new task.

Critical thinking, then, requires that we to take responsibility for our own minds and put them to work. Working a problem with the intention of focusing single-mindedly on the task will by its very nature call up the demons of distraction that haunt us. But just what are those demons? From a psychological perspective, our demons might best be understood as beliefs we have about ourselves fused to the feelings we experienced around the time (or times) we took in the lessons, formed our beliefs, and made the overall association, i.e., "I'm bad at math," or "I can't sing," or "I'm a terrible writer." Other beliefs underlie these, and can be debilitating, for example, "I'm an idiot," or "I'm worthless," or "I always fail." It should be noted we do not say these things to ourselves so much as we assume them to be true, and thus act accordingly to fulfill them.

## The importance of unlearning

Set about your task. There is an old saying that we should "serve the task, not the master." The master in this case is whatever idea we have of achieving, winning, losing, succeeding, failing, seeking attention, going viral, and so on. The task shorn of these agendas becomes a much simpler endeavor. It requires a process, that is, a way of going about things—we do not have to invent a new way, only adapt traditional ways to meet our own needs.

Begin each task by taking full responsibility for time. What is your history with time? Deadlines? Punctuality? For example, it is almost surely a challenge for young people raised in a school system that requires us to be awake and alert when science now tells us that we should have been sleeping a bit longer. What might we believe about our ability to do math if math class was at 8 a. m.? Consider that the problem may be bigger than any individual student's interest or ability. The adolescent brain is not really awake until 10 a.m.,[10] but we demand early morning classes to suit a system at odds with the young people it purportedly serves. The challenge going forward is to accept responsibility for our time, that is, for the present moment, as we experience it. Accept each day mindfully; start with a clear, focused intention. Get out of bed, breathe deeply, and drink a glass of water—your brain and body need hydration.[11] Intentionality means that we ask ourselves in no particular order:

- What am I doing today?
- How am I feeling right now?
- What do I need?
- What time is it?
- How long do I have before my next contact with work, people, the world at large?
- What should I be doing now in order to be ready for what is next?

The goal is to cultivate habits of mind so that intention, focus, and agency find their way into all of our activities. That said, this is not an argument to become a slave to our schedules. A timetable is not a prison house; it is a road map that outlines the selections we may face based upon the choices we make in the present.

Practically speaking we need periodic breaks from the internet and our devices when we have scheduled study or work time. We recommend reading books whenever possible rather than digitized text. Reading a book helps us to focus on one thing at a time. We might consider scheduling our screen time and set an hours-per-day limit for ourselves if only because our relationship to our screens has become something of an addiction. "The average adult spends close to 11 hours looking at a screen per day and checks their phone every 10 minutes."[12]

In such a screen-filled environment, it is unrealistic to try and live without them. Consider that critical thinking requires substantial screen time in order to do research, to read, to write, and to take in information in the form of images, music, and so on. Nevertheless, the issue at hand is not whether we should use our screens or not, but that the screens, when used inattentively, engage us shallowly. To develop deeper, long-form habits of focus we need to practice *the kind* of attention we give to our screens.

Even so, "knowing thyself" can be a task best undertaken with a quiet mind. Taking the time to clear and focus our minds away from screens will enhance our ability to critically engage with a screen for the task at hand. We will initially struggle to focus because our brains have adapted to the demands we have put on them: our brains have "learned the language" of our technological world and our habits of attention have been shaped accordingly. While getting to the bottom of our anxiety, fear, and insecurity is important, it also helps to take stock of how much time we spend online or in other activities that do not help us achieve our goals. To take the path of critical thinking is to question, perhaps even unlearn, many of the habits of mind encouraged by society and a digitized world.

Time, as they say, is money. Time management functions in precisely the same way as money management. In order to help people take control of their money, finance experts recommend keeping a record of all spending, no matter how trivial. People discover that what they think they spend is quite a bit less than what they actually spend, which is why we tend to live beyond our means, sometimes wracked in debt. This is another example of the Dunning-Kruger effect at work that illustrates how we are capable of living in a state of denial rather than how things really are.

## Mindful meditation: developing the capacity for meta-cognition

To focus on the present moment means to take a break from worrying about the past or the future. This alone can alleviate some anxiety. The long tradition of mindfulness meditation holds that mindful awareness has the potential to bring us into closer contact with our humanity. Developing our focus and attention helps us to discover that life is lived as a series of present moments. By taking responsibility for each moment we develop our intellectual and emotional agency. Meditation is a tool that facilitates meta-cognition.

Jon Kabat-Zinn, Executive Director of the Center for Mindfulness in Medicine, Health Care, and Society wrote, "Mindfulness is the psychological process of bringing one's attention to the internal and external experiences occurring in the present moment, which can be developed through the practice of meditation and other training."[13] The term, mindfulness, comes from Sanskrit, *smrti*, which means to remember, to recollect, to bear in mind. So the idea of mindfulness meditation is to pay attention purposefully and, crucially, without judgment to our thoughts. In practice, the meditator assumes the role of the observer—that the basic ground we walk on, speak in, and act in is neutral. Working in neutrality, we learn to be less judgmental of ourselves and others, and this opens up a window for critical thinking and meta-cognition. The research tells us that meditation practice gives us the tools for applied rational, balanced thinking because it is a practice of awareness and understanding of our own thought processes. Indeed, mindfulness meditation is highly correlated with meta-cognition.[14]

By sitting quietly and doing nothing we meet ourselves in the form of the feelings that rise up within us and the thoughts that come with them. By practicing empathy and non-judgment with ourselves first we develop the ability to practice it with others. Too often acts of hate and violence are undergirded by ignorance and self-loathing. We often hate in others what we reject about ourselves.

Our goal is to make peace with ourselves. As we learn about ourselves and accept all that we are, we are more able to sit with a ready, steady, quiet mind. In this sense, a quiet mind is useful precisely for its emptiness. Like a cup, it stands ready to receive and serve, only to be emptied and made ready again for the next task. If our mind is full of thoughts, fears, and opinions, it does not leave much room for critical thinking nor does it allow us to focus on the task at hand.

Research done using MRI scans of the brain have revealed what happens in our brains when we meditate.[15] In the first few minutes of meditation, our ventromedial prefrontal cortex becomes active. In fact, this part of the brain is always active but jumps to life when we pause to pay attention. The ventromedial prefrontal cortex is responsible for our mind springing from one thought to the next. We might dwell on something someone said, or something we said, and give in to worry and anxiety. If we push through the first few minutes of activity by focusing our attention on our breathing, the lateral prefrontal cortex becomes active and overrides self-centered thinking such that we can understand things more rationally and see things more objectively, less personally. All of this is a positive feedback loop that helps us settle into our meditation and clears the path for critical thinking. The more we sit quietly in mindful meditation, the more awake the lateral prefrontal cortex becomes—and the less active the ventromedial cortex becomes.[16]

If we continue with our practice, after two or three months of daily meditation our dorsomedial prefrontal cortex lights up and helps us experience empathy. "It's why the more we meditate, the more compassionate we become in life," says Rebecca Gladding, psychiatrist and author. "This part of the brain becomes more active, more of the time."[17]

To begin a journey into mindfulness, start by asking:

- "How do I feel?" Feelings are physical, unlike thoughts. Beware of thinking about your feelings, rather endeavor to "have" them by breathing and making room for them. Support your right to feel what you feel.
- Sit, lie down, or even stand in a comfortable position with your spine straight and your body relaxed.
- Take a deep breath in. Pause before you exhale. When you exhale, count silently to yourself, "one." As you continue to inhale and exhale, continue to count each exhalation until you reach the count of four.
- Continue counting your exhalations in sets of four for five to ten minutes. You might notice your mind and body physically relaxing. If your mind drifts and you lose track of what number you are on, this is not a problem. Simply and intentionally start over with "one" and continue counting each out breath.
- Use this meditation anywhere and at any time to calm your mind, such as standing in a check-out line at a grocery store; to refocus on a task before you; or even while lying in bed before you start your day.

Mindfulness meditation asks us to focus on breathing in a quite involved, formal way. We count our breaths, or watch our in and out breaths, and in so doing, this brings us more deeply into contact with the pulsations that define our humanity and everyone else's. As we focus on our breaths we may feel our posture become tense, and intrusive thoughts can come galloping in to our minds. We may lose focus. If so, we simply start back at "one" again and let go all self-recrimination. This is a practice of compassion. When we find ourselves overly critical of our performance, let us consider this a valuable piece of information that mindfulness practice has brought to our attention. If we are overly concerned about "getting it right," or "winning" or other "gaining" ideas, sitting quietly and practicing mindfulness will be more difficult. The practice is not to master any particular process; the practice is taking care of ourselves, and this is precisely why we call it "practice."

By placing our mind on our breath, we relax the whole body. When relaxed, body and breath become synchronized. Sometimes we may find that our mind becomes quite busy with discursive thoughts, and if this happens, we can label the thoughts, "thinking" to stop them and then return our focus to our breathing again. It may be helpful to mouth the word, "thinking," to cut off the distracting thoughts.

Practicing mindfulness opens up our awareness to the present moment as something more than our thoughts, something to be experienced by our entire being. And so we regard our thinking as transient thoughts and we let them go without judgment, clinging, or pursuit. This certainly does take practice. We learn that we can attend to our thoughts later if they require it, but for five or ten minutes we practice consciously letting go in order to be.

The beauty of such a compassionate, mindful practice for ourselves is that we develop the skill to pay attention to the present moment anywhere and at any time. We can take any moment through the day to reflect on how we are feeling and practice breathing and letting our thoughts alone for a few moments. As we breathe, we can practice non-judgment with ourselves especially when we feel triggered, discouraged, or frustrated. Taking a moment to feel our anger and to accept it allows us to avoid acting in ways we might later regret, for ourselves and others. By accepting that we feel we build rapport with ourselves.

Many of us have forgotten how to be alone, and instead search for reassurance, recognition, and support from outside ourselves, especially via social networks. Such external reassurances simply cannot take the place of self-love and self-acceptance. When we sit quietly, we create an opportunity to learn about ourselves with no distracting interventions. This is how we hold our seat when times get stressful, or we are triggered by something someone said or did. The idea of holding your seat means that we can remain calm when difficult emotions and conflicts arise in our daily lives: It is an opportunity for reflection, growth, and development.

We practice any skill in order to apply what we learn to our day-to-day activities and over time improve our skills. Musicians practice scales not simply to get good at playing scales, but so that they might improve their ability to play music, alone or with others. Fortunately we can practice mindfulness anywhere. Nearly every human activity we engage in benefits from our attention and focus. When engaged in a task, we should think of nothing else, pay attention to nothing else. As we go along we will need to sort through the distractions that interrupt our focus, and with mindfulness practice, we can become acutely aware of procrastination, feeling stressed out, and potential conflicts before they happen. Distracted minds make mistakes, get into accidents, and feel too overwhelmed to take responsibility for themselves and their actions. Thankfully mindfulness practice can help.

When we look back at ourselves from a place of meta-cognition—a position of awareness from which we can see ourselves—we open up the possibility of recognizing patterns in how we feel, what we think, and how we act. Psychiatrist and author Jacques Lacan tells us our two basic drives are for recognition and for love.[18] Might this simple observation lie behind so much of our addictive behavior online? Are we hunting for recognition? For love? For support? It seems so. When we do not get enough of either as children, we spend the rest of our lives looking for it. In this way our developmental needs inform our day-to-day desires and activities, but unconsciously.

Consciously we passionately pursue an idea—say, even a xenophobic ideology based on a conflict we had with someone else, an "us" versus "them" way of thinking. Maybe life would be so much better without "them" around, although in fact we are most likely working out our own terror and rage at those who treated us badly in the past, i.e. as if we were "them." Lacan would say that we betray others as a reenactment of our own betrayal; we mistakenly take the abuser's position in the reenactment, and re-traumatize ourselves in the process, thus doing the abuser's work for him. When trapped in a cycle like this, we need an inner-reconciliation in order to avoid the unconscious reproduction of our suffering over and over again.

Though we hope to practice mindfulness in most everyday activities, we also need time to practice alone. Mindfulness meditation brings the deliberate effort to make time and space to work on ourselves. Perhaps most challenging for some of us will be to unplug from our digital devices while we sit quietly doing nothing. The tension we might feel when unplugging from our digital networks in order to quiet the mind is analogous to the challenge of what psychologists call "letting go of the ego." Unplugging from the digital cloud means that, for a time, we practice letting go of our digital egos as they exist online. We let go of, for a time, the hope for recognition and love, and instead we sit patiently with how things are in the present moment.

Even such a small act of acceptance might lead to the ego's resistance. The ego resists precisely because it is that part of our mind that has been taught explicitly *not* to accept us as we are, but to strive to turn us into someone different, someone "better," someone more acceptable. If noisy thoughts arise, we just breathe through it and accept everything as it is for the moment, doing nothing. Some egos are timid, others are bullies, but they all want the same thing: to be recognized and loved. By sitting and accepting ourselves we learn to love ourselves.

This is a key point, especially if we are particularly hard on ourselves. If we accept our thoughts, but not cling to them, and if we recognize our feelings without judgment, we are in essence practicing empathy with ourselves. When we understand and accept our whole self, compassion for others becomes genuine. When we hate or reject ourselves, on the other hand, hating and rejecting others seems reasonable. Scientific research has shown that mindfulness, when undertaken as a daily practice, reduces aggression, dishonesty, and the need to manipulate others.[19] Our ability to sit quietly doing nothing will help us to handle stress more effectively too, and this leads to numerous health benefits.[20]

Taking responsibility for our mental and emotional awareness is a discipline that helps us develop a connection to our essential core self, our personal integrity, and our fundamental humanity. From such an inner place we can see the logic of social justice. It takes courage and honesty to look within. According to Nelson Mandela, "the first thing is to be honest with yourself. You can never have an impact on society if you have not changed yourself. … Great peacemakers are all people of integrity, of honesty … and humility."[21]

## Checking narcissism

To practice critical thinking in order to work for social justice requires that we take responsibility for our own behavior and to understand why we do it. In this way we develop our understanding of others as well as ourselves. Practicing mindfulness is one way to generate the kind of reflexive self-awareness that we need now more than ever in our complex, digital world.

Sociology professor and political adviser Anthony Giddens has written that our modern way of life moves us further from mindfulness and practical consciousness and into what he describes as "non-conscious" discourse, that is, we do things and think about things on "auto pilot.[22]" Such habits of mind are the opposite of mindfulness and short-circuit critical thinking and meta-cognition. If follows then that if we forget how to trust our own minds, we become vulnerable to beguiling and manipulative ideologies rooted in fear and insecurity. The point then is this: social injustices thrive when we forget our-selves and ignore the better spirit of our nature.

Self-awareness, the awareness of the present moment, intellectual competence, and meta-cognition combine to put a check on narcissism. When we live narcissistically, we tend to think about ourselves and forget how to empathize with others, or worse, believe that everyone thinks the way we do, and so *they* should be thinking about *our* needs. Narcissistic traits include the belief that everything "happens" to them. "Why is this happening to me?," we say when feeling put upon, targeted, or victimized. The truth of any situation, however, is multi-dimensional with many different con-tributors. We are both a cause and an effect in every situation.

Meta-cognition offers the mind a way to outgrow narcissism; however, we must first realize the *need* to outgrow our narcissism otherwise we are like the dog that chases its own tail. The fruits of meta-cognition and self-knowledge, at least according to Socrates, grow from the recognition of humility and a felt sense that to live an authentic, fully-human life we need to nurture the critical faculties of our minds. But like any potential, the higher mind does not emerge without effort, discipline, and regular practice.

---

## REFLECTIVE EXERCISE: *WHO AM I?*[*23]

How do you answer this question? How would you describe yourself if someone asked? Is it important to you to be appreciated for who you really are, without titles, games, or roles? There are probably many things about yourself that you are proud of and would not want to lose. Yet there are probably other things that you might not like about yourself. Is there a true self that you can always trust?

This exercise can be done in class or on your own. Be as honest as possible; no one will see your reflections except you.

You need ten small scraps or strips of paper.

To begin, write down ten different words or short phrases, one on each strip, that answer the question, "Who am I?" When you have written down town all ten, rank order them, with the most important to you on top. Now turn the pile over so the most important answer to the question, "Who am I?" is now on the bottom.

Take a deep breath. Slowly turn the first strip of paper over and read it to yourself, saying, "I am _____." Take a moment to imagine the impact this quality has on your life, your family, and friends. Take another slow breath and contemplate what you wrote and really think about this role or quality in your life. Second, ask yourself how this quality or role impacts others or what it might mean to other people with whom you interact.

Now imagine that this quality is totally gone from your life. Wad up the strip of paper and throw it down on the floor by your feet. Take a moment to feel this loss. How does it make you feel?

Now repeat this process nine more times. When you have gone through all ten strips of paper, and they are crumpled at your feet on the floor, take a moment to contemplate what you would be like if you were none of these things anymore. Who would you be? Who are you? Can you glimpse your true self under all these labels you and others place on yourself?

Now collect all the discarded strips of paper at your feet and read them again. This time pick ones that you want to keep and ones you want to throw away. Did you keep the one that you identified as the "most important" at the beginning of the exercise? Would you order the strips any differently now?

Take one more deep breath and reflect on who you are now in this moment.

## Critical thinking: test case

Critical thinking represents a crucial set of intellectual moves that can be achieved only by deliberate effort in the form of training and practice. The different skills that comprise critical thinking each reinforce and presume the other. On the one hand we need the intellectual ability that allows us to understand what it means to "take a step back" from an argument in order to analyze its structure, to question its content, and to be sure it meets the standards of intellectual competence. It takes an emotional self-awareness to recognize that the "others" in a conflict feel as confident, emotional, and committed as we do. They even have evidence that they believe in as firmly as we believe in ours. Importantly, critical thinking does not exist without the skills that comprise intellectual competence and an understanding of ourselves. As prominent sociologist George Herbert Mead (1863–1931) wrote, the way we think, our attitudes and opinions, constitute the construction of the self; therefore the self is a social process, always unfinished.[24] So as we engage with the world, on line or *in vivo*, by interacting with certain groups, these exchanges condition our consciousness, our mind, and construct the self. The important point is how critical the process of self-reflection and our interactions are—they turn us from being *reactive* to events to *acting*, analyzing, and interpreting what we are confronted with as critical thinkers.

The essential moves we make in order to critically think about how we should respond to a problem or conflict can begin by questioning:

- What is our connection to the issue, question, or problem—what are our feelings about it? Why are we pursuing it? What is at stake? Who cares? Why bother?
- What we have been taught to believe about the issue, if anything, during our childhood?
- How do we characterize the nature of the conversation about the information we and "they" are interested in? Who has been saying what about it? When? Where have they been communicating? Are they engaged in a discussion of evidence? Are they using sound logic to make their points?

- Assess the quality of information we have regarding the issue, question, or problem: who or what are the source(s) of information? Is the information part of a vested interest? Who paid for the research to be done in the first place?
- What do we believe now and why? How did we come to believe what we do?

## Test case: climate change

Climate scientists from across the world have concluded that climate change and global warming are effects of human emissions. They cite overwhelming scientific evidence from decades of observations to prove causation between heat trapping emissions and the overall rise in global temperatures.[25] Nevertheless, scientists still struggle to win the hearts and minds of ordinary citizens in the United States, who may claim the danger of global warming is overstated in a conspiracy to destroy energy companies.[26] Many choose to believe that climate change and environmental degradation are *not* the result of human activities. Whatever is happening to the climate, they say, is part of a natural cycle.

While we may not have perfect mastery over the many varieties of logical reasoning, we may still engage in critical thinking by deploying a basic understanding of *cause and effect*. Cause and effect governs the processes that drive the material world. This means that there can be no observed effect without a cause; however, causes can be difficult to identify and measure in order to prove that one event caused the other. Many events may only be correlated, which is what climate deniers basically argue. They claim only an association between human activity and climate change, thus denying causation.

It is true that the earth's geographical environment combined with human society comprise a fantastically complicated whole, all of which makes it very difficult to discover the specific cause of some specific effect. Some effects, maybe most, have *multiple* causes so one-to-one correspondence is often difficult to prove even when confidence is high that causation has been determined. For example, cigarette smoking causes cancer, but not always and in the same way for everyone who is diagnosed with it. For others, a habit of smoking 20 or 30 cigarettes a day leads to lung cancer, while for still other smokers there may be no cancer at all in spite of the myriad ways that science has demonstrated that the chemicals in cigarettes are known carcinogens. There are variables at work that science does not fully understand even though the causal link between cigarettes and cancer is real.

Critical thinking requires suspicion of simplistic one-on-one cause and effect statements. Like tobacco companies before them, the fossil fuel industry has led a decades-long misinformation campaign that effectively questioned evidence in favor of a fantasy, all in order to gorge on private profit at the expense of public good. The poor and disenfranchised around the world are inordinately hit by the effects of climate change, while the rich protect themselves using resources previously coopted from the public commons. We already see the effects of climate change, and it promises to be one of the greatest social injustices ever perpetrated on the world.

In order to practice intellectually competent habits that serve critical thinking, part of that process means that we must at some point decide to trust second-hand information. In other words, we must trust *others* who have gathered evidence, and then analyzed it, interpreted it, and communicated their findings. But what if those we choose to trust have gathered information incorrectly, or in other ways made it unreliable? What if the assessment of the evidence was incorrect or otherwise confused? While we have no choice but to trust experts and the information they provide in order to critically think as intellectually competent people, at the same time we have to be skeptical. Sometimes experts get it wrong, or worse, misinterpret, misrepresent, or simply make up their findings: this was the case for one medical doctor who published a study that claimed children's vaccinations caused autism *based on the evidence*, only he had none.[27] This falsified study helped to drive forward the anti-vaccination movement that continues in spite of all the evidence that proves the overall safety and necessity of vaccinations. So while we may place our trust in experts, we also have to question them. One way to question and confirm our information is to seek second opinions (and third opinions) from the scientific community.

Yet we have multiple sources of evidence documenting human activity's devastating impact on the environment, including climate, yet America remains a "hotbed" of climate science denial. Nevertheless, most Americans accept that human activity has led to climate change, and that a changing climate represents a threat to our way of life. Meanwhile, we do nothing to stop it. In fact, carbon dioxide ($CO_2$) levels in the atmosphere continue to increase at an alarming rate, breaking through one record after another. Recent increases indicate that we are burning fossil fuels at an even greater rate, too. So while more people accept climate science, there is still "no political path forward."[28]

Meanwhile, many leaders in the United States—leaders in the White House, the Congress, and across the country—continue to deny climate science in the most audacious and offensive terms imaginable. There is no evidence to support the view that the majority of climate scientists across the world are in a conspiracy or have conspired together to misrepresent their data.

Returning to fallacious reasoning about climate change, consider the following argument and the logic, advanced by the fossil fuel industry, to deny human activity as the primary cause of climate change today:

- Premise one: The climate has changed in the past through a natural process as part of a cycle.
- Premise two: The climate is currently changing.
- Conclusion: The climate is currently changing like it always has, naturally, and as part of a cyclical process.

Is the example above an inductive or a deductive argument? Remember that inductive statements proceed from specific examples that result in a generalized statement or conclusion that makes sense of the specific examples. Deductive logic, on the other hand, begins with a general truth, like "all humans are mortal," that we accept as a true premise.

An effective deductive argument requires that we accept the first premise as true: in this case, the premise states that scientists agree that the earth's climate has changed in the past as part of a natural cycle that repeats. The second premise addresses a more specific concern: "today, the climate is changing." This too appears to be an accurate claim according to nearly all climate scientists. According to deductive logic, if the first two premises are true, then the conclusion must be true. But in this case something appears to have gone wrong for we have arrived at a misleading conclusion that appears, while logical, does not mean that the rapid rate of climate change is part of a natural process.

What went wrong? Let us look again at the first premise: "the climate has changed in the past through a natural process as part of a cycle." Note that the premise does not claim to explain *all* possible effects of climate change, only those that occur naturally. It does not claim anything about human activity at all, in fact. Logic can be sound *and* invalid. Furthermore, because the premise ignores the possibility of *unnatural* climate change, the second premise does not follow from the first in any sort of cause-and-effect relationship, and so together the two premises do not support the conclusion.

One might make such an argument out of ignorance, or wishful thinking, or worse—in aid of those who seek to protect our fossil fuel burning culture. When we seek to analyze an argument, we work to identify its main claim, then reduce it into the simplest language possible, but no simpler. This might be made more difficult by a badly written, badly reasoned argument. We may have to carefully research in order to fully satisfy intellectual competence that an argument's premises are accurate and true, or probably true, or as in the above example, incomplete and not true.

Once we identify an argument's main claim, we need to determine whether it is a deductive argument's first premise, or if it is a conclusion reached by inductive thinking. When we analyze an argument our goal is to find the logical the structure in order to question it, one part at a time. In this way we can learn to identify if cause and effect breaks down, or if the argument depends on a hidden, unarticulated premise, often called mediating or moderating variables. The *form* of the argument, in other words, reveals an argument's invalidity even before we read the information for ourselves.

Knowing how deductive and inductive reasoning function can help us unknot difficult arguments in order to determine the soundness of the reasoning and the likelihood that the conclusions reached are true. Remember that inductive reasoning draws conclusions that are strongly probable, as indicated by patterns of evidence; deductive reasoning, on the other hand, is the logic of proof.

Consider another example:

Premise one: In the past, racism was normal.
Premise two: There is racism in the world today.
Conclusion: Racism is normal.

In this case, the argument's conclusion assumes its own truth without proving it, a fallacy known as "begging the question." In other words, the fact that there was racism in the past, or racism in the present, has nothing to do with whether "racism is normal." The ambiguity of the language also bears close analysis. What do we mean by normal? What do we mean by racism precisely? Arguments collapse around weak logic and imprecise language.

It is difficult to correct ambiguous or misleading claims unless we have a confident hold on the information in question. Critical thinking requires not only an open and ready mind, but a commitment to intellectual competence. Only then can we identify and effectively assess an argument based on misleading information, false premises, or vague generalizations, all of which fail to prove cause and effect.

Though we may eventually come to agree with a popular explanation of some social or natural phenomenon, we may not learn the truth unless we take responsibility for what we believe. For example, some politicians advocate for a policy that calls for police to "stop-and-frisk" anyone whom they deem suspicious, all in the name of reducing the crime rate. Such a policy may seem to make sense: police stop and search "suspicious-looking" people so that they can deter criminal activity before it happens. But the question remains: is this an example of effective public policy, or a social injustice based in bad inductive reasoning informed by systemic racism?

Examples as evidence: seven out of ten "stop and frisk" interventions resulted in arrests for previous criminal activity. Inductive conclusion: criminal activity can be reduced by stop-and-frisk police work. Critics of stop-and-frisk police work label such activities as an example of systemic racism because police enact the policy almost exclusively against people of color. A logical question to ask is what makes them look "suspicious?" How is that term defined?

## Fallacies and other risks

Consider again our "stop and frisk" police policy example and whether it meets the test of logic. We might be able to assemble data on crime rates and "stop and frisk" policies, and *deductively* argue that "stop and frisk" leads to crime prevention. (Everywhere stop-and-frisk is used, crime rates have dropped. Therefore, stop-and-frisk in our city should result in decreased crime rates here.) But like an artificial intelligence algorithm, inductive and deductive logic provide no defense against a user who is *already* inclined to racist, sexist, homophobic, or xenophobic beliefs and behaviors. Like AI, logic has no moral compass, no soul. We must provide the ethical dimension to all of our critical thinking, which means that critical thinking must take into accounts the limits of logic.

And so, a "stop and frisk" policy might make perfectly good sense to someone who is frightened and insecure, and who has been taught to be especially frightened by, say, people who look different from them in urban communities. Frightened and insecure thinkers will likely accept a "stop and frisk" policy because they believe that they "have nothing to hide" from authorities, though they might also enjoy the cultural privilege that makes them invisible to law enforcement, and so will almost never experience "stop and frisk" first hand. Is stop-and-frisk effective crime deterrence or an example of systemic social injustice?

Stop-and-frisk police work requires a world that presumes guilt by association based upon the way we look. Too often inductive reasoning hides racist profiling. And so the critical thinker must challenge the logical assumptions at work in such a social policy, or risk losing their own civil rights, and beyond that, their human dignity.

---

## EXERCISES

- What evidence can you find that demonstrates causation between "stop-and-frisk" and reduced crime rates? If there is no causation, then who argues for correlation between crime rates and stop-and-frisk? Have crime rates actually dropped? Who claims this and why? What do we mean by "crime rates?" What sorts of crimes are included? Excluded? Are the percentages, graphs, and charts used to prove the value of "stop-and-frisk" correct?
- Finally, is it reasonable to stop-and-frisk people because police suspect they *might* be the type to commit a crime? What have the United States federal courts ruled about stop-and-frisk policing?

---

## Collaboration is key

Sometimes critical thinking begins with an analysis of an argument's logic, or perhaps in the breakdown and inaccuracy of a key piece of data, or perhaps the critical thinking process begins with a gut feeling, a pre-knowing insight about a question, issue, or problem related to social or cultural practice; sometimes situations simply *feel* wrong, and so we need to find the evidence that supports our insight. Sometimes, however, when we reason through the evidence we cannot support our gut feelings. We would be wise then to apply the logic of our conclusions consistently, especially when we feel an emotional connection.

In his work for the National Geographic Society's Climate Change Bureau, long-time climate reporter Andrew Revkin interviewed sociologists and psychologists who helped him realize that his own attachment to his beliefs about climate change made it impossible for him to help others to think critically about it; deep down, he wanted others to see it his way and this interfered with his ability to be empathetic and mindful. He also realized at the same time that compromise for him would be unthinkable, and that his opponents almost certainly felt the same way.[29]

His dialogues with colleagues helped him understand that in his aggressive certainty, he was missing an important psychological component to his understanding of his conflict with deniers, leaving him with little desire to find empathy for "alternative facts" and oppositional science paid for by big industries. Nevertheless climate change deniers have had a profound effect on politics and policy. Revkin had to acknowledge that people still gravitate toward the idea that all those climate scientists could be wrong. How can science not be enough?

Revkin learned that if he was to make any progress in changing hearts and minds, he had to contextualize the climate science he offered to his opponents. That is, he had to talk about climate from the perspective of his opponents' experiences and understandings. Knowing *where* an argument comes from can help our analysis of why people believe what they believe. If we want to change hearts and minds, we have to know our own and be willing to know our opponents'.

Revkin began to work on a new approach to the climate change debate by thinking about how he could connect with people who appeared uninterested in the problem of climate change, maybe even committed to continued burning of fossil fuels and other big industry polluters. So in Tennessee he decided to talk about the wildfires in Tennessee. In California he talked to deniers about drought. In these exchanges, Revkin learned to argue for the economic benefits of using clean energy and was easily able to justify its development and use for both purposes: savings and climate.

For Revkin, thinking critically about the challenges he faced in trying to fight against climate change led him to a kind of critical awareness that rose above and beyond climate change as an issue. Revkin realized that while data are crucial, and logic must be sound, and conclusions evidence-based, it is equally important to find empathy and understanding for the persons and their historical and cultural community. Given the situation, Revkin reasoned that the only way to approach the problem of civil social discourse as it relates the question of our culture's impact on climate and climate change, was through collaboration. The only way forward was in finding some common ground that could begin a dialog. He actively sought to remove the "us" versus "them" thinking.

Revkin's approach helped to create a dialog with climate deniers because he was able to discuss the cost of heating and cooling their homes, especially in the extreme seasons. Through discussion and collaboration, Revkin helped his historic opponents meet their needs in a cost-effective way by demonstrating the affordability of air conditioning when powered by electricity generated via solar panels. Cheap electricity became the common ground for climate change where instead of conflict, he achieved collaboration; instead of losers and winners, he fashioned a win–win scenario.

But to achieve such an outcome, Revkin realized that he needed to break out of his personal comfort zone. This meant he had to question and even surrender his hold on his political identity (held by himself and others) as a left wing radical environmentalist. To think clearly about his challenges, he realized he had to have an open mind, and that meant letting go of his ego, and his need to "win" and "be right."

Collaboration of the sort Revkin achieved requires the ability to compromise— no small task. Collaboration is an expression of empathy and critical thinking, and is the fruit of critical awareness. There can be no collaboration without mutual respect for each other's humanity. When it works, collaboration yields results because it involves empathy, defined as compassion for the other's humanity, an open mind, and a self-conscious commitment to understand the other's point of view *without judgment*. Collaboration is a challenge precisely because when we come from different cultural traditions, languages, and social practices we are often weighted with the freight of judgment, of history, and of suffering. Recovering from all of this requires *restorative justice*, the topic of Chapter 6.

## Putting it together

While critical thinking is a capacity endemic to the human mind, like any potentiality, it requires effort, regular practice, and competent feedback to develop. When we pair mindfulness with critical thinking, and critical thinking with cultural competence, we create the conditions for critical awareness to emerge, a way of seeing and thinking that uses critical thinking as a tool for social justice. Critical awareness includes a moral and ethical dimension that reason and logic can only comment on tangentially, but not serve as a source. The source for critical awareness is empathy, a central theme of Chapter 5.

Along with the rise and spread of conservative politicians, has arisen the cynical use of "alternative facts" as a parody and mockery of the fruits of critical thinking. The truth has to feel right. It must meet the conditions of reasonableness born of evidence. While it may be an approximation, or a provisional assessment, the truth should include the ability to update itself as conditions require. Indeed, critical thinking often leads us to the conclusion that the "truth" of any situation is a difficult thing to determine amid a host of competing claims. In this context, critical thinking is as much about finding the most reasonable solution to an issue, problem, conflict, or question, as it is about understanding the nature of truth.

Meta-cognition is the state of mind that drives the critical thinking process. Mindfulness and the practice of quieting the mind helps us exercise that part of the mind capable of self-examination, reflection, and change. This amounts to a culti- vated skill that will always represent a challenge to the cultural and ideological status quo. At its heart is skeptical inquiry and doubt intertwined together with an almost idealistic faith in truth and won by intellectual courage and rigor. Critical thinking challenges anything not founded on evidence, or that claims authority via revealed knowledge and secret teachings.

"Thinking about thinking" is as good a way as any to describe meta-cognition. But there are more effective ways than others to take a step back from our thoughts so that we can gain perspective about them. Such a "stepping back" serves as a check on the discourse of our media ecosystem, our "bubble." It opens the way to reflection. Even this is not a perfect guarantee of knowledge, but it represents a crucial step in becoming aware of what we believe, and why.

Social injustice depends upon a cultural narrative divorced from evidence, assess- ment of cause-and-effect, and commitment to reason. Critical thinking, on the other hand, allows us to impose intellectual standards on our own way of life in order to expose the assumptions, fears, and irrationality that undermine social justice. Submit- ting our assumptions, beliefs, and values to critical scrutiny allows us to begin to assess our own thinking. But humility must be part of this process, and skepticism as well, for there is no part of the reflective thinking process that is fixed and absolute. Even the process of reflection needs to be reflected upon from time to time, and submitted to others for comparison, for sharpening, and perhaps correction. From there the possibility of a social justice born of critical awareness emerges. More on what we mean by "critical awareness" and how it relates to critical thinking when we take them up in the following chapters.

## Notes

1 "How Religious Commitment Varies by Country Among People of All Ages." *Pew Research Center, Religion and Public Life*. https://www.pewforum.org/2018/06/13/how-religious-commitment-varies-by-country-among-people-of-all-ages/. Accessed July 20, 2019.
2 "Blanshard, Brand (1892–1987)." *Encyclopedia of Philosophy*. https://www.encyclopedia.com/humanities/encyclopedias-almanacs-transcripts-and-maps/blanshard-brand-1892-1987. Accessed July 20, 2019.
3 Brand Blanshard. *Reason and Analysis* (La Salle, IL: Open Court, 1962).
4 Ralph D. Ellis. "Moral Hermeneutics, Coherence Epistemology, and the Role of Emotion." *Kilikya Felsefe Dergisi, Cilicia Journal of Philosophy*, Vol. 3 (2015): 24–36.
5 Jeremey Donovan. *What Great Looks Like: Leadership Best Practices for General Managers* (North Charleston, SC: Create Space Independent Publishing Platform, 2011).
6 Charlie Warzel. "He Predicted the 2016 Fake News Crisis. Now He's Worried About an Information Apocalypse." *BuzzFeed*. https://www.buzzfeednews.com/article/charliewarzel/the-terrifying-future-of-fake-news. Accessed July 20, 2019.
7 Chris Bailey. *Hyper-focus: How to Be More Productive in a World of Distraction* (Toronto: Random House, 2018).
8 Katie McBeth. "The Infocalypse Is Coming." *International Policy Digest*. https://intpolicydigest.org/2018/03/08/the-infocalypse-is-coming/. Accessed July 20, 2019.
9 Mihaly Cszikszentmihalyi. *Finding Flow: The Psychology of Engagement in Every Day Life* (New York: Basic Books, 1997).
10 "The Teen Brain: 6 Things to Know." National Institute of Mental Health (NIMH). Transforming the understanding and treatment of mental illnesses. https://www.nimh.nih.gov/health/publications/the-teen-brain-6-things-to-know/index.shtml. Accessed July 20, 2019.
11 Glenn Berger. "The Healthy Brain: A Glass of Water in the Morning." *HuffPost*. https://www.huffpost.com/entry/the-healthy-brain-a-glass-of-water-in-the-morning_b_58cf1bb3e4b07112b6472f26. Accessed July 20, 2019.
12 Katie Moritz. "Should Adults Have Screen Time Limits, Too?" *Rewire*. https://www.rewire.org/living/adults-screen-time-limits/. Accessed July 20, 2019.
13 Christopher Shea. "A Brief History of Mindfulness in the USA and Its Impact on Our Lives." *PsychCentral*. https://psychcentral.com/lib/a-brief-history-of-mindfulness-in-the-usa-and-its-impact-on-our-lives/. Accessed July 20, 2019.
14 Robert Wright. *Why Buddhism Is True: The Science and Philosophy of Meditation and Enlightenment* (New York: Simon and Schuster, 2017).
15 Tom Ireland. "What Does Mindfulness Meditation Do to Your Brain?" *Scientific American*. https://blogs.scientificamerican.com/guest-blog/what-does-mindfulness-meditation-do-to-your-brain/. Accessed July 20, 2019.
16 Deanna Michalopoulos. "This Is Your Brain on Meditation: What's Actually Happening to Your Brain When You Meditate?" *Yoga Journal*. https://www.yogajournal.com/meditation/brain-on-meditation. Accessed July 20, 2019.
17 Ibid.
18 Owen Hewitson. "What Does Lacan Say About … The Mirror Stage?—Part I." *LacanOnline*. https://www.lacanonline.com/2010/09/what-does-lacan-say-about-the-mirror-stage-part-i/. Accessed July 20, 2019.

19  Paul Blancka, Sarah Perleth, Thomas Heidenreich, Paula Krögera, Beate Ditzen, Hinrich Bents, and Johannes Mander. "Effects of Mindfulness Exercises as Stand-Alone Intervention on Symptoms of Anxiety and Depression: Systematic Review and Meta-Analysis." *Behaviour Research and Therapy*, No. 102 (March 2018): 25–35. Accessed July 20, 2019.
20  Rebecca Fix and Spencer Fix. "The Effects of Mindfulness-Based Treatments for Aggression: A Critical Review." *Aggression and Violent Behavior*, Vol. 18 (2013): 219–27. Accessed July 20, 2019.
21  "Nelson Mandela > Quotes > Quotable Quote." *Goodreads*. https://www.goodreads.com/quotes/75630-as-i-have-said-the-first-thing-is-to-be. Accessed July 20, 2019.
22  Anthony Giddens. *Modernity and Self-Identity: Self and Society in the Late Modern Age* (Redwood City, CA: Stanford University Press, 1991).
23  Adapted with permission from "Who Am I?" Alternatives to Violence Project. https://avpusa.org/. Accessed July 27, 2019.
24  George Herbert Mead. *Mind, Self and Society* (Chicago: University of Chicago Press, 1934).
25  Andrew Revkin. "Climate Change First Became News 30 Years Ago. Why Haven't We Fixed It?" *National Geographic*. https://www.nationalgeographic.com/magazine/2018/07/embark-essay-climate-change-pollution-revkin/. Accessed July 20, 2019.
26  Karen M. Douglas, Robbie M. Sutton and Aleksandra Cichocka. "The Psychology of Conspiracy Theories." *Current Directions in Psychological Science*, Vol. 26, No. 6 (2017): 538–42.
27  Paul A. Offit. "Do Vaccines Cause Autism?" *Children's Hospital of Philadelphia*. https://www.chop.edu/centers-programs/vaccine-education-center/video/do-vaccines-cause-autism. Accessed July 20, 2019.
28  Robinson Meyer. "The Unprecedented Surge in Fear about Climate Change." *The Atlantic*. https://www.theatlantic.com/science/archive/2019/01/do-most-americans-believe-climate-change-polls-say-yes/580957/. Accessed July 20, 2019.
29  Andrew C. Revkin. "Is the Climate Problem in Our Heads?" *New York Times*. August 5, 2009. https://dotearth.blogs.nytimes.com/2009/08/05/is-the-climate-problem-in-our-heads/. Accessed July 21, 2019.

# 4

# CULTURAL COGNITION

## "Getting" others

Cultural cognition refers to the ability to interact effectively with people who come from different socioeconomic, cultural and linguistic backgrounds, who are different from each other and different from the professionals who engage with them. Cognition is the mental action or process of acquiring knowledge and understanding through thought, experience, and the senses. When we understand and practice cultural cognition effectively, it means we are *culturally competent*, and so we are able to practice reflective self-awareness without defensive posturing.

According to Jonathan Stacks, social worker and researcher, cultural cognition moves beyond what some have labeled as "cultural awareness," that is, the knowledge of another cultural group, or the notion of "cultural sensitivity," which refers to the knowledge as well as experience with another culture. Instead, cultural cognition acknowledges and responds to the unique worldviews of different people and communities. To understand the individual, Stacks maintains, we must understand the individual's lived experiences.[1]

Stacks argues that cultural cognition is vital to every program's effectiveness, not just to those serving "minority" groups. Indeed, the benefits of cultural cognition are many:

- Developing cultural cognition helps professionals interact more effectively in the field, whether our work takes us to the street in a patrol car, behind a desk writing a character reference for a judge, or into victim advocacy services and other social work-oriented careers. In the field of criminal justice and related social services, an awareness of (and a sensitivity to) peoples and cultures different from our own can make the professional work environment more dignified for everyone.

- Cultural cognition mitigates institutional prejudices and helps to resolve conflict. Ultimately, utilizing a cultural cognition approach in our professional work allows us to better meet the needs of the individual, the group, and the communities in which we work and live.
- Cultural cognition helps professionals steer clear of acting on unconsidered or biased assumptions.

To begin to develop cultural cognition is to begin to explore the contents of our own minds. If we remain critically *un*aware of what we learned about the world in childhood, then we risk repeating the traumas and injustices we seek to redress as responsible adults, as professionals, as citizens. For example, child abuse is a great social injustice, even as it stands as a kind of road map to the ways in which the powerful treat the powerless in societies all over the world. Inequality in all of its myriad forms is a social distortion of our potential as human beings. Yet, too often the ideological status quo has a vested interest in maintaining social inequality by exploiting ignorance and fear. We must address our fear so that we might inform our ignorance.

To be culturally competent, as the social sciences define it, means to recognize the behavior of people as an expression of their culture. In order to do this, then, the critical thinker committed to social justice must understand what makes up the culture of different communities, including issues related to gender, race, age disparities, and especially the economic realities experienced by them.

The concept of "otherness" is a fundamental organizing social category that implicitly teaches us to perceive ourselves in opposition to an "other." When identity depends upon a dichotomy, a hierarchy of insiders versus outsiders, social groups, as well as individuals within them, will be polarized, at odds, and locked in a social conflict *sui generis.* [2] Because different social groups have unequal access to power as well as resources, systemic inequality results, all of which confirms predisposed beliefs in the inferiority of some, and the superiority of others, based upon their access to power and resources. Such a way of thinking is a self-fulfilling ideology that serves to maintain the cultural status quo.

To authentically engage with others—rather than to placate, condescend, or "manage others," we must first accord individuals their rights to respect and dignity, something difficult to do if we have already judged them in our minds. It is no surprise that a fundamental idea to initiate cultural cognition comes from a social worker, whose training includes "active listening."

To practice "active listening" requires mindful attention to the verbal and non-verbal messages that help us to understand their choice of words, the idioms they use, the social contexts of the communication, and so on. "Active listening" is empathy at work. If we accept the fact that all communication has meaning, we open the door to understanding others and the nature of their realities even when (and especially when) they differ from ours. We do not have to be social workers to develop this awareness. When we resist stereotyping others, or projecting our fears and prejudices, we can focus and actively listen. When we understand ourselves more authentically, we are able to recognize and re-own our projections and so enhance authentic contact with others.

The challenge to empathy and authentic contact is that discrimination comes in myriad forms; nowhere is the Dunning-Kruger effect more operative than in unconscious bias we often carry towards others. We believe one thing while remaining unaware of our deeper assumptions about the world. In other words, we most often respond to others the way our role models taught us in our most formative years. We learn from an early age from things said and unsaid by family members—who think children are not listening or are oblivious. But children absorb the values of their environment as sure as they breathe the air. In school, in the media, on the internet, at the dinner table, even in religious programs like Sunday school, children need no formal education about how to treat others. They learn it exactly as they learn language—by immersion, by osmosis. This is no small idea. The very notion of human dignity and the possibility for social justice begins with childhood. If adults treat children with dignity, authenticity, non-violence, and fairness—while living and speaking these values for others—the world might actually change for the better. Childhood is a laboratory of environmental conditioning.

To understand "cultural cognition" and to practice it requires critical thinking skills. But it is *not* true that critical thinking might end in "cultural cognition." In fact, critical thinking might lead to artificial intelligence, for example, and the coding of increasingly sophisticated algorithms that do our thinking for us. Research has shown that the creators of artificial intelligence hardware and software build into them their own unexamined cultural biases, racism, and other ideological values that systematically disenfranchise others. We take this issue up in later chapters, but it is worth noting again how critical thinking must be combined with self-awareness and empathy in order to turn it towards social justice. Even so, critical thinking and cultural cognition require self-awareness and the ability to self-assess via meta-cognition. Crucial, too, is the ability to take in and act upon the feedback from colleagues and others.

The first step towards recognizing others as part of a community that differs from our own is to first recognize our own culture and become aware of how it operates. The challenge here is that our own culture, our language, and our social practices of all kinds seem entirely "normal." Others are different. The experience is precisely like that of listening to others speak: we hear their accent, but we do not hear our own. In fact, often we believe that we have no accent—only other people from other places have accents. We speak "normally." This is a great, yet common error that underscores the problem of privilege.

To study our own culture requires that we practice meta-cognition, that is, we need to step back from our environment and learn how to "hear our own accent." Remember that "normal" might be defined in a multitude of ways, and it has throughout history, and many of which history has condemned. How do we live? Is there anything "normal" today that history may condemn us for later? We learn what "normal" is from our families, as well as from our screens, TVs, computers, cell phones, etc. But our families come first, and so it behooves us to explore our own history. What did we learn about wealth and money from our primary caregivers, especially from their role-modeling? What did we learn about work? Did anyone value education? Who held power in the family? How did the powerful use their power against others? Who expressed anger? When? Under what circumstances? The question of violence is a difficult one, for violence is often defined by those in power. Was there violence in the home growing up? What kind of violence? Verbal? Emotional? Physical? Was their drug and alcohol use? Were family conflicts resolved, or did they go on without resolution? If resolved, how so? If not, what do we learn as children in such a situation?

Exploring questions like these is crucial for social justice; meta-cognition combined with cultural cognition add up to what we are calling *critical awareness*, discussed in the next chapter. For now, it is enough to define *critical awareness* as the amalgamation of intellectual competence, meta-cognitive awareness, and cultural cognition, which together inform what we consider to be a robust and transformative way to understand social justice.

## Discussion and writing exercises

- How does/did your parent(s) and/or other adults in your family behave towards others who appear racially or ethnically different from you?
- What are some of the things you have heard your parent(s) and/or adults in your childhood say about people who held different religious beliefs from your family? What does your family's religion teach and practice that may be different from other religions? How is/was the difference handled?
- Has anyone in your family presented themselves as a non-conforming gender? Has anyone shared their non-conforming sexual orientation? How did your family respond? How did you feel? What do you believe today?
- How are children and the elderly treated in your family?
- Do you know anyone who is living with a disability of any kind? How are they treated or talked about in comparison to others? Do they receive the support they need? How easily are you able to integrate people with disabilities into your family, schools, and communities?
- Try to imagine what it would be like to live with a physical disability. Precisely how would your life change from the way it is?
- What life experiences might you hold in common with your enemies?

As we can see from these questions, cultural cognition and critical thinking go hand in hand. Our pre-judgments about others inform our thinking in a way that makes our biases seem natural, obvious, and nearly impossible to "hear," like our accents when we speak. In order to become aware of our judgments and the routinized thinking that goes with them, we have to claim our humanity and commit to the work required to become more fully human. Confucius (551 BC–479 BC), China's most famous philosopher, said: "To see what is right and not to do it is to want of courage, or of principle."[3] Moral fortitude brings sharpness of mind, courage, and honor. Exploring what all this means is the topic of this book.

## The problem with otherness

When we live in an entrenched ideology that posits "otherness" as a reality defined by those in power, then social injustice becomes the norm. In Michel Foucault's famous work, *Discipline and Punish: The Birth of the Prison* (1975), he addresses how power structures have created "docile bodies."[4] Foucault's "docile bodies" represent an antithesis to the notion of individual agency. Examples of docile bodies are prisoners, soldiers, hospital patients, and even school children. According to Foucault, the institutions that house docile bodies manage the people in their charge based upon the social category assigned to them by culture and social practice. While seemingly benign, Foucault argues that in a society where institutions make bodies submissive and meek, knowledge becomes an instrument of power. Foucault argues that the goals of social power and the goals of social knowledge cannot be separated. Our job then, as responsible agents combatting injustice, is to identify social and historical formations of power and the knowledge that perpetuates them.

Because we were all children once, nearly all of us have been raised as compliant and pliable precisely because when we were young, we were powerless, dependent creatures. As very young children we internalize social norms along with the language we acquire simply by listening to it, a process that begins in infancy. We have no choice but to participate. But later, as we grow, we enter into the possibility of awareness of both ourselves and others along with the understanding of how knowledge is socially constructed. It follows then that the notion of "otherness" is an example of a socially constructed idea, not really "real," that is, not biologically necessary for one racial group to dominate, enslave, torture, or kill another group. Nevertheless, social practices informed by tradition and history make such beliefs seem real and necessary. By this historical process, culture "creates" knowledge and creates categories of "other" within a given society by race, by gender, by socioeconomic class, by immigration status, by age, by sexual orientation, by ability versus disability, or by religion. These so-called "others" wield far less power than those who shape the dominant cultural discourse and have far less access to opportunities or social resources. Built in to the concept of "otherness" is a self-justifying belief that the "other" probably deserves their condition because they are somehow responsible for their poverty, misery, illness, and so on.

Durkheim argued that there are independent facts, *sui generis*, that exist outside of society and that exist outside of every individual, all of which simply compounds the problem of what is socially "normal." Our ideas pre-date us, our parents, and our grandparents. But consider the fact that the African slave trade went on for well over 400 years: that means slavery, colonialism, the idea of superior and inferior humans, and that buying and selling of other human beings was perfectly consistent with a Christian civilization that persisted for over 20 generations.

We should be mindful then, and skeptical, of social "norms." The ideologies and social practices that usually pre-date our arrival in the world, and that will likely exist after we depart, is not proof of their "rightness" and in no way validates the vast social injustices that persist. It is no small task to investigate the effects of our social practices on our minds and the values we hold. We have been molded from birth—before birth even—by categories that have shaped generations.

As children we have little choice but to adopt the social categories the world offers us, and so we become passive and tame in exchange for an identity and a group that offers us a sense of belonging. Our need for identity and belonging seems harmless enough at face value, but such is the root of the problem that can challenge our growth and build cultural cognition. Our identities are constantly reinforced by the groups we spend time with; every social exchange reinforces our sense of identity and our sense of self-worth.

We become more human when we understand how much of who we are has been shaped by social and historical forces that we generally do not think about, yet they are all around us in the form of gross social inequity, routine violence, and a wide range of undesirable, unhealthy behaviors, policies and circumstances—all normalized by our routinized social practices. Cultural cognition begins when we address our own personal assumptions about others which are almost always misinformed as a result of ideology supported by ignorance.

---

### RESEARCH EXERCISE

Interview a member of a racial or ethnic minority group different from your own who has had experience with law enforcement. Interview another person from a more privileged group (e.g., white, middle-class man or woman), and ask him or her about their experience with the police. Ask each what she or he feels when a police officer enters her or his space, such a convenience store or on the street. Ask about traffic stops: how often each respondent is stopped, for what offenses, and what were the outcomes? Compare the similarities and differences between the respondents.

---

## On race and culture

By now it should be obvious that we believe no one is born a racist. In fact, science tells us no one is born a "race." "In 2003 scientists completed the Human Genome Project, making it finally possible to examine human ancestry with genetics.[5] Geneticists have discovered that race cannot be biologically defined due to genetic variations among populations. An older but still-prevalent belief in identifying someone's "race" is a collection of five distinct race categories that no longer have a biological basis in reality: African, Asian, European, Native American, and Oceanian. According to this disproven typography, there is a wide variation among "races," each a separate category unto itself. "Additionally," Vivian Chou, doctoral candidate at Harvard University, writes, "individual races are thought to have a relatively uniform genetic identity," but this is not true.[6] In fact, genetic variations among different populations around the world are very small, contradicting the concept of five distinct racial categories. "Furthermore," Chou said, "that the study revealed many genetic variations within small geographical regions, which indicates that there is no uniform genetic identity for any single 'race.'" Genetic evidence "points to the fundamental similarity of all people around the world—an idea that has been supported by many other studies."[7]

The consensus then among a wide variety of scientists is that the concept of race is a social construction and not a sign of some inner biological essence. The idea of biological essence refers to what some believe are indicators of racial "superiority"—stronger, smarter, for example, and that some "races" are superior to others because of their racial lineage. From this nonscientific interpretation, we are more different than we are the same; therefore, it makes sense that some races should dominate—perhaps even eradicate—other races because of their "inferiority."

Scientific evidence indicates that race is part of our nurture, not our nature, despite the concept that race continues to inform ideological beliefs and social practices. The question of race and the associated issues of privilege and power, or lack of privilege and power, that go along with different racial categories have long been determined and defined by ideologies and social practices formed by a European patriarchy. Using the idea of race and one's racial superiority to justify the power they sought to exert took place all over the world in the form of a colonial empire.[8] Racist ideologies, informed by both religious and pseudo-scientific rationalizations, were used to endorse the African slave trade and slavery along with other genocides of the modern era. The malignant desire for power, privilege, and wealth justified (and continues to justify) gross social injustices.

At one time Europeans thought of race and national origin as one and the same thing, so if we asked people about their race in Europe and in many other parts of the world it was akin to asking them about their country of origin. But over time, particularly in the United States with its history of African slavery and property rights, the terms "race" and "ethnicity" came to yield political and cultural associations that perpetuate institutionalized discrimination, racism, and prejudice, which is indeed ironic when considering the United States historically considered itself a "classless" society compared to Old Europe.

Today the term "ethnicity" refers to the state of belonging to a social group that has a common national or cultural tradition. Our ethnicity plays a large role in standardizing our behaving, perceiving, evaluating, and acting; our verbal and nonverbal communication skills; the food we eat and the clothing we wear; the rituals, celebrations, and the religious customs that we participate in. All these traditions help us piece together our self-concept. And although we inherit these traditions from our ancestors, our ethnic culture is diverse and constantly changing.

The term race, on the other hand, is much less straightforward and infinitely more problematic. Yet, discrimination against people of color continues as a consequence of cultural practices informed by ideologies of race going back hundreds of years, and with *no basis* in biology. Fundamentally, we are one species with only superficial differences. Understanding the difference between our biology and our ethnicity and cultural traditions opens up the possibility for critical awareness, that is, of seeing into and operating from insights that could unite us as a species.

Cultural cognition involves our ability to harness intellectual competence and critical thinking to become aware of and to take action against issues of systemic social injustice. The false notion of racial superiority or inferiority as a function of "nature" lies behind notions of the "other." The good news is that it can be unlearned. We can use critical thinking skills to become aware of our conditioned responses to social practices and reclaim our humanity. We can become active agents for social justice.

## Class, culture, and ethnicity

Socioeconomic diversity tells an interesting, albeit sobering, story about the problem of social stratification and the imbalance of power between the rich and the poor. As we discussed in Chapter 1, the income gap between the haves and the have-nots, within and between countries, has steadily increased at an accelerating rate over the past decades.[9] What does this mean in terms of real life experiences? According to the US Bureau of Justice Statistics National Crime Victimization Survey, the data report that individuals living at or below the poverty line are more than twice as likely to become victims of violent crime, and in economically poor households they experience a higher rate of violence with a firearm compared to middle-class households. [10] According to the US Census Bureau report, minority populations experience the highest national poverty rates[11]: 27 percent of American Indian and Alaska natives live below the poverty line, followed by Blacks or African Americans at 25.8 percent. By comparison, only 12 percent of people who identify as white live below the poverty line. Overall, income inequality—the gap between the rich and the poor—has steadily increased since the 1970s. From 1970 to 2016, the income gap increased 27 percent and continues to rise. More disturbing is the rise in inequality within racial and ethnic communities.[12] Why does this matter? Racial and ethnic groups experience diminished economic opportunity, restricted upward mobility, and have less political influence. Growing inequality also leads to geographic segregation based on income. These economic disparities also brings with it a limited investment in education, and education predicts—or is causal—to median family wealth and is also highly correlated with health and well-being, mortality and morbidity.[13]

Economic insecurity leads to struggles with employment and under-employment, and it can create material conditions so demanding that individuals are unable to emotionally cope with their situation. Having to choose between eating and paying the rent defines what it means to be in a "stressful situation." To blame an individual for being "lazy" in such a situation seems at best inadequate, and at worst maliciously neglectful.[14]

For centuries the poor in the United States were unable to vote, apply for a bank loan, qualify for an advanced educational degree, or effectively manage an encounter with the criminal justice system. Some things have changed, but many things have not. Racial profiling is common across societies. Too often our physical features seem to confirm for others who they think we are without anyone saying a word. Racism is lazy; it is organized around ignorance and fueled by fear. That mere physical differences among some groups have been used to create and perpetuate racial castes in the United States and in other regions of the world remains an ideological source of social injustice.

According to sociologists, poverty is a self-fulfilling cycle not because its victims embrace it, but because the poor have minimal access to resources that would lift them out of poverty. When such a cycle exists in a community for generations, social injustice takes on the form of "blaming the victim," or in other words, the dominant social group blames the poor for their poverty because they are "lazy." Such beliefs eliminate the need to take into account the systemic social issues that lead to generations of poverty, and instead fall back on racial and ethnic stereotypes to justify inequality. While it is true that "life is unfair," this does not mean that life *should* be unfair—we can make it fair. That is what it means to work towards the humanization of our society.

To practice *cultural cognition* means to recognize cultural difference without judgment and recognize our own awareness of difference as a product of social conditioning. To understand that race is a social construct, and racism is the outcome, means that we understand the misuse of power and must question the ideological justification that oppresses large groups of people. Blaming the victim misdirects attention from the causes of poverty and rationalizes perpetual discrimination.

Should a baby born into poverty be cursed for life by her environment? By bad nutrition? By inadequate educational resources? By instability, violence, and prejudice? As infants and children, our developmental environment affects our overall physical, emotional, and mental health for the rest of our lives. Researchers from the Centers for Disease Control (2016) released a report on the impact significant childhood deficits have on our mental and physical health later in life.[15] For example, they report that

> Those who lived in poverty as young children are more at-risk for leading causes of illness and death, and are more likely to experience poor quality of life. This growing problem costs the United States billions of dollars annually … Interventions that support healthy development in early childhood reduce disparities, have lifelong positive impacts, and are prudent investments. Addressing these disparities effectively offers opportunities to help children, and benefits our society as a whole.

It is easy to see how socioeconomic inequities lead to basic kinds of suffering, while planting the social and biological seeds for greater suffering in years to come.[16] Consider that our socioeconomic realities inform the most basic life decisions adults make for children. Because of generational poverty, we may have no choice but to live in a community that has no access to a supermarket, adequate schools, or safe and secure housing. Instead, we may live in what researches call a "food desert" with only fast food chains, liquor stores, and billboards that encourage us to play the lottery. We may live month to month, pay check to pay check, work for minimum wage; perhaps with a threat of eviction months or weeks away.

For others, socioeconomic insecurity often triggers incidents of domestic violence, including incidents that involve children who witness domestic violence, or who themselves become victims.[17] Recent research has discovered that the trauma of violence that we experience in our childhood can last a lifetime if left unaddressed, and in some instances these traumas are the building blocks for criminal behavior later on in life.[18]

According to the Bureau of Justice Statistics, 41 percent of the nation's incarcerated do not have a high school diploma or a GED, and another 31 percent of those on probation do not have a high school diploma or its equivalent.[19] The BJS data show that over half the prison population in the United States are incarcerated for either using or selling drugs. Meanwhile, of those who never completed high school, a third of them live below the poverty line, set in 2019 as $25,750 per year for a family of four.[20] When there are no or limited opportunities like education to climb the socioeconomic ladder, economic and personal hardships later in life are likely to follow.

The data indicate that the lack of education is a predictor of poverty. According to the US Department of Education, people who work full time without a high school diploma can expect to earn an average annual income of $23,900.[21] Important to note that living in poverty does not predict delinquent and criminal behavior, although the two factors are strongly correlated due to other risk factors besides poverty. Sociological research has demonstrated that the stressors associated with not having enough to make ends meet explains why we might find a disproportionate representation of people living in poverty filling hospitals beds, police cars, courtrooms, and prison cells. In sum, the many scientific studies which find that at-risk groups of people *from birth* are more likely to develop anti-social or criminal behavior notify us of the myriad social injustices they experience.

Before we move on to privilege as a correlate of dominant group membership, we need to complete our analysis of non-dominant group status. So far, our picture is bleak: poverty, discrimination, criminal justice system involvement, demonization, minimal educational, economic, and social opportunities and so on. But the helping professions, such as those in the medical field or social work, have long recognized that all social groups have strengths, which come in many forms. Think about the growth of single-parent families, usually mothers. Deficit-based blaming-the-victim assessments point to single moms as evidence of inferior culture, and the prominent cause of inter-generational poverty. Strength-based analyses recognize changing family structures as adaptations to environmental stressors, such as the over-representation of men of color in the prison system (primarily for offenses for which white major-group males receive very little or no prison time). Social workers and other trained professionals know to look for and build on the strengths they find among people experiencing social stressors, as an application of rigorous empathy.

## Breakout writing assignment: check your privilege

Privilege refers to a type of narcissism. Because of our class-cultural identity, along with our community memberships, "dominant group" members (typically white,

Christian, middle-aged, wealthy, straight, able-bodied) are spared from having to think about how others with fewer favored characteristics experience the world. Often privilege is largely unearned, but because of it we have access to resources, both materially and socially, that are only readily available to advantaged group members. Being born with privilege is an advantage, just as being born poor means that you are part of a disadvantaged group. Privilege is often invisible to those who enjoy it, though sometimes this status comes with arguments that attempt to justify it. We use the term narcissism because dominant groups get to determine ideas about what is "normal," and place themselves as examples of normality. Typically, to be white, upper middle class, able-bodied, and heterosexual means to have the most access to resources and power; this is how advantaged groups perpetuate themselves as the ideological status quo.

Writing is an opportunity to organize our thinking, and record key ideas, quotes, and questions. We use writing as an opportunity to step back and consider our world and our place in it. Questions to consider and respond to in writing are:

- How privileged are you? On what basis? Do you belong to a dominant group that claims, and is accorded, a superior social position? What groups have more or less privilege than yours?
- Identify some benefits (and/or) liabilities that come from your relative privilege, or lack thereof. Think about your education and access to higher education, your housing, your safety, your security, your transitions among life's developmental stages, your career opportunities. Think about lunch and dinnertime growing up. Choose three examples from your life experiences to answer this question.
- What do members of your group think of groups with less privilege than yours? What do members of your group think about groups with more privilege? What assumptions or caricatures do members of your group hold about those with more or less privilege?
- Do you enjoy access to resources that enhance your chances of leading a comfortable, productive and secure life? How much of this is due to privilege?
- Do you belong to a social group that has been in the past, or in the present, considered inferior, different, or abnormal in some way?
- Because of your community or personal identity, have you experienced limited access to resources and social power?
- To finish your writing, define "privilege" in your own words, and identify groups in society today who you believe have more or less privilege than you do.

According to social philosopher and sociologist Jürgen Habermas (1929–) and other experts, privilege allows us to live in a world at odds with reality.[22] To be unaware of the effects pollution has on the environment is an example of privilege. To be unaware of myriad social injustices caused by pollution is another. Privilege insulates us from having to think about others, sometimes the consequences of our own actions, and privilege keeps us unaware of the material conditions and social injustices that others experience every day. For example, environmental reporter Sharon Lerner, who writes for *The Intercept*, provides an account of what has happened to a small town outside of New Orleans, Louisiana.[23] The little town of St. John "has been overloaded with carcinogens" from a colorless gas called chloroprene, a byproduct emitted by a nearby synthetic rubber factory that has been in operation since 1969. This community is 80 percent African American and per capita income is under $18,000 per year, and individuals living in the community have a risk of developing cancer at an outstanding rate. The nationwide risk of developing cancer from chemicals in the air is assessed at 30 per million people while for those living in St. John it is 800 per million. Needless to say, this community of 46,000 people has an urgent need to get their government to put more regulations in place, but the Environmental Protection Agency supported the companies in the area by simply changing the classification of its assessment of polluting gases from "probable" to "suggestive" and replaced the safety limit for chloroprene with one that is 156 times higher. Despite the community's best efforts, regulation of these industries that emit cancer-causing chemicals largely falls on deaf ears. Chloroprene and other industrial chemicals make St. John the highest locality of cancer in the nation. While the Environmental Protection Agency knew about St. John's unusually high cancer cluster, they decided not to change the industrial regulations. As Lerner states,

> In an administration that has been defined by its science denial and regulatory rollbacks, the assessments that haven't led to enforceable protections—or have been kept from the public entirely—are in one sense just another example of a government captured by industry.

For the people of this small town, the lack of government protection is a matter of life and death.

When we join the people who "are like us" within a particular socioeconomic circle and think like us, we can easily obscure, even hide, the important discourses that need our attention and debate. Habermas (1993) wrote, "I would in fact tend to have more confidence in the outcome of a democratic decision if there was a minority that voted against it, than if it was unanimous … Social psychology has amply shown the strength of this bandwagon effect."[24] Habermas laments our lack of independent thinking, so like cows to slaughter, we copy what others in our group have said is the right thing to do, what to buy, or whom to vote for. He and other researchers argue that our bubble is too comfortable, so much so that we are lulled into a kind of obliviousness to other bubbles in the world, drastically different from our own, and perhaps can open our mind to engage in a more enlightened and mindful way. The minority in opposition to a majority often demonstrates that critical thinking and dissent are part of a truly democratic process.

## Cultural cognition and the science of the brain

Neuropsychology helps us to understand how brains develop within the cultural horizon of our childhood environments. We begin to learn language by hearing language, much of which is not directed at us as the primary target. We simply absorb the sounds of the words, the emotional tenor of the voices, and a host of other environmental factors as we learn our native tongue. Language comes at us as ambient sound waves that shape our brains from our earliest moments. As children we even begin to form unconscious bias against individuals who are rejected or feared by our primary caregivers.[25] In such a way, our biases and prejudices—and the traumas and strains that inform them—are passed down generationally, so much so that we may never know precisely where our own beliefs come from or how they seem to preexist us.

Medical techniques like functional magnetic resonance imaging (fMRI) have allowed neuropsychologists and other scientists to see the brain function in real time.[26] From this research, we know that the brain's neural pathways develop stronger and hardier networks in some areas and have less developed networks in other areas. Research confirms what may seem obvious: the more of one kind of interaction we have, the more likely it is that our behavior related to that interaction becomes a conditioned response. We stop thinking or reflecting on it, and instead we respond automatically, that is, as a conditioned behavior not unlike Ivan Pavlov's dog experiments.[27] Psychologists call this "classical conditioning." We do it, think it, and believe it automatically and without reflection.

Why? Because when stimulated, the brain is learning and growing, expanding its dendrites into a well-connected neuron superhighway.[28] As our childhood environment continues to inform our brain development, our brains also adapt to the culture, language, and social practices all around us. How we interact with others, how others interact with us, and how we witness others cooperating with each other informs how we learn to relate to the world and all its relational parts. Our classical, pre-conditioned responses strengthen over time as our brains continue to develop.

Neuroscience also tells us the brain has the ability to change, so while we may have learned one thing as children, it is certainly possible to grow and develop. Cultural cognition requires us to have the willingness and the courage to explore our own learned assumptions about the world. The more we are willing to consider and sort out the contents of our own minds, the more likely it is we will be able to identify debilitation, alienating fears, prejudices, and outright discrimination. From here, we become more capable of finding the humanity in other people. Our brains can and do adapt to the new demands we put on it. With exposure to new people, new communities, and different cultures, we learn and we change.

Though the brain is capable of self-awareness and change, we often fail to realize the need. The Implicit Association Test, "Project Implicit," by Harvard University illustrates that we are often not aware of our own prejudices.[29] Project Implicit has been found reliable in its ability to measure implicit or unconscious attitudes and bias about cultural issues pertinent to professionals, and the results have shown that we are often unaware of our implicit or unconscious biases toward some person or groups of people. For example, in a study of 2,156,053 participants, Hehman, Flake and Calanchini (2018) demonstrated that only subconscious racial prejudices and stereotypes among Whites approved of police using lethal force.[30]

Some other forms of bias and prejudice are more deliberate and manifest themselves with actions and words. Such an overt display is known as "explicit bias," a conscious intention to behave differently toward a particular person, social group, or social situation. This type of blatant (mis)behavior might be observable as signs of social disrespect that include a shrug of indifference, dismissal, or more aggressive verbal insults that can even culminate in acts of violence.

Neuroscientists tell us that many of the brain's judgments actually come from one small and oldest part of the brain, the amygdala.[31] The amygdala has left and right almond-shaped sections and is located deep within the temporal lobe and plays a primary role in the process of memory, quick decision-making, and emotional reactions. Neuropsychologists have discovered that the right side of the amygdala helps us to process negative emotion, and this is how we unconsciously link our experiences in the world with fear or anxiety, and we project these emotional qualities on to other events, people, and places. This is known as "fear conditioning," or the "fight, flight, or freeze" response and accounts for how neutral stimuli can cause us take on disagreeable, aversive behaviors. Thankfully, also within the amygdala's charge is its ability to help us grow and change. In fact, when neuropsychologists study the brains of violent criminals, they have found that their amygdalae are significantly smaller, indicating less empathy, than those of adults in the general, non-incarcerated population.[32]

The good news is that by providing cognitive behavioral therapy and supportive social skills programs, violent criminals can be helped—the amygdala in their brains actually changes. Such cognitive behavioral programs help their amygdalae to grow with amazingly positive results, and with this growth, their ability to think critically and competently grows.[33] Over time, these inmates showed improvement on social and emotional behavior development scores and were better able to suppress and control their anger.[34] Compassion for themselves and others was quantitatively measurable and showed improvement. (Such research suggests an argument to do away with solitary confinement.) Needless to say, the brain has an amazing capacity to grow and expand our minds and change our behaviors at any age and under difficult circumstances.

As critical thinkers, we must train ourselves to the reality that all people and circumstances are neutral; it is how we respond to each and every conflict that matters. We can choose to respond to any difficulty with anxiety and fear, bias and prejudice, or outright discrimination, or we can be mindful of what our reactions might be and take an approach of neutrality before we even open our mouths to respond.

## Discussion exercise: is this racism?

At the grocery store in a suburb of a major US city, a white woman busily placed her groceries on the checkout belt when she looked at two women standing in line behind her and she frowned. They were brown. Their long hair was brown. They looked Mexican, or something, she thought. The white woman grabbed for her purse from her carriage, and slung it around her so that she was between it and the two brown women. She noticed their clothing now and thought their hair was too long and made them both look squat and dark. They were out of place in her supermarket and she immediately felt suspicious, a bit fearful of the impending walk to her car after paying for her groceries.

The two brown women both noticed the white woman's behavior. The first one felt a wave of anger course through her body as she stood there. She stared at the white woman. The second young woman looked down at her feet. One of the women was a graduate student studying sociology, visiting the United States from Central America. They were both in town for a nearby academic conference. The first met the white woman's eyes and said politely, "Don't worry, we won't steal your purse. It's beautiful, though. Kate Spade has great designs." *What a racist* she thought to herself. The white woman laughed nervously. "Oh, no!" was all she could manage to mumble. "*Oh, yes,*" the sociology student thought to herself, but said nothing more. She felt that she had called out the white woman with her not so subtle display of prejudice and was glad that she made the cutting remark about the woman's purse. That was enough, she thought.

- Is the white woman guilty of racist behavior? What else might be going on here? What do you make of the brown woman's comment about not stealing the purse? Was it an innocent statement or did it carry more meaning?
- Could more have been accomplished in this encounter? Who is responsible for moving the dialogue forward between privileged and non-privileged people?

More complicated than "implicit bias" and "explicit bias" is something called "aversive racism." Aversive racism is a type of cognitive dissonance or conflict that occurs when we find our conscious thoughts at odds with our unconscious conditioning. For example, aversive racism is a form of bias that can manifest as every day "put downs" and insults that psychologists describe as microaggressions.[35] Negative evaluations of racial and ethnic minorities, for example, might lead to a continual avoidance of interaction with individuals from these social groups. An internal processing conflict occurs in the brain when we deny that we hold any explicit bias against a person or group while at the same time we hold unconscious, negative feelings and beliefs against that person or their community. In these instances, we are indeed the perpetrator and the individual or group we are biased against is the victim. Aversive racism describes what happens to the brain, and subsequently how we respond, when we are trapped between "explicit" and "implicit" bias.

To resolve the contradiction would require a serious exploration into the feelings and thoughts inherent in bias and prejudice. But rather than a deep dive into our own values, feelings, and beliefs by exploring where our thoughts come from, we step away—we might think that this is too threatening to our fragile egos to analyze. And so we reject, that is, we dissociate from ourselves as a defense mechanism to protect our sense of self and to reduce the fear and anxiety our inner conflict has provoked. It is not uncommon for people who do not consider themselves racist, sexist, etc. to harbor these beliefs against another without recognizing their beliefs for what they are.

Aversive racists and sexists are typically more diffuse than overt racists; they tend to express this personal prejudice with feelings of uneasiness and anxiety or avoid eye contact and perhaps blink more.[36] For example, someone might be an aversive racist when she or he has uncomplimentary things to say about a stigmatized group, as defined by race, age, ethnicity, religious preferences, physical disabilities, or sexual orientation, and so on.[37] It should come as no surprise that the aversive racist may be an avowed anti-racist, but such a person will struggle with inter-personal relations when trying to demonstrate her or his understanding. Individuals such as this who remain dissociated from themselves will have problems with communication, cooperation, and trust-building. Aversive racists bring negative consequences to our workplace relationships and other social situations. Unfortunately, aversive racism, sexism, and classism are all too common and continue to represent a fundamental challenge to social justice.

We believe all people have judgmental feelings toward "others" as a consequence of being members of society. We must recognize and challenge our prejudices and focus diligently on trying to overcome them. To deny that we do not have those feelings while articulating anti-racist, anti-sexist, anti-ageist sentiments, etc., is to live in the averse trap. Being mindful that we might get trapped means we are able to practice cultural competency. Being culturally competent is indeed a constant practice where we seek to identify and understand our culturally-grounded differences in a manner that is both congenial to persons of diverse cultural outlooks and consistent with social justice. The term for this is "cultural cognition" and the lack of it refers to the tendency to accept behavior and activities that we and our peer group deem honorable for the good of society, and we reject behavior by others that we perceive as dishonorable and hurtful to society. These "world views" produce hierarchies of "in-groups" and "out-groups" with serious social and personal consequences.

If we are to pursue social justice, we must spot the importance of cultural cognition as the politicization of intellectual competence and critical thinking, themselves largely apolitical and without agendas. With cultural cognition, however, a political agenda is enjoined to critical thinking. In the following chapter, we will explore how intellectual competence, critical thinking, and cultural cognition combine to inform what we are calling *critical awareness* as a moral, ethical, and political agenda for social justice. To unlearn our biases requires that we recognize our associations, our identifications, and our memories from a network of learned behavior, woven together into our personalities complete with threads from our ancestral histories and present day groups with which we associate.

Consider the terms "in-group" and "out-group" to explain racism, classism, sexism, ageism, and bias based on sexual orientation. According to sociologists, the in-group and out-group terms categorize our social environment into manageable units that designate those groups in which we feel accepted and the "other" groups to which we feel we do not belong. To develop our cultural cognition, it helps to sort out our beliefs about what we think we know about "out-groups" and to *seek direct experience at every opportunity* to learn from them. It is rare for an avowed racist to know, or even meet, a single person who identifies as the out-group they so despise.

If we slow down the speediness of our automatic thoughts, particularly when the thoughts harbor bias, stereotypes, and prejudice, we are practicing a habit of mind necessary for cultural cognition. Cultural cognition requires a moment to reflect and become aware of our own internal processes that lead up to our feelings, our language, and our actions. The research that we have mentioned earlier in this chapter shows that culturally competent individuals who are highly motivated to reduce their implicit biases have learned strategies that strengthen and build new and improved neural networks in the brain. These new neural networks reduce implicit bias and aversive racism.

Up until this point we have mainly focused on racism that has serious, life-long negative effects. Gender bias is also an area that, whether you identify as a boy or a girl, goes far beyond biological identifiers. Our differences are with the *idea* of our differences, for other than our ideas, there are no important, actual differences. Keeping this in mind opens the way to critical awareness and movement toward social justice.

We all have biased assumptions we learned in our early development years. Meta-cognition offers a way of recognizing where these beliefs come from and helps us sort out the ones based in fear, ignorance, and inherited prejudices. In this way we reduce our biases to ideas that are subject to analysis via intellectual competence. Developing cultural cognition is an organic process; it is not without its emotional challenges. Many insights about privilege, for example, might challenge the awareness we have of ourselves. All we need is the willingness of an open mind.

## Breakout writing assignment: check your brain

Spend 30–45 minutes writing responses to the following questions:

- Where did you grow up? Describe the neighborhood.
- What did you hear about race, or sexual orientation, or other prejudices and biases growing up?
- Who did you hear it from?
- How would you describe your own beliefs, assumptions, feelings and interactions with people who are different from you?
- Based on this chapter, so far, how might you take steps to undo your prejudices?

## Practice

Aversive racism can be an extremely difficult challenge, particularly in the heat of the moment when quick decision-making is necessary. Quick judgments are necessary in some work professions, so let us take a look at the issue of racial profiling through the eyes of a police officer.

## Exercise

Read the following transcript of an actual exchange between a white police officer and a suspect that happened at 1:00 a.m. in a strip mall parking lot, in an American urban area during the month of January. The officer had been sent to check out suspicious activity of a young black male at the strip mall. Read the exchange below and assess whether the officer is an explicit racist. Is he the product of aversive racism? Or does he navigate the situation with critical thinking? Is he mindful of how the stop may appear to the suspect?

SUSPECT: You're stopping me because I'm black.

OFFICER: Well, yeah, I kinda am. But not really.

SUSPECT: This is racial profiling shit … You're only stopping me because I'm black!

OFFICER: Hey, come here. I want to show you something.

[The young man reluctantly walks over to the police cruiser.]

Take a look at what the description is here that was called in to HQ. Seriously, come here and sit in my police cruiser and read what dispatch told me to check out. Come see what it says on this screen.

SUSPECT: No way, man.

OFFICER: OK, I'll read it to you then. It says that I am to check out suspicious activity at this address, suspect is a black male, about 6 feet tall, and wearing a dark sweatshirt. OK … so if you were me, who would you stop? Is there anyone else at this location on this cold winter night with all the stores closed who is male, about 6 feet, and wearing a sweatshirt? There isn't anyone else here in this strip mall but you. So, am I really stopping you because you're black? Or am I stopping you because you're the only person at this location at one in the morning, and you happen to match the description dispatch sent me? And just what *are* you doing here when all the stores are closed?

SUSPECT: I'm waiting for a ride home.

OFFICER: You're waiting for a ride … here? Out in the cold? Where are you coming from?

SUSPECT: My cousin's house.

OFFICER: Your cousin's house. Where's your cousin's house?

SUSPECT: Over there.

OFFICER: Let me get this straight. You're waiting for a ride, but you were at your cousin's house just over there. It's like 10 degrees out here, so why didn't you wait for your ride there? Why did you walk all this way without a coat to wait for your ride? Let me see some I.D.

SUSPECT: [shrugs]: I don't have it on me.

OFFICER: You don't have any I.D? No wallet? What's your name?

SUSPECT: I left my wallet at my cousin's.

OFFICER: So you're headed home but say you left your wallet just over there. And you're not going back to get it?

SUSPECT: [shrugs]: You're profiling me, man. I ain't done nothin'.

[The officer notices that he keeps putting his hands inside his sweatshirt pocket]

OFFICER: Look, if you were me, you'd probably say to yourself that something just doesn't add up here. Yes? Am I really stopping you because you're black? What do you have in your sweatshirt pocket? Why do you keep touching what you've got in there?

[At that moment, another vehicle pulls into the strip mall parking lot, but sees the interaction, and quickly speeds away. The officer then decides to do a Terry frisk, which is a justifiable, quick search based on suspicious behavior, and finds a small scale and just less than an ounce of marijuana in the front pouch of his sweatshirt.]

So do you think the officer seemed concerned and aware for the potential of racially profiling the individual? Was this encounter police profiling rather than racial profiling? Did he confront it in a professional manner? This officer tries to impress upon the young man that his skin color had very little to do with the stop, while at the same time he acknowledges the suspect's comment about racial profiling. By acknowledging the historical and systemic discrimination African Americans face, do you think this officer was aware of the bias? Did he convey a sense of understanding? Are there additional or different ways the officer could have been culturally competent?

## Conclusion

We study ourselves not to judge ourselves, but in order to accept what we find, and then change for the better. We must begin with our own biases before we seek to affect institutional change. The work of cultural cognition requires that we remember where and when we internalized our prejudices, biases, and beliefs about the world and the people in it. Remember, they all started at a very early age—even before we could talk. We absorbed our sense of reality exactly the way we learned our primary language— passively from family, from exposure to popular culture and our entertainment mythologies, from school as social practice, from work place interactions, and so on. We may not even remember where many of our assumptions have come from or why we hold on to them so steadfastly. Recognizing that our assumptions and stereotypes about people do not develop in a vacuum or some privilege-neutral environment is a crucial insight that informs cultural cognition. It helps us to realize and to understand where we have been so that we can understand better where we are now.

To practice *cultural cognition* means:

- To accept difference without judgment and to recognize it as a product of social practice;
- To understand that race is a social construct and racism is the outcome;

- That no one is born a racist, a sexist, a homophobe, or someone who discriminates against people with disabilities, and so on.
- Prejudice justifies the misuse of power by serving as the ideological justification for the oppression of varying groups of people.

To purposefully work to counteract institutional or individual acts of bias, prejudice and stereotyping is the work of social justice. We can undo the unconscious bias that has built up along the brain's neural pathways by making real connections to real people in spite of our preconceived notions or "fear conditioning" to do otherwise. Over time such contact becomes less fraught as we become more accepting of ourselves and of others through practice. Let us reiterate: it does take practice.

Like critical thinking, cultural cognition requires self-awareness and the ability to self-assess via meta-cognition as well as getting feedback from others. Cultural cognition requires that we have an understanding of human nature, our own especially. Anything less will lead us to a widespread practice of cultural psychopathy, that is, we may find that we live in a world in which we have learned not to care about others or what others experience as human beings.

## Notes

1 Jonathan Stacks, Andrés Meléndez Salgado and Sara Holmes. "Cultural Competence and Social Justice: A Partnership for Change." *Advocates for Youth.* http://racialequity tools.org/resourcefiles/stacks.pdf. Accessed July 21, 2019.
2 *Sui generis* is a term that French sociologist Emile Durkheim (1858–1917) used to express his theory on social existence: a society's culture exists long before any one person is born into it, therefore any society is independent of all individuals. See "In Durkheim's Concepts, What Does Sui Generis Mean?" *Enotes.* https://www.enotes.com/homewor k-help/durkheim-concepts-what-does-sui-generis-249495. Accessed July 21, 2019.
3 "Confucius." Quotes. https://www.quotes.net/quote/50135. Accessed July 21, 2019.
4 Michel Foucault, *Discipline and Punish: The Birth of the Prison* (London: Penguin, 1975).
5 "15 for 15: Human Origins and Ancestry." *National Human Genome Research Institute.* https://www.genome.gov/dna-day/15-for-15/human-origins-ancestry. Accessed July 21, 2019.
6 Vivian Chou. "How Science and Genetics Are Reshaping the Race Debate of the 21st Century." *Harvard University, The Graduate School of Arts and Sciences. Science in the News.* http://sitn.hms.harvard.edu/flash/2017/science-genetics-reshaping-race-debate-21st-cen tury/. Accessed July 21, 2019.
7 Ibid.
8 Between the 18th and 20th centuries the British Empire held more territories than any other nation in the world. The writer John Wilson, under the pseudonym Christopher North, composed a serious of articles for a column called "*Noctes Ambrosianae.*" Wilson wrote, "His Majesty's dominions, on which the sun never sets," was changed to the more commonly held phrase, "The sun never sets on the British Empire." The British had established colonies in Africa, Asia, Europe, the Americas, and many islands across the globe. Historians estimated that approximately 25 percent of the earth's land mass was controlled by the British. See: "What Does The Sun Never Sets On The British Empire Mean?" *World Atlas.* https://www.worldatlas.com/articles/what-does-the-sun-never-sets-on-the-british-empire-mean.html. Accessed July 21, 2019.
9 Emily Guskin, "Is America Divided between the 'Haves' and 'Have-nots'? Most People Say No." *Washington Post.* April 4, 2019. https://www.washingtonpost.com/politics/

2019/04/04/is-america-divided-between-haves-have-nots-most-people-say-no/?utm_term=.e0e0e67108d2. Accessed July 21, 2019.

10 Erika Harrell, Lynn Langton, Marcus Berzofsky, Lance Couzens, and Hope Smiley-McDonald. "Household Poverty and Nonfatal Violent Victimization, 2008–2012." *U.S. Bureau of Justice Statistics, National Crime Victimization Survey, Poverty Crime and Violence.* https://www.bjs.gov/index.cfm?ty=pbdetail&iid=5137. Accessed July 21, 2019.

11 Rakesh Kochhar and Anthony Cilluffo. "Key Findings on the Rise in Income Inequality within America's Racial and Ethnic Groups." *Pew Research Center.* https://www.pewresearch.org/fact-tank/2018/07/12/key-findings-on-the-rise-in-income-inequality-within-americas-racial-and-ethnic-groups/. Accessed July 21, 2019.

12 Rakesh Kochhar and Anthony Cilluffo. "Income Inequality in the U.S. Is Rising Most Rapidly Among Asians: Asians Displace Blacks as the Most Economically Divided Group in the U.S." *Pew Research Center.* https://www.pewsocialtrends.org/2018/07/12/income-inequality-in-the-u-s-is-rising-most-rapidly-among-asians/. Accessed July 21, 2019.

13 William R. Emmons. "Education and Wealth: Correlation Is Not Causation." *Society for Financial Education and Professional Development.* https://www.stlouisfed.org/~/media/files/pdfs/hfs/assets/emmons-education-and-wealth-27oct2015.pdf?la=en. Accessed July 21, 2019.

14 Michelle Alexander. *The New Jim Crow: Mass Incarceration in the Age of Colorblindness* (New York: The New Press, 2010).

15 "Addressing Health Disparities in Early Childhood." Center for Disease Control and Prevention. https://www.cdc.gov/grand-rounds/pp/2016/20160315-childhood-development.html. Accessed July 21, 2019.

16 For a more personal and up-close account of these socioeconomic disparities, we suggest the classic, Jay MacLeod. *Ain't No Making It: Aspiration and Attainment in a Low-Income Neighborhood, 3rd Edition.* (New York: Routledge, 2009).

17 F. Blair, J. McFarlane, A. Nava, H. Gilroy, and J. Maddoux. "Child Witness to Domestic Abuse: Baseline Data Analysis for a Seven-Year Prospective Study," *Pediatric Nursing,* Vol. 41, No. 1 (2015): 23–9. https://www.ncbi.nlm.nih.gov/pubmed/26281272. Accessed July 21, 2019.

18 Tonya Glantz, Jill Harrison, and Adam Cable. "Trauma and Recidivism: Informing Assessment and Treatment Options for Incarcerated." *International Review of Modern Sociology,* Vol. 43, No. 1 (2017): 95–118. http://serialsjournals.com/index.php?route=product/product/volumearticle&issue_id=116&product_id=387.

19 Caroline Wolf Harlow. "Education and Correctional Populations." Bureau of Justice Statistics. https://www.bjs.gov/content/pub/pdf/ecp.pdf. Accessed July 21, 2019.

20 See this site for additional poverty threshold incomes: "U.S. Federal Poverty Guidelines Used to Determine Financial Eligibility for Certain Federal Programs." *U.S. Department of Health and Human Services, Office of the Assistant Secretary for Planning and Evaluation.* https://aspe.hhs.gov/poverty-guidelines. Accessed July 21, 2019.

21 "What Is the Annual Income for Someone Without a High School Diploma?" *Google.* https://www.google.com/search?rlz=1C1GCEA_enUS798US798&q=non+high+school+graduate+salary&sa=X&ved=2ahUKEwiz-4uopMbjAhUm1VkKHcs0AYoQ1QIoAXoECAoQAg&biw=1280&bih=578. Accessed July 21, 2019.

22 Jürgen Habermas. *On Society and Politics* (Boston: Beacon Press, 1989).

23 Sharon Lerner, "When Pollution Is a Way of Life," *New York Times.* June 22, 2019. https://www.nytimes.com/2019/06/22/opinion/sunday/epa-carniogens.html.     Accessed July 21, 2019.

24 Craig Calhoun (Ed.). *Habermas and the Public Sphere* (Boston: MIT Press, 1992).

25 Tobias Raabe and Andreas Beelmann. "Development of Ethnic, Racial, and National Prejudice in Childhood and Adolescence: A Multinational Meta-Analysis of Age Differences." *Child Development,* Vol. 82, No. 6: 1715–37. https://onlinelibrary.wiley.com/doi/abs/10.1111/j.1467-8624.2011.01668.x. Accessed July 21, 2019.

26 C. Hohenfeld, N. Nellessen, I. Dogan, H. Kuhn, C. Müller, F. Papa, S. Ketteler, R. Goebel, A. Heinecke, N. Shah, J.B. Schulz, M. Reske, and K. Reetz. "Cognitive Improvement and Brain Changes after Real-Time Functional MRI Neurofeedback

Training in Healthy Elderly and Prodromal Alzheimer's Disease." *Frontiers in Neurology*, Vol. 8: 384. https://www.ncbi.nlm.nih.gov/pubmed/28848488. Accessed July 21, 2019.

27  For a short review of Pavlov's work, see "How Pavlov's Experiments with Dogs Demonstrated That Our Behavior Can Be Changed Using Conditioning." *Psychologist World*. https://www.psychologistworld.com/behavior/pavlov-dogs-classical-conditioning. Accessed July 21, 2019.

28  Jenna Koschnitzky. "Neurons—a brain superhighway!" *Hydrocephalus Association*. https://www.hydroassoc.org/neurons-a-brain-superhighway/. Accessed July 21, 2019.

29  Take a test at "Project Implicit." *Harvard University*. https://implicit.harvard.edu/implicit/. Accessed July 21, 2019.

30  Eric Hehman, Jessica K. Flake, and Jimmy Calanchini. "Disproportionate Use of Lethal Force in Policing Is Associated with Regional Racial Biases of Residents." *SAGE Ocean*. https://journals.sagepub.com/doi/abs/10.1177/1948550617711229. Accessed July 21, 2019.

31  Daniel Reisel. "The Neuroscience of Restorative Justice." Ted Talks. https://www.ted.com/talks/daniel_reisel_the_neuroscience_of_restorative_justice. Accessed July 21, 2019.

32  Sofi da Cunha-Bang, Patrick M. Fisher, Liv Vadskjær Hjordt, Erik Perfalk, Anine Persson Skibsted, Camilla Bock, Anders Ohlhues Baandrup, Marie Deen, Carsten Thomsen, Dorte M. Sestoft, and Gitte M. Knudsen. "Violent Offenders Respond to Provocations with High Amygdala and Striatal Reactivity." *Social Cognitive and Affective Neuroscience*, Vol. 12, No. 5: 802–10. https://www.ncbi.nlm.nih.gov/pmc/articles/PMC5460055/. Accessed July 21, 2019.

33  Rebecca Umbach, Adrian Raine, and Noelle R. Leonard. "Cognitive Decline as a Result of Incarceration and the Effects of a CBT/MT Intervention: A Cluster-Randomized Controlled Trial." *SAGE Ocean*. https://journals.sagepub.com/doi/10.1177/0093854817736345. Accessed July 21, 2019.

34  Haochang Shou, Zhen Yang, Theodore D. Satterthwaite, Philip A Cook, Steven E. Bruce, Russell T. Shinohara, Benjamin Rosenberg, and Yvette I. Sheline. "Cognitive Behavioral Therapy Increases Amygdala Connectivity with the Cognitive Control Network in both MDD and PTSD." *Neuroimage: Clinical*, Vol. 14 (January, 2017): 464–470. https://www.ncbi.nlm.nih.gov/pmc/articles/PMC5331144. Accessed July 21, 2019.

35  Brenda Major, John F. Dovidio, and Bruce G. Link (Eds.). *The Oxford Handbook of Stigma, Discrimination, and Health* (New York: Oxford University Press, 2017).

36  John F. Dovidio and Samuel L. Gaertner. "Aversive Racism." In M. P. Zanna (Ed.), *Advances in Experimental Social Psychology*, Vol. 36 (2004): 1–52. http://www.psych.purdue.edu/~willia55/392F-%2706/Dovidio&Gaertner.pdf. Accessed July 21, 2019.

37  Anthony G. Greenwald and Linda Hamilton Krieger. "Implicit Bias: Scientific Foundations." *California Law Review*, Vol. 94, No. 4 (2006): 945–68. https://www.researchgate.net/publication/275736251_Implicit_Bias_Scientific_Foundations. Accessed July 21, 2019.

# 5

# CRITICAL AWARENESS

## The lift equation

If we are to engage with information competently we need to know how to acquire reliable information, and assess its validity. There is no way to guarantee we might not be fooled, or allow ourselves to be misled, but intellectual competence combined with critical thinking offers a way to self-correct: routinely consider the evidence and adjust our behavior and beliefs as required. While we have argued that intellectual competence is largely a neutral, or apolitical, activity, some still might contend that our belief in "facts" as reliable information is in itself a suspect premise. The attack on science, in fact, and on reason, has used the very tools of reason against itself. The challenge is real and significant if we are to find our way to a more socially just and sustainable society.

Once we identify and accept a premise, ideas informed by what we consider to be reliable information, we need to understand how to make meaning from it. Our goal is to identify possible cause and effect relationships indicated by the evidence. We must also scrutinize the arguments made by others, based on their data and interpretations, and compare our own analyses and interpretations by deploying our self-correcting meta-cognitive abilities. By asking a question at the beginning and also at the end, we strive to understand cause and effect in this world. Understanding basic structures of logic helps us to more effectively improve our own thinking and separate it from our emotions, like fear and anger. Having a basic understanding of how numbers, charts, and graphs function plays no small part in our analysis of others' data and in determining what we believe. The truth of the matter may be lost in the details.

While *intellectual competence* and *critical thinking* together imply an ethical mandate, one might argue that, according to the evidence, certain abhorrent social practices are perfectly in line with the law, and with social practices of the past. Issues of race, class, gender, sexual orientation, age, disabilities of all kinds, and other defining characteristics have been used—and are still used—to determine someone's place in the social order, and the kind of resources—the kind of justice—they are to receive.

Arguably we are reasonable beings, but only to a point. While we have the capacity to reason, and for meta-cognition—many do not use it or achieve it, and many still might use their intellectual capacities to build bigger bombers, or develop more profitable fracking operations for oil and natural gas. Something is missing in this picture if social justice is to emerge from a critical analysis of the evidence. We need *cultural competence* in order to recognize, identify, and understand the systemic and historic cultural ideologies and practices that for centuries have given rise to myriad social injustices. When cultural competence functions as a product of intellectual competence and critical thinking, it informs critical awareness which we believe is the heart of social justice. Critical awareness refers to that state of mind achieved when intellectual competence, cultural cognition, and critical thinking are illuminated by empathy.

## Empathy and reason

There are a great many things we know for certain, like the effects of gravity for example, and that in space bodies with larger masses draw things with smaller masses towards them. Or the certainties of the laws of nature, as they have been observed for centuries or perhaps discovered through experiment. As we discussed in Chapter 3, evidence leads us to the recognition of cause and effect relationships: one event is the direct, or indirect result of another (or combination of others). Consider the cause and effect relationship between thrust and wings: if we combine forward thrust with an aerodynamic wing, we achieve lift. If a law of nature—an experiment repeated many times with essentially the same results, or by hundreds of hours of observation to test a specific hypothesis—we know that we can trust that information time and again.[1] Unfortunately ordinary language does not function quite so precisely as a rarified physics hypothesis or the equations needed to test it, nor does the information with which we must challenge play out so easily in our day-to-day lives.

While critical thinking is a tool available to anyone no matter their motives, critical awareness applies the tools of critical thinking to social goals—rooted in the belief that every person has an inalienable right to human dignity. As we've said elsewhere, critical thinking skills might be employed to help feed the hungry just as well as to build smart bombs. Critical thinking takes on an ethical direction when the critical thinker chooses *empathy*. Empathy serves as the ethical and moral compass in a world of relativistic and uncertain cardinal points. Empathy points the way to our most basic value: dignity and social justice for all. Through an understanding and a practice of empathy, we can see and act in the world with critical awareness .

In the previous chapters, we have linked the need for critical thinking skills with a number of ongoing social crises, including climate change, the growing inequality between rich and poor around the world, international immigration, and fake news, along with the rise of autocratic governments that coincide with attacks on historically marginalized groups, including people of color, women, the LGBTQi population, and people living with physical and psychological disabilities, among others.

Coincident with the rise of nostalgic ideological discourse has been the increasing proliferation of misinformation. Social networks around the world have been host to ever-more sophisticated armies of trolls, bots, and artificial intelligence, set to churn out a miasma of misinformation expressly designed to challenge our ability to discern fact from fiction. The result: a further erosion of the intellectual skills we need to deal with these challenges. The misinformation that is out there leads to a dangerous and reactionary retreat, perhaps even into a perverted way of thinking, that normalizes a society ever more devoted to social division, social hierarchies, and relations of power.

Critical awareness leads to social justice, but what, precisely, is social justice? For us, social justice includes a political, economic, and cultural philosophy that embraces a collective humanity: people are, from birth, entitled to equality and dignity regardless of age, ability, religion, sexual orientation, ethnicity, race, gender, and so on. Practitioners of social justice make a personal commitment toward enriching the common good in these three ways: socially, economically, and politically. A socially just society is defined by social relations that expand human rights. It is a philosophy both personal and global that champions the realization of a fundamental equality among all peoples. Economic justice is an obvious component of social justice, with its focus on creating economic opportunities, employment, and resources sufficient for each person to have a productive and dignified life. Lastly, political justice requires that members of a society can straightforwardly participate in a democracy in which morality and ethical behavior of political agents and elected officials work in their best interest to create laws and policies that support economic and social justice.

In this context of social, economic, and political justice, empathy and compassion are our guides. For empathy to have meaningful expression, critical thinkers must agree to an honest inventory of their own condition and then subject their findings to self-inspection. Why? Because we tend to withhold empathy from others when deep down we believe we have never received our fair share in the first place. Rather than connection or understanding of the human dignity of others, we feel resentment, jealousy, perhaps even anger towards them.

Critical awareness involves looking into our own minds in order to sort out how we know what we know—and to discern the difference between an abstract idea versus a physical feeling. Too often our feelings seem to justify our ideas, though our ideas about the world can often be demonstrably false. Unfortunately the solution to this is not as simple as "just the facts." For example, studies have shown that even when individuals are introduced to an evidence-based idea drawn from facts, facts that disprove their beliefs and prove how inaccurate their understanding is, something curious happens:[2] rather than change and adapt to this new information, people have the tendency to retrench and dig in to what they think they know by simply rejecting evidence.

If we grant ourselves empathy and understanding, we can more effectively address our basic emotional needs which can support others as they try to do the same. If, on the other hand, we fail to address our emotional needs, or worse, remain unaware of them, we will be subjected to the tyranny of our unconscious as it pours out of us in the form of compulsions, mood disorders, and self-defeating ways of thinking and acting. In fact, we may be so consumed with our discursive thoughts that we might think that we do not have time to deal with "someone else's problem" and the injustices they face.

Our values guide how we apply critical thinking to problem-solving, and what remedies, if any, we choose to pursue. In the previous chapter, we explained how we learn our values as children in our primary environment by simply living and learning with language and participation in social practices as they present themselves to us. The process of becoming a critical thinker, however, involves deliberate skill development, e.g., intellectual competence, along with growth of our capacity for self-awareness, e.g., the ability to reflect on and take stock of our values, prejudices, social blind spots, and fundamental beliefs about the world that inform some of the deepest layers of our personalities.

## The United Nations and human rights

What is the inherent worth of the individual human being? Such a question begets another question: who has the right to determine an answer? Is it not somehow inhumane to discuss human life in terms of what one life, or one person, is "worth"? To determine the value of a human life using the language of economics in and of itself is decidedly disrespectful. Even language works against us at this point, for if we are not all, in the end, equal, then we are forced to resort to social hierarchies based on cultural norms that are far from universal, bolstered by economic and political systems that reward some with material wealth while punishing others living in poverty. The end result is that groups with and without power are sorted into "winners" and "losers."

After hundreds of years of economic and political inequality, some children born into such a world might find themselves cursed not by their biology, but by the society they find themselves a part of, with a belief system that has labeled them "losers" even before they can walk or talk. This is decidedly unfair—a key element of social injustice. If social justice is to prevail, critical awareness allows us to arrive at an understanding that beyond our cultural attachments, we are, all of us, the same in fundamental ways. Social justice establishes the idea of biological rights that we inherit at birth.

Empathy for the other is an understanding that the other is, in reality, a version of us all. We are all reflected in the faces of everyone we meet. Would we want to be born into a state of competition and chance, labeled a failure because of the color of our skin, our perceived gender, our religious affiliation, our disability, or our family name, or where we live? Should our need for dignity and security depend upon the luck of the draw? Some might say "yes," but then the reasons given are blamed on God, or the gods, or fate, or some divine power beyond human knowledge. But empathy demands that in an apparently unfair social universe we strive to make fair what nature has left incomplete. If we accept our responsibility to make the world fair—or as fair as possible—for all, then we must believe that each person should be accorded the same fundamental human rights from the moment we are born.

After the genocidal atrocities of the Second World War became known, the United Nations moved to establish the Universal Declaration of Human Rights (1948) in order to protect the powerless from the worst crimes of misguided social practices.[3] According to the United Nations, the Universal Declaration of Human Rights is the most translated document in the world. It has been translated into 500 different languages and stands as a testament to the global resonance of its core principles: a yardstick by which we measure right and wrong in a relative and secular world. It is not a religious document, though its values are widely shared by most religions. It provides a foundation for a just and decent future for all, and has given people everywhere a powerful tool in the fight against oppression, impunity, and affronts to human dignity.[4]

According to this Declaration, each and every child, upon birth, has a right to life in a world that prohibits slavery and torture. We have a birthright to spiritual, public, and political freedom, including the freedom of thought, of religion, and of conscience. In Article 25, the Declaration takes on economic conditions, stating that "everyone has the right to a standard of living adequate for the health and well-being of himself [sic] and of his family, including food, clothing, housing, medical care, and necessary social services." It also makes additional accommodations for security in case of physical debilitation or disability, and makes special mention that care should be given to mothers and children.[5]

The Constitution of the United States does not go as far as this Declaration. In fact, some scholars believe that the US constitution enshrined slavery by arguing that the 13th Amendment that abolished slavery actually permits it by allowing for involuntary servitude of convicted criminals. Under the 13th Amendment there is an exclusion clause which reads: "Neither slavery nor involuntary servitude, *except as a punishment for crime whereof the party shall have been duly convicted*, shall exist in the United States, or any place subject to their jurisdiction" (emphasis added). Once the Amendment was ratified and signed into law in 1865, new legal offenses, or "black codes" were generated in mostly southern states to keep "others" in check, such as charges like "malicious mischief" and showing disrespect.[6] Depending on the severity of the act, such behavior could result in a misdemeanor or a felony for the individual, usually a person of color, who could be sent to prison. By the 19th century, incarceration became a way to handle all sorts of "others" and resulted in the country's first "prison boom."[7]

In today's world, contemporary scholars, activists, and prisoners argue that the exclusion clause is still used to disproportionately incarcerate more black men and women—at five times the rate of whites—that stem from these historic, yet on-going practices.[8] In turn, public and private prisons profit from prisoners' unpaid or underpaid labor.[9] At the 50th anniversary of Dr. Martin Luther King's "I Have a Dream" speech in 2013, it was summed up in this way by former President Jimmy Carter who said, "I think we all know how Dr. King would have reacted" to the large numbers of African-American men in prison.[10]

Mothers and children also have very little claim on a society's vast resources and routinely are victims of discrimination. In the US, employers may legally discriminate based on family responsibilities (and these responsibilities disproportionately fall on women and mothers),[11] or an employer may deny them a comparable wage that their male colleagues earn. During the nineteenth century, for example, both women and children worked long hours in factories while they were paid on average about one-third less than any male worker.[12] Today, not much has changed: women earn about 80 cents to every dollar a man makes.[13] Across the globe, children routinely work for their families rather than going to school, and are routinely obligated into forced and bonded labor.[14] According to Human Rights Watch, over 70 million children worldwide are victims of child labor, and nearly half (48 percent) of these children are between the ages of 5 and 11.[15]

When the United Nations Universal Declaration of Human Rights was unanimously approved by all eligible voting members, the agreement was to stop any atrocities like the Holocaust and to support human rights initiatives all over the world. When delusional ideas, such as Hitler's and those of many other dictators, distort our humanity and cause us to misrecognize who we are, we are vulnerable to beguiling ideologies that teach us to value a human life according to a phony, racist and sexist hierarchy based on pseudo-science, all of which serves to sort humanity into "good" people and "bad" people. The "bad" people are dehumanized and turned into scapegoats for all that goes wrong in a society, and the impulse to eradicate them is tragically ever-present. Since World War II and the signing of the UN human rights declaration, there have been over a dozen well-documented genocidal wars that include, but are not limited to: Sudan, Rwanda, Tibet, Guatemala, Bangladesh, Bosnia & Herzegovina, Myanmar, and Indonesia.[16]

Under the cover of warfare in the twentieth century, genocidal atrocities were carried out against the unlucky, but especially against those who were deemed inferior, less than human, and unworthy of the life into which they had been born. Prisoners of war were starved, physically and emotionally abused, over-worked and marched to death, and subjected to cruel medical experiments. Whole communities were annihilated. In Europe, Nazi Germany methodically destroyed 11 million civilians, 6 million of them Jews, precisely because they had been deemed inferior. Jewish families, homosexuals, communists, Romas, and other so-called undesirables were methodically rounded up and transported in cattle cars to death camps located all over Europe. Thousands were killed every day, mostly with poison gas. Other unlucky ones were used to examine the limits of human agony, and still others were used to "prove" theories of racial superiority. It was from this grotesque history that the United Nations enacted the Universal Declaration of Human Rights.

What is a human right? After the Second World War, revulsion and shame led to an international examination of the concept in order to define "a human right." There were no previous truths such a study could rely upon—the scope and scale of the Holocaust forced the United Nations to start from scratch if such a human catastrophe were to be prevented from ever happening again. The UN defines a human right as a right that justifiably belongs to every human being, regardless of race, ethnicity, gender, sexual orientation, disability, age, language, religion, or any other status.[17] By accepting the set of ideals embodied in the definition of a "human right," countries agreed to work toward the long and important list of human rights over time by teaching and otherwise promoting these universal rights through decrees, and passing national laws. Signatories agreed to a shared and common understanding of the individual and their rights in society, an understanding that is not enforceable by law unless adopted and enacted at the national level, yet the eagerness and earnestness of UN member countries made the Declaration the most radical, yet unenforceable, document in the world.

The Declaration made clear that human rights are inherent to all human beings, and we are all equally entitled to our human rights without discrimination. These rights are all interrelated, interdependent, and indivisible.[18]

We take the Declaration of human rights as a fundamental premise for understanding critical awareness and its application to social justice.

- All human beings are born free and equal in dignity and rights.
- No law or tradition can erase our fundamental birthright to life, liberty and security of person, including race, color, gender, language, religion, political affiliation, place of birth, or economic status.[19]

According to the UN Declaration, we all have the inherent and inalienable right to dignity and respect along with the right to due process and equal protection before the law; freedom to travel; freedom from slavery; the right of free speech, free association, free expression, and more. It is worth noting two other principles specifically emphasized in the UN Declaration that have yet to be realized in the United States:

- Everyone has the right to a standard of living adequate for the health and well-being of himself and of his family, including food, clothing, housing, medical care, and necessary social services, and the right to security in the event of unemployment, sickness, disability, widowhood, old age, or other lack of livelihood in circumstances beyond his or her control.
- Everyone has the right to education. Education shall be directed to the full development of the human personality and to the strengthening of respect for human rights and fundamental freedoms. It shall promote understanding, tolerance, and friendship among all nations, racial or religious groups, and shall further the activities of the United Nations for the maintenance of peace.

The Declaration of Human Rights serves, then, as a ground floor for social justice as well as a text born from the failures of reason, the failures of religion *and* science, the failures of politics and culture, of law and order. The Declaration of Human Rights was not so much born in 1948 as it was reborn from the ash heap of our traumatic history, all in an attempt to set the post-World War II world on a more compassionate path. It is not a new idea, nor a set of new ideas, but rather, it represents a gathering together of human values, moralities, and ethics that have their roots in secular as well as religious traditions dating back thousands of years.

The principles articulated in the UN's Declaration of Human Rights remain a seminal definition of what it means to be a human being in this world. To deny the universal applicability of the United Nation's Universal Declaration of Human Rights is to allow individuals occupying positions of god-like power to suppress, condemn, and alienate certain groups of people in society. Social justice demands that such positions of power and hubris be exposed and the systemic violence built into their ideas overthrown. To become critically aware is to embrace the Declaration, the epitome of social justice. Such a society defines itself by its social relations that exist in order to expand access to dignity, liberty, and security for all. Social justice champions the realization of a fundamental equality among all peoples.

## Critical awareness: a thought-problem

According to 2017 data, 257.7 million people, or 3.4 percent of the world's population, are on the move and migrating from one country to another. Factors contributing to migration include general social unrest up to and including incidents of famine, warfare, violence of all kinds, and even genocide. The UN's Declaration would appear to justify the rights of people to travel in order to protect their lives and well-being. Countries who erect barriers to migration are guilty of violating the Declaration that they signed, in the absence of evidence that migrants represent a threat to national security.[20]

What is an immigrant? What is a refugee? A migrant? An émigré? An expatriate? How we use words to describe people uprooted from their home country "has been shaped by the historical forces of colonialism, globalization, immigration and war," writes one expert.[21] It is possible, then, that issues related to immigration have their roots in social injustice. What rights do immigrants have when approaching a sovereign country's border? Before we attempt to answer a question like this, we need to put into action our intellectual competence skills. We gather information relevant to the question so that we might begin our deliberation with the ability to consider what others have said along with our own opinion and research on the subject. A preliminary review of respectable authorities on the subject of immigration leads first to information related to language and vocabulary, and then to a few immigration facts:

- An immigrant is someone (of any origin) pursuing long-term residence or citizenship in another country.
- A refugee is someone forced to flee their country of origin, especially because they were being persecuted for reasons of race, religion, membership of a particular social group, etc.
- A migrant is any person living outside of their country of origin, but especially a non-skilled worker moving for economic reasons. This word frequently has a negative connotation.
- An expatriate is someone staying abroad temporarily or of an undetermined period, especially a white-collar professional or someone from a wealthy or English-speaking country. This term is also commonly used for long-term guest workers in Asian countries that naturalize few foreign citizens.[22]
- In recent years more than 5 million people have actively fled their homelands in search of life, liberty, and security. Destinations have included Europe, Asia, North America, parts of Africa, the Caribbean, and Latin America.

- Almost 1 percent of all people globally "are either an asylum-seeker, internally displaced, or a refugee."
- "By the end of 2017, 68.5 million individuals were forcibly displaced worldwide as a result of persecution, conflict, violence or human rights violations. That was an increase of 2.9 million people over the previous year, and the world's forcibly displaced population remained at a record high. This includes:
- 25.4 million refugees in the world—the highest ever seen;
- 40 million internally displaced people; and
- 3.1 million asylum-seekers."[23]

What should a potential host country do with uninvited visitors who appear at a border hoping to enter? What does the law say? What does public opinion say? What does the current political party in power say? Finally, from a position of critical awareness and social justice, how might we address the challenges of immigration posed to host countries? Should immigrants be barred entry and turned away? Or, on the other hand, should they be welcomed and provided with the resources and comfort they need to relocate successfully? Should immigrants be required to make allowances for their impact on host communities? Should they be granted preliminary citizenship? Should they enjoy the same legal rights of legal residents?

Critical awareness as it informs social justice requires that we establish what we believe about the importance of one child's life as part of our attempt to address any social crisis. If we avoid or disavow this first step in the journey towards social justice for all, we risk reproducing systemic violence in prettified political verbiage that obscures and denies many in their desperate plight for security and basic human rights.

As we consider immigration as a thought-problem, we need to remember that most countries around the world tacitly acknowledge dignity and respect as a basic human right. How best to implement such human rights, though, is often reduced to a political and economic equation—who is most deserving of our attention? Do both men and women deserve the same dignity and respect? This politically false standard of who deserves our support depends on hierarchies and comparative worthiness of one group over another and often informs our thinking without our even being aware of it. This is why it remains crucial for us to assume an original position of neutrality that unilaterally establishes the inherent equality of all; otherwise we may lack the empathy needed for critical awareness to emerge, and to possibly arrive only at "solutions" that seem cold, calculated, and geared toward bureaucratic efficiency. With empathy, critical awareness—illuminated by critical thinking—leads to the pursuit and defense of human equality and human dignity as birthrights.

## Social justice and empathy

Although the UN Declaration is non-binding in any court of law, perhaps its significance affords us the opportunity to see clearly whether we have been living up to our most widely established statements on the rights of the human being, in this or any country. The Human Rights Watch (2019) annual report lists violations perpetuated in all 91 countries for which the organization could obtain data and includes every country that has agreed to the UN's Universal Declaration of Human Rights. The report identifies egregious atrocities that include these human rights abuses:

- Violence against citizens (sometimes related to government forces fighting insurgents), including police brutality.
- Violence against girls and women (by governments, communities, and families) including failure to report abuse and neglect of girls and women. The criminalization of abortion and restrictions of women's reproductive rights.
- Detention, torture, and extra-judicial killings.
- Violations of free speech, association, assembly and press, including violence against government critics and journalists (e.g., exclusively state-owned or controlled media).
- Violence against children, including forced military service, sex trafficking, and slavery.
- Prosecution of minorities: religious, philosophical, cultural, and sexual, especially regarding gender identity, sexual orientation, and the criminalization of homosexuality.
- Violence against immigrants and refugees.
- Election interference, including voter suppression and election violence.
- Inhumane conditions in prisons and detention facilities.
- Prosecution of indigenous populations by a judicial system designed to disenfranchise them.
- Corrupted courts, the denial of due process, the denial of equal protection under the law, in part due to a politically biased judicial system.
- Discrimination against people with disabilities, including imprisonment rather than treatment.
- The death penalty.
- Environmental destruction that leaves the air unfit to breathe, the water unfit to drink, and the food unfit to eat.
- Slavery, forced labor, including child labor, denial of labor rights, and other forms of human trafficking, including sex trafficking.[24]

With the UN Declaration unenforceable, it became clear that no country would sacrifice its sovereignty to the United Nations or bow to its proposals. Instead, sympathetic governments around the world characterized the Declaration as "a common standard of achievement for all peoples and all nations."[25] It is an aspiration and a guide—nothing more.

However, the story of the Declaration aptly serves our discussion of critical awareness in manifold ways. It stands as a fundamental example of how social justice might be gained—by first acknowledging that we have birthrights that include social, economic, and political justice issues, matters that cannot be legislated away by a temporary expression of human greed or power, and that if our birthrights are threatened, we have a duty and an obligation to mindfully and steadfastly work against their oppression.

Obviously human rights abuses did not end when the UN adopted the 1948 Declaration. But since then, countless people have gained greater freedom as a result of its aspirations. Human rights violations have been prevented; in some cases, independence and autonomy not otherwise imaginable have been attained, too. In fact, many people have been able to secure freedom from torture, release from unjustified imprisonment and detention, and due process rather than summary execution, or enforced disappearance, unjust persecution or discrimination. Still other examples abound with more access to education, economic opportunity, and health care. More people have obtained justice because of the Declaration than would have been the case if it did not exist.[26]

Some experts have claimed that fully understanding the threat posed by climate change, environmental pollution, a rising global population and so on, is simply beyond the human mind's capacities. We are selfish, or so the argument goes, and we will go on being selfish to get *our* needs met. It is simply impossible to expect an individual—and so a government—to operate from anything other than selfish, local concerns. As a result, social justice will be impossible to achieve in spite of the fact that it encompasses all aspects that concern the health and well-being of a society's members, things as basic as the air, water, and soil we need to live.

The changes required by social justice require soul searching and courage, but the stakes are enormous. Why? Because social *in*justice promotes economic inequality and political inequality—the rich and powerful remain in a position to protect their interests and assets while putting at serious risk the vast majority of the world's population. So many of the toxic consequences of profit-driven big businesses hit the poor, marginalized, and disenfranchised while the privileged minority remains oblivious, or worse still, simply does not care.

In the previous chapter, we explained that we understand empathy only tangentially when we do not know it ourselves. Empathy and the empathetic response can often come off as half-baked, insincere, and manipulative—an expression of dysfunction in the form of misguided selfishness. While such motives cannot be banished or denied, they might be mitigated with an equal portion of mature reflection. Why do we feel the way we do about the situation? What motivations are at work in our need to attack a problem or a person? Sorting out how we feel aids in our effort to respond with, at least in part, an empathetic face. Must we all experience tragedy first before we can become empathetic to the tragedies of others? Or might we discover empathy through critical awareness ?

Recall that empathy refers to our ability to see and to feel how the other sees and feels, because we recognize that beyond our differences, our feelings, needs, and fears, that human consciousness itself and the burden of mortality—is shared by every living person. To have empathy for the other's experience means to first have empathy for our own experience.

Empathy fails when we cannot understand ourselves cognitively nor support ourselves emotionally. Empathy fails when we try to offer the other what we refuse to offer ourselves. An empathetic response has a much better chance of connecting with another person or group when we understand and accept ourselves as we are, not as how we wish to be. This is easy to say but difficult to achieve.

The hard work of empathy and the courage required is the work of self-reflection. To surrender to something larger than our individual selves—it is the moment of compassion—it is the moment that we realize that everyone is in the same boat. That is we are all cursed with self-awareness, stress, disease, and death. It comes for us all, but some have the resources to put it off longer than others. But make no mistake—the iron tissue of life has not changed since the first cave paintings 40,000 years ago. Accepting our own mortality, then, is the first and last step in empathetically relating to another human being no matter how different they, or their plight, seem. They are, like us, adapting to the chaos of life as best they can with the tools their world gave them.

Empathy, according to science,

> seems to have deep roots in our brains and bodies, and in our evolutionary history. Elementary forms of empathy have been observed in our primate relatives, in dogs, and even in rats. Empathy has been associated with two different pathways in the brain, and scientists have speculated that some aspects of empathy can be traced to mirror neurons, cells in the brain that fire when we observe someone else perform an action in much the same way that they would fire if we performed that action ourselves. Research has also uncovered evidence of a genetic basis to empathy, though studies suggest that people can enhance (or restrict) their natural empathic abilities.[27]

Empathy does not necessarily lead to compassionate action, but compassionate action is impossible without empathy. Without empathy, compassionate action risks becoming the very thing it seeks to redress. Empathy is the kernel of truth at the heart of compassion that aptly fosters critical awareness, critical thinking, and cultural awareness.

Empathy allows us to think in terms larger than our own back yards. For example, climate change and the environmental crises are no more or less deadly than the threat of the Cold War when the former Soviet Union and the United States almost slipped into a nuclear tête-à-tête during the 1980s. It is not too much to say that humanity's future hangs in the balance for every generation. To think about the world the way the other thinks about the world is to empathize with the other. Empathy goes beyond judgment. In the empathetic moment we ask for nothing from the other.

## Critical awareness and non-violent communication

Critical awareness represents a way for us to work for social justice causes without inadvertently re-enacting the very same sorts of violent actions that social justice seeks to end. To practice critical awareness means to become aware of ourselves in the most basic of ways. First we focus on our language. By waking up to the language we use, and the language that informs who we are and what we believe, we can become responsible and empathetic agents who relate to others without violence, either intentional or unconscious.

Non-violent contact with others (and with ourselves) is a mode of reflection and awareness that emerges into social practice at the level of language. To be mindful of how we use language requires us to have an understanding of how we feel in the moment, what our needs are, and how respectfully we can articulate ourselves as a request, rather than a demand, to others in our lives. When we are in touch with our core feelings, we can open up to the possibility of becoming aware of the fact that others feel much the same way about their beliefs, communities, children, and so on. In other words, by understanding ourselves, we understand others as well, and what others may be experiencing. When we recognize our shared humanity, we open up to the possibility of empathetic communication with others.

Confrontational language may serve our emotional need to "be right" and prove others wrong, to dominate others in order to pass moral judgments, but non-violent language seeks connections and understanding, "win/win" scenarios based upon common human needs. We try to substitute non-violent communication, based on intrinsic feelings and needs, that is, from one's own deep felt experience of our shared humanity. We connect with others empathically when practicing non-violence in our language and in our lives.

Non-violent communication is simple as an idea, but difficult to put into practice precisely because of the way we rarely notice how we speak, so much of it is on autopilot. Non-violent communication requires vulnerability and the willingness to, first, think about our language, and second, to express our feelings and needs without blame or judgment. If we can do this for ourselves, we can then listen to others as an act of empathy and respect for their feelings and needs. If we cannot do this for ourselves, or if we feel stymied or blocked, we may feel equally frustrated and seek to blame someone other than ourselves for our condition. Non-violent communication is an expression of non-violent relationship. In this way non-violent communication represents an expression of social justice at the level of language.

The language of violence, on the other hand, glorifies violence, speaks in absolutes, depends upon a hierarchy of "us" and "them," and that "they" must be by definition "less" than "us." Because of this, we believe we should hold on to the power and get our way. Such a way of thinking is all too common. It is rooted in a narcissistic view of the world that lies at the heart of intellectual *in*competence, that is, self-centeredness, willful ignorance, and intellectual intransigence. In such a state we are driven by fear and judgment, self-defense, anxiety, anger and alienation. Perhaps because we feel trapped in such a state we secretly want others to experience it too.

It may seem obvious to say, but it is worth underscoring: how we speak represents how we think. Our judgments find their way from our minds to our mouths, and we may hardly realize that the language we use can dehumanize people, and frequently turns them into objects.

Non-violent communication still requires that we make value judgments about what is important to us, but it is when we judge others for not living the way we do, or believing what we believe, we fall into moralistic judgment which is almost always informed by fear, ignorance, and oftentimes, anger. We compound a situation like this when we lack empathy or understanding for the situation of the other, and as a result we find it easier to see others as annoying objects worthy of scorn and rejection.

According to psychologist Marshall Rosenberg, "our language obscures awareness of personal responsibility."[28] Through habits of communication we communicate our refusal to accept responsibility for our speech or that our speech has any material consequences. Instead, social problems are the result of forces outside ourselves, as if we are merely victims, or puppets, and powerless to change anything.

Non-violent communication, on the other hand, replaces the language of passive irresponsibility with an awareness of language that accepts and acknowledges our need to take active responsibility for who we are in the world. When we take responsibility for our speech, we take responsibility for our lives.

Indeed, should someone call us out on our violent speech, we may become defensive about it. We get defensive because we feel poked somehow, accused, and so we defend ourselves from our own weakness and insecurity, often with self-righteous emotion. While we might put on a show of indignity for ourselves and others by way of defending our wounded pride, one of the functions of our defensive performance serves as a way to avoid considering the possibility that the feedback from others may, in fact, be accurate.

For Rosenberg, non-violent communication begins with taking responsibility for what we observe. So, when in contact with others, we observe from the point of view of the first-person. He recommends using phrases like, "I see," or "I hear you saying," or "I notice." Any sentence that begins with "you" is almost certain to initiate or perpetuate antagonistic communication. Avoid speaking for others. Speak for yourself.

In order to speak for ourselves, we first need to honor our own feelings, surface them, and come to understand what they mean. Anything less may lead to emotional incontinence at inappropriate times, resulting in bouts of rage, or sobbing, or panic attacks. Consider how "I feel angry" transforms the more threatening, "you piss me off!" The latter example uses anger to justify blaming the other—all the while provoking anger—while the former example owns the feeling of anger, names it, and lets the other know the state of things. Understanding how we feel in any given moment helps us to understand what we need from ourselves and from others in the world. To speak and live non-violently is leads to a life spent in the protection of human dignity and the practice of social justice.

## Language of love

How difficult it is today to make connections, even with those we are close to. Consider the phenomenon sometimes called "phubbing," the experience of having someone close to us snub us by using their smartphone instead of spending time together face-to-face.

Here is an example of "phubbing" with a couple out on a dinner date:

"You're always on that thing!" I complain, but my date does not quite hear me, for the smartphone takes all her attention in that moment, and so I get more annoyed and say something hurtful to get her attention, and it works. She looks angry and now I am too.

"It's like a disease with you," I mumble.

"Whatever."

"You need to get off your phone."

"You need to shut up."

"Yeah, uh, no," I declare, and I get up from the table and stand there like I might want to get into a fight. Instead, she leaves me standing there and I feel self-righteous indignation, a little confused, but defensive and angry. I replay the moment again in order to prove to myself that I was right and her behavior was totally unreasonable.

From a non-violent communication point of view, the possibilities for transformation, connection, and intimacy become obvious quickly, but from the point of view of the two speakers, finding connection requires a break from their ordinary habits of communication, and this will be tough to achieve in their current state of mind. To avoid making judgmental accusations we should observe the situation and tap into our feelings before we speak.

An alternative scenario:

I see her on the phone typing away energetically making contact with someone else while I sit there and feel abandoned. I feel angry, but underneath my anger actually I am scared—scared that I am boring company and she would rather be with someone else. Seeing her on her phone makes me feel insecure and inadequate. If the truth be told, I want her to make me feel adequate, which is, perhaps, an unrealistic need to put on her or anyone.

"I'm feeling a little abandoned over here," I might say, owning my feelings and not projecting them onto her. And knowing that I value our relationship built as it is on the idea of connection, trust, and honesty, I tell her what I need as a request, not a demand.

"Would you be willing to go without phones for an hour so we can hang out and talk?"

"Sure, I was just replying to my boss. Phone's off now."

Now we have something to talk about. "What's going on at work? What did your boss need?" I have the opportunity to listen without judgment and avoid trying to fix things. My focus is to work on listening to see how the other feels, what the other needs, and what the other's requests might be.

Blaming others blocks us from connection, as does blaming ourselves. We might instead become aware of our own feelings and needs, and then listen intently for the other's, observe them, and acknowledge them. If connections are made, solutions will follow as a dialectical process rather than one that is forced. Non-violent communication is not so much about "getting it right" as it is about creating a space in which we can move more effectively toward the connections that we seek.

## How do you feel?

"How do you feel right now?" It sounds like an easy question, but it may be more complicated than it first appears. We often struggle with articulating our feelings; some struggle more than others.

So it is a good idea to take a moment now, and every day, to set aside a few minutes to check in and figure out how we feel: consider the moment and where we are, where we have been, and how the last few days have been, the last few weeks, months, and so on. We experience our feelings in our bodies, so quieting down and taking stock of how our bodies *literally* feel is a good first step: Is there tension in my back? My neck, shoulders, chest, legs? How is my breathing? Can I take a full breath or do I restrict myself? If I am not sure how I feel, I might consider some breathing exercises in order to open up my upper torso and imagine I am expanding my capacity, making room for what I carry, and inviting it to my awareness. Maybe even take a few moments for a short session of mindfulness meditation.

Our day-to-day feelings can be obscured by older patterns, stored responses, controlled energy (because we have been taught that holding in emotions is what we are supposed to do). If so, feelings of anger or sadness may, for some, be difficult to express because anger is off-limits, or too dangerous, or we have been told that expressing sadness is for weaklings. Even happiness and joy can be side-tracked by child-rearing environments that teach guilt and fear as motivating drives for growing up.

Knowing how we feel also includes knowing how we handle our feelings, and what we did with the ones we have had, especially traumatic ones growing up. If we stuff our feelings away and fail to express them, our capacity to experience the present moment becomes less because we spend so much energy holding on to the past. If we are unaware of how we feel in the present, how recent events have made an emotional impact, and how the past has informed our relationship to our feelings, it will be more difficult to empathetically connect with others because we remain disconnected from ourselves.

Exercises: (1) So, let us ask you: How are you feeling? Make a list of feeling words that articulate how you are feeling now, how you have been feeling, and where you come from emotionally. And remember: feelings are not thoughts—there is a difference between experiencing our feelings and thinking about our feelings. Feelings are felt in the body, along with our intuition, while our thoughts are once-removed abstractions of the brain.

Hint: If you have difficulty identifying feelings, think about any of the crises we have addressed in this chapter: immigration, oppression, extreme poverty, the deteriorating global environment. What are your feelings about the issue? (2) What do you need? Right now? From this moment? But also more broadly, from this time in your life? Make a list of words that articulate human needs. What do *you* need? Do not limit yourself to material needs, such as more money, a better apartment, a more rewarding job. Think about your personal well-being needs also.

Consider that to know what you need is to know who you are. To know who you are requires you to know how you feel, why you feel the way you do, and how best to address your unquiet mind. All of this is a process by which we practice moment to moment taking responsibility for our feelings, our needs, and generally speaking, our lives. Our feelings are connected to our bodies, and so by checking in with our feelings we connect more deeply to who we are and what we need. If we feel scared and frustrated, perhaps it is because we are disconnected from ourselves and are afraid of missing out. (3) What have you learned growing up about needs? Consider a childhood memory of a time when, without realizing it, you learned a powerful lesson about what you should do with your feelings and your needs.

### Benefits of self-awareness

Authentic contact with oneself and with others is deeply rewarding, yet deeply challenging. Authentic connection with another person is often interrupted when we remain conflicted and upset by feelings that we may or may not have access to or identify, and so we have little or no ability to sort them out and address them effectively. The more we seek connection, the more challenged we may feel by our inability to stay committed to vulnerability, honesty, and empathetic awareness. Knowing how we feel and what we need, and being an advocate for ourselves, frees our mind to be open so that when we are in contact with another we might listen empathetically and with our full attention.

Worse, we often project our feelings onto others in the unconscious demand that they help us sort out our feelings for us. It is a relational style burdened by narcissism, the need to make everything about us, and this is especially so when we do not even realize we are doing it. Understanding our own feelings, needs, and beliefs defines self-awareness and helps us to recognize that others might feel just as we do about the causal events in their lives. In this way then, self-awareness helps us to develop empathy for the other.

### The dangers of automatic pilot: artificial intelligence and the illusion of objectivity

While critical awareness for social justice invites us into a deeper, more reflective understanding of what it means to be human, what it means to be human is changing even as we speak. New technologies, such as computer interfaces with human intelligence, the widespread availability of virtual reality, and the explosion of artificial intelligence, are all already ubiquitous aspects of contemporary life. Who has access to such resources, and what rights we might expect in a world governed by algorithms, will change the world. The concept of universal human rights will be under duress as artificial intelligence (AI) evolves and grows more sophisticated, putting pressure on how we understand the nature of human consciousness.

It is, in fact, human consciousness that cuts across every other form of difference. No matter our class, our place of birth, our cultural affiliations, our gender or sexual orientation, or our religious traditions, we all—each and every one of us— share a state of consciousness, an awareness of being in the world with thoughts, desires, and so on. Our thoughts and desires may differ, but the fact that we think, live, and die in precisely the same ways helps to illustrate just how much we all share in spite of perceived differences.

Known as the "oracle of AI" in China, CEO and author Kai-Fu Lee believes that compassion and love cannot be programmed into artificial intelligence.[29] Rather, the human capacity for empathy, compassion, and love goes beyond an algorithmic calculation; the human mind is more than an organic computer.[30] Although Lee recognizes that AI will continue to change the world, more than electricity changed the human condition, it will never be human. Critical thinking and critical awareness , or what he calls "deep learning" is not intelligence so much as it is our ability to use "brute force" on "big data."

Lee describes AI technology as the "sharp weapon" of the modern state, capable of violence and with the capacity to initiate myriad social injustices in all types of platforms. AI technology could be something that governments use to crush dissent, control their people, and/or to reproduce existing biases, prejudices, and systemic injustices socially, economically, and politically. For example, if an algorithm incorporates "residing in a minority, low-income neighborhood" as a marker for poor social support, it may recommend patients from this neighborhood go to a nursing facility rather than receive home-based health care, such as physical therapy. Worse yet, a program designed to maximize efficiency to lower medical costs might discourage operating on those patients altogether.[31]

Experts like Lee predict that upwards of 40 percent of the work force will be replaced by AI by 2040. His prediction is that food service personnel, including chefs, waiters, as well as fast food workers will become automated within 15 years. Displacing many individuals out of work, this may be simply the inevitable effect of technological progress.[32]

At the same time the likelihood that robots will replace many human workers makes current economic issues of inequality even greater. Even now, food workers and other laborers cannot afford to live in the cities in which they work. Rather than address the fundamental inequality underlying our economic system and affordable housing, in the scenario in which AI and robots go to work in Boston or San Francisco or Manhattan, the employees who had already been displaced by economic disparity are now literally abandoned by a system driven by ideologies that are consistently anti-human.

Lee believes that human wisdom will overcome these great challenges posed by the current technological revolution, but the challenge of AI is that it is coming faster than in previous industrial and technological revolutions. Our challenge is to retain, and develop, our humanity even as what it means to be human evolves and adapts to the technological times in which we live.

Computer scientists like Zeynup Tufekci have warned about the possible challenges we might face when sharing the world with machine intelligence.[33] While algorithms are powerful predictors, they are essentially amoral, or, in effect, psychopathic in their behavior if only because, like psychopaths, AI can only pretend to understand how someone might *feel*. Allowing artificial intelligence to make choices for our businesses, school communities, and law enforcement agencies should not be left to private companies or technology. Ethics and morality are too important to leave up to corporate engineers and software programmers, yet that is what many schools, police departments, and other important service agencies are doing.

Some experts maintain that artificial intelligence will help us to eliminate bias and racism in our social lives, but this, too, is in dispute.[34] Maybe someday an algorithm will be able to prevent racial profiling, but we are certainly not there yet. Conversely, facial recognition software can identify individuals and their locations, although there is still quite a bit of work left to do before we can claim this technology for facial recognition is reliable. The danger is that if this kind of software is used in policing, officers will use the information to know who belongs where, and who looks to be suspicious. In a sense, AI could produce racial profiling on steroids.

Who programs the machines? Who writes the algorithms? The technology from which artificial intelligence continues to emerge is driven less by altruism or social justice and far more focused on a way to manipulate a wide array of human behaviors, especially the need to sell new things to an ever-distracted mass of consumers. If the dominant capitalist model becomes the basic cognitive infrastructure of artificial intelligence, social justice—including environmental, economic and political justice—may slip further out of reach.

There is little doubt that the surveillance state has benefited greatly from technology and artificial intelligence. In fact, computer technology can now reliably determine human veracity, emotional states, and at times individual faces. For example, smart cars are transmitting driver habits to databases at up to 25 megabytes of data per hour, and this information is for sale to any buyers who can afford it.[35]

Perhaps, however, by allowing machines to think for us we might become truly "colorblind" in society. If an algorithm-based artificial intelligence that sifts only abstract data and ignores racial and gender bias made recommendations for us at every level of scale, it is conceivable that incidents of social injustice may disappear. However, a colorblind society is still far off because the algorithms AI uses are only as good as the computer programmer's lack of bias and prejudice when she or he writes the computer codes.

For example, suppose for a moment that a company uses an artificial intelligence program to decide whom they should hire and fire. Turning over to AI such difficult and challenging tasks—rife as they are with interpersonal interactions that invite all kinds of superficial misunderstandings—might sound like a good way to remove conscious and unconscious biases from the equation, and remove the possibility of nepotism. However, proxies for race and ethnicity, such as name, school attended, employment history, etc., may intrude into AI equations because programmers are unaware of their ignorance of these markers.

Our software is getting more powerful, but it is also getting less transparent because of its complexity. In the past decade, complex algorithms have made tremendous advancements, along with the ability to decipher handwriting and other very personal characteristics of a group it seeks to understand. The technology is always awake, ready to detect credit card fraud, to block spam, to translate between languages. AI has detected tumors in medical imaging when human doctors have not.

How did artificial intelligence get so smart? Much of the progress achieved in developing AI has come from a method called "machine learning." While traditional computer programming relies on inputting detailed, exact, painstaking instructions as software code, machine learning is far less linear. Machine learning involves inputting lots of data, including unstructured data (the kind we generate in our digital lives on line), into the AI system, and the system is programmed to autonomously search for patterns in the information. It learns to recognize and put together facts and information into usable data points, for example in order to sell us a new car, join a new club, or even change our opinion on a political candidate.

Crucially, AI systems do not produce a simple answer to a question or problem: AI offers a more probabilistic set of responses engineered by the programmers. Even with powerful machine learning, the AI system is only as sophisticated and knowledgeable as the engineers who are designing and programing it. For example, an AI program might conclude that one event, outcome, person, or group, is more likely to offend based on a risk assessment of the data engineers have made available to it. AI software is already very potent, but even the head of Google's AI team admits that they do not really understand how the AI system learns beyond its initial programming, or how it arrives at its answers. One chief engineer of Google's AI team calls this "the unreasonable effectiveness of data"![36] This statement begs the question, can AI learn to be *critically aware* as ordinary people, you and I, can learn to become critically aware? Can a machine learn empathy? At best, at least for now, perhaps a form of game theory can teach AI that the best scenario is always one where everybody wins. The use of big data and AI certainly does not focus on that now and perhaps it never will.

Consider a company now using a machine-learning system to hire its employees.[37] Such a system was trained on previous employees' data and instructed to find new hires that appear to be the equals of high performers in the company. While all of this sounds good to company management, there are, problems with the way AI interprets the data it has access to. While employers are excited to use an AI system to avoid bias, i.e., giving women and minority candidates a way around racially or gender-biased hiring managers, its outcomes are only as good as the data they draw from to do its analysis. In other words, if there are already biases about "high performers" built into the system, it is unlikely that AI will produce a different set of criteria to eliminate prejudices to hire women and minorities.

At the same time, though, AI can pick up on hiring the kind of employees that hiring managers are not legally allowed to ask about, information that is inferred from the digital crumbs we leave behind online. AI can determine sexual orientation, political preference, and dominant personality traits with high levels of accuracy. What if, unbeknownst to management, AI decides to weed out people it deems unfit, for example, people who score as having a high future likelihood of depression, or who may become pregnant, or have a pre-existing health condition, or have a violent offender as a family member, or any other problematic biographical detail? AI can use our digital crumbs for these kinds of queries—questions that are illegal to ask in a job interview. The hiring manager uses the AI data in her decision-making but does not know how the program achieved the results that it did.

Cathy O'Neil, software engineer at the Columbia Institute for Data Sciences and Engineering, maintains that currently AI has been programmed to score individuals according to privately owned algorithms. [38] Perhaps we earned a favorable score for paying our car insurance on time and maintaining good credit. AI does not allow us to understand how or why it included or excluded what it did in order to come to a decision. These kinds of data are summed up and maintained in secret and often by private companies that can sell the data they collect to other companies. While such a system may be less biased than a human hiring manager in some ways, prejudice and favoritism can persist because AI is only as informed as the people who program it, at least at first. Unless AI is specifically programmed to bring a *critically aware* perspective to the hiring practices of a company, it is unlikely that unbiased outcomes will remove themselves on their own.

The apple, as they say, does not fall far from the tree. AI, in other words, cannot help but reflect human ideological biases already present in the data. The clear danger is that AI may very well throw our prejudices and dislikes back to us in a way that makes such biases seem objective and neutral. This is indeed unsafe and perilous territory, at least in part because we are likely to give AI-generated information more credibility than our human reports.

Suppose we use AI data to establish crime patterns in a section of a city populated only by persons of color. Compared to other sectors of the city comprised of white, or diverse ethnic and racial populations mixed together, AI predictions for crime would disproportionately and negatively impact the black residents of this city sector by demonstrating that blacks have more arrests by race than any other. The AI information is biased because there is no racial group for comparison, and every crime from that sector is committed by a person of color. Based on the information at hand, it seems fair to infer from the arrest data that a person of color in that community will commit the next crime, and the next, and so on. Now, armed with the AI results, we ask an AI risk assessment algorithm to predict details about the next crime in this sector of the city and the algorithm accurately tells us that a person of color will commit the next crime in the black community. The data allow a police department to over-patrol the area, concerned that the next crime will come from this sector as opposed to other sectors of the city. And the police department goes even further by initiating "stop and frisk" searches on innocent members of the black community under the guise of protecting (not harassing) those who live in the area. Based upon the "objective" data then, police departments conclude that persons of color everywhere are more likely to be criminals than white or other racial or ethnic groups of people who live in more diverse neighborhoods around the city. But the dire reality is that AI steers the police department into this type of uncritical assessment and residents of the community feel harassed, unsafe, and racially profiled.[39]

Another example of the profound impact of AI comes from a source we are likely to know: Google. Researchers found that when we use Google online to search for employment, Google's AI software detects the gender of the user. Software engineer O'Neil claims that the gender component alone results in more men likely to see advertisements for high paying jobs than women. Is this because AI is sexist or believes women are worth less than men? In a similar troubling study, when an individual searches for African-American names Google's AI is more likely to direct advertisements related to criminal histories and criminality based upon inferences it draws from the search words as a predictor of the family history of the user.

ProPublica, an independent research organization, examined a recidivism-risk algorithm in Florida that impacted a sentencing decision made by the trial judge.[40] Two people, one black, one white, were brought in together for sentencing for a drug possession conviction. They both had prior jail time, although "Bernard," the black defendant, had no felony charges on his record, while "Dylan," the white defendant, did. But in spite of this, Florida's sentencing algorithm labeled Bernard at "high risk" for reoffending and Dylan at "low risk." One researcher calls this an example of "weapons of math destruction" where machine bias produced the disparity in sentencing.[41] Certainly there is a pattern of social injustice that persists through the artificial intelligence supply chain.

Such hidden biases and black box algorithms are widespread and can have life-changing consequences. In the case of *Wisconsin v. Loomis*, Eric Loomis was sentenced to six years in prison for evading the police in relation to a drive-by shooting that he did not do.[42] After sentencing, Loomis wanted to go back to court to know why he was given a six-year sentence. In court, his lawyer argued that the AI risk assessment tool, Correctional Offender Management Profiling for Alternative Sanctions (COMPAS) violated his due process rights. During the trial it was ascertained that the private company that owns COMPAS calculated Loomis' fate and determined the six-year sentence based upon its proprietary methods using group, not individual, data. As the trial played out, the judge relied on COMPAS for determining his sentence.

The company that made COMPAS, Equivant, refused to have its algorithm challenged in court, so ProPublica, an investigative non-profit company, was granted access to audit the "black box" risk-assessment tool. They discovered that COMPAS labels black male defendants as future criminals at twice the rate of white male defendants—in spite of the fact that the algorithm does not have the ability to predict future outcomes.[43]

In its 2016 findings on COMPAS, ProPublica claimed that the bias in criminal risk scores is inevitable using artificial intelligence because of the way the formulas are written. In ProPublica's analysis, Equivant claimed that the COMPAS algorithm produced equally likely results for whites and blacks, so it was impossible that the scores could be racially biased. So intriguing was this question of how an algorithm could simultaneously be fair and unfair generated a plethora of the nation's top machine-learning researchers from Cornell, Stanford, Harvard, and Carnegie Mellon universities to explore the seeming dilemma.[44] The scholars set out to address this question: since police re-arrest blacks more often than whites, is it possible to create a predictive algorithm that is fair to people, that is, fair to individuals with their own individual history, and not as a "*race*" group? Four different sets of scholars, working independently, determined that no, it is *not* possible with this technology. The Stanford group concluded that it is impossible for a risk-of-re-arrest score to satisfy fairness criteria if race is part of the algorithm's data base. In the end researchers agreed that the COMPAS tool could not fairly generate accurate predictions for individuals because it cannot see through its own racial bias. It computes an assessment of an individual's likelihood to re-offend based on group identification only. Despite these analyses, Eric Loomis lost his case that went all the way to the Wisconsin Supreme Court and his six-year sentence remained unchanged.[45]

Now let us consider how biased AI systems inform commonly used online social networks. The news items in a Facebook news feed comes to the user the way they do, thanks to Facebook's AI algorithm. Should the user see a picture of a group of friends at a party? An advertisement for a vacation? A pair of shoes? Or how about a sad news story? Recall that on August 9, 2014 Michael Brown, an 18-year-old African American, was shot and killed by a white police officer in Ferguson, Missouri under questionable circumstances. Protests ensued, but on Facebook many individuals did not get the news because the story was filtered out by the news feed algorithm, perhaps based on not wanting to upset its users.[46] Twitter's news feed, on the other hand, was not filtered, and so anyone who was on Twitter could see friends talking about the story, and suddenly the events that took Michael Brown's life were everywhere, horrible and haunting and in real time. How can one online platform be so drastically indifferent? The answer is that an algorithm for Facebook had determined that the story of Ferguson—and others like it—was not important enough to show its users. Why? Because responding to gun violence, or police use of force with "likes" and "dislikes" is essentially inadequate, even disrespectful, when a user must click "like," etc. So when Facebook users failed to respond to the Ferguson story initially, the algorithm used that information to show it to fewer and fewer people because, it seemed, users were not interested in sharing it with others. By comparison that same week Facebook's algorithm highlighted the Amyotrophic Lateral Sclerosis (ALS) Ice Bucket Challenge, and the story went viral. In sum, Facebook's AI determines what we see based on the choices it makes for us. The problem of who—or what—controls what we read online remains, and it promises to have a profound impact on society as artificial intelligence expands into more and more aspects of our lives. Thinking for ourselves is difficult enough. We must beware of those who want to relieve us of that responsibility.

As in all crucial questions, the challenge of algorithms and AI in contemporary life means that we must question authority, cultivate algorithmic suspicion, scrutinize the AI systems that find their way into our lives, and take responsibility to learn and investigate. Unless algorithms and artificial intelligence begin from the position of empathy and equality for all human beings, we need to accept that AI just might represent an intensification of social injustice, and does not offer a solution. Artificial intelligence too easily allows us to abdicate and outsource our responsibilities to one another, and as we ignore the human dimensions, we allow

AI to do the work for us. And so, while it seems that machine intelligence is here to stay, it will be even more difficult to awaken to critical awareness .

## Capitalism and AI

According to Shoshana Zuboff, Harvard Business School professor emerita and author of numerous books, we live in an "an age of surveillance capitalism that requires us to fight for a human future."[47] She compares smart devices like Alexa and Google to ivory poachers: we are the elephant, and the digital assistants harvest our personal information like "ivory tusks ... and we are the abandoned carcass."[48] Her argument is that we are losing control of our lives to AI because AI is controlling us. The cliché is that if we are not paying for a product in a store with cash, face to face with another human being, then we humans are actually the product that big technology companies are buying. The amount of data that big technology companies currently collect dominates our lives in the simplest but most evil of forms. AI capitalists collect our behavioral data, our human experiences, and use it to predict our consumerism. With constant tracking and analysis, tech giants profit by being able to predict our every move and market to us.

On the surface, perhaps many of us could argue that AI capitalism seems efficient and helpful, but Zuboff and other researchers state that AI's crunching of big data increases inequality and threatens our rights, our freedom, and even our conscious thought.[49] For example, Google introduced its Nest Secure anti-intrusion device for our homes that works in tandem with the voice-activated Google assistant service. The company never disclosed that Nest Secure had a microphone placed inside it. Google claimed that the microphone was "never intended to be secret," and that the microphone "has never been turned on."[50] Amazon Alexa devices also listen to us, and in fact have sent our data back to thousands of paid listeners around the globe, who, says Amazon, are using the information to make Alexa smarter.[51]

It is not too much of a leap to wonder what digital threat could arise when these giant tech companies decide to activate their microphones, invade our privacy, and manipulate our social relations with one another. In fact, this happened during the US 2016 presidential race when Facebook sold its data to political extremists who generated fake news to help sway the election. As CEO Mark Zuckerberg testified before Congress, "It's clear now that we didn't do enough to prevent these (dis-information) tools from being used for harm ... Fake news, foreign interference in elections, hate speech, as well as developers and data privacy."[52]

Big and small machine learning companies deploy their AI technology in other ways that are far from harmless. In 2011, Brooklyn high school teachers were scored with a secret algorithm that rated their success as teachers, and teacher-shaming became public in print and on the internet for all to see. In all, 200 teachers were fired because of their scores on the assessment, an algorithm tool that the *New York Post* retrieved via the Freedom of Information Act, to analyze precisely how teachers were scored.[53] The case went to court, and the AI company provided the teacher assessment algorithm but refused to release its source code or formulas for determining teacher success. The courts forced the company to comply, and a research team evaluated the data only to find that the algorithm's results were no more reliable than a random number generator. That is to say, worthless. Nevertheless, based upon the algorithm's spurious calculations, over 200 teachers were fired from the school district despite favorable recommendations from principles, students, and parents. We can only ask what "neutral" and "factual" pieces of data were used in their algorithms to justify the mass exodus.

Another compelling example of the social injustice that sometimes results from an uncritical acceptance of AI comes from Fox News. In 2016, CEO Roger Ailes left the company as a result of the many claims of sexual harassment against him. After he had left Fox, more than 20 women came forward to complain of systemic sexual harassment and unfair promotion practices. The women alleged that they were not allowed to succeed at Fox News despite the fact that Ailes left the company in 2016. Ailes had been blamed as the cause of Fox News' unfair working conditions for women.[54] Yet when Fox News acquired a machine-learning algorithm as a way to root out and rid the company of gender bias, they merely replicated the problem, this time via an AI algorithm. It turns out the algorithm had been programmed to define "successful" people at Fox News as those who had worked there for at least four years and had been promoted at least once, and this it turns out was mostly men. Women, according to the algorithm's analysis, were simply not as successful as men, all the while under the guise of objective and neutral algorithms used to correct the workplace environment gender discrimination continued.

According to Dhruv Khullar, if left unchecked, AI

> could create self-fulfilling prophesies that confirm our pre-existing biases, especially when used for conditions with complex trade-offs and high degrees of uncertainty. If, for example, poorer patients do worse after organ transplants or after receiving chemotherapy for end-stage cancer, machine learning algorithms may conclude such patients are less likely to benefit from further treatment—and "logically" recommend against it.[55]

The unfeeling, uncaring AI might would likely recommend a richer patient that it has determined will be more "successful" after transplant surgery.

These examples serve to build our critical awareness : AI promises to intensify the conditions within which social injustice occurs. Critical awareness depends upon our understanding of ourselves, our social and cultural context, our ability to reason from evidence, and our empathy for the experience of others. The danger of artificial intelligence lies in its implicit threat to human agency and autonomy. Can we afford to surrender ourselves to a virtual reality created by algorithms and artificial intelligence?

To practice critical awareness means we must confront our world with our minds competent, awake, and fully engaged in order to act effectively upon it. If we are too swift in surrendering our intellectual agency to AI, the biases that exist at the level of language will undeniably find their way into artificial intelligence. We will have encoded an almost imperceptible language of injustice into the fabric of our digital—and so our real—lives.

# Notes

1 "The Life Equation." *NASA*. https://www.grc.nasa.gov/www/k-12/airplane/lifteq.htm l. Accessed July 12, 2019.

2 Hugo Mercier and Dan Sperber. *The Enigma of Reason*. Cambridge MA: Harvard University Press, 2017.

3 "Universal Declaration of Human Rights." *The United Nations*.https://www.un.org/en/universal-declaration-human-rights/. Accessed July 12, 2019

4 Ibid.

5 Ibid.

6 Becky Little. "Does an Exception Clause in the 13th Amendment Still Permit Slavery?" *History*.https://www.history.com/news/13th-amendment-slavery-loophole-jim-crow-prisons. Accessed July 12, 2019.

7 Michelle, Alexander. *The New Jim Crow: Incarceration in the Age of Colorblindness* (New York: The New Press, 2010).

8 John Gramlich. "The Gap between the Number of Blacks and Whites in Prison Is Shrinking." *Pew Research Center*. https://www.pewresearch.org/fact-tank/2019/04/30/shrinking-gap-between-number-of-blacks-and-whites-in-prison/. Accessed July 12, 2019.

9 In 2018, prisoners in the United States were paid as little as 14 cents per hour. For more information, see Daniel Moritz-Rabson. "Prison Slavery." *Newsweek*.https://www.newsweek.com/prison-slavery-who-benefits-cheap-inmate-labor-1093729. Accessed July 12, 2019.

10 John Gramlich. "The gap between the number of blacks and whites in prison is shrinking." *Pew Research Center*.https://www.pewresearch.org/fact-tank/2019/04/30/shrinking-gap-between-number-of-blacks-and-whites-in-prison/. Accessed July 12, 2019.

11 "Family Responsibilities Discrimination." *Workplace Fairness*.https://www.workplacefairness.org/family-responsibilities-discrimination. Accessed July 12, 2019.

12 For more information on the wage gap in the 19th Century see "The Wage Gap between Men and Women." *History at Normandale*.https://historyatnormandale.wordpress.com/2018/11/16/the-wage-gap-between-men-and-women/. Accessed July 12, 2019.

13 "Pay Equity and Discrimination." *Institute for Women's Policy Research*. https://iwpr.org/issue/employment-education-economic-change/pay-equity-discrimination/. Accessed July 12, 2019.

14 "Child Labor." *Human Rights Watch*. https://www.hrw.org/topic/childrens-rights/child-labor. Accessed July 12, 2019.

15 "Child Labor Facts." *Compassion*.https://www.compassion.com/poverty/child-labor-quick-facts.htm. Accessed July 12, 2019.

16 "ICD Program for Human Rights and Global Peace." *Inter-parliamentary Alliance for Human Rights and Global Peace*. www.ipahp.org/index.php?en_acts-of-genocide. Accessed July 12, 2019.

17 ""Human Rights." *The United Nations*. https://www.un.org/en/sections/issues-depth/human-rights/. Accessed July 12, 2019.

18 "What Are Human Rights?" *United Nations Human Rights: Office of the High Commission*. https://www.ohchr.org/EN/Issues/Pages/WhatareHumanRights.aspx. Accessed July 12, 2019.

19 "Universal Declaration of Human Rights." *The United Nations*. https://www.un.org/en/universal-declaration-human-rights/. Accessed July 12, 2019.

20 "Total Number of International Migrants." *Migration Data Portal*. https://migrationdataportal.org/?i=stock_abs_&t=2017. Accessed July 12, 2019.

21 "Language Reports." *Druide*. https://www.druide.com/en/reports/migrant-refugee-immigrant-and-expatriate-what-difference. Accessed July 12, 2019.

22 Ibid.

23 "Total Number of International Migrants." *Migration Data Portal*. https://migrationdataportal.org/?i=stock_abs_&t=2017. Accessed July 12, 2019. https://www.unrefugees.org/refugee-facts/statistics/

24 "World Report 2018." *Human Rights Watch.* https://www.hrw.org/sites/default/files/world_report_download/201801world_report_web.pdf. Accessed July 12, 2019.

25 "The Declaration of Human Rights was only a common standard of achievement for all peoples and all nations. To the end that every individual and every organ of society, keeping this Declaration constantly in mind, shall strive by teaching and education to promote respect for these rights and freedoms and by progressive measures, national and international, to secure their universal and effective recognition and observance, both among the peoples of Member States themselves and among the peoples of territories under their jurisdiction." Declaration Handbook. *Universal Declaration of Human Rights.* www.un.org/en/udhrbook/pdf/udhr_booklet_en_web.pdf. Accessed July 12, 2019.

26 Declaration Handbook. *Universal Declaration of Human Rights.* www.un.org/en/udhr book/pdf/udhr_booklet_en_web.pdf. Accessed July 12, 2019.

27 "What Is Empathy?" *The Greater Good.* https://greatergood.berkeley.edu/topic/empa thy/definition#what-is-empathy. Accessed July 12, 2019.

28 Marshall B. Rosenberg, Ph.D. *Nonviolent Communication* (Encinitas CA: Puddle Dancer Press, 2015).

29 Kai-Fu Lee. *AI Superpowers: China, Silicon Valley, and the New World Order* (Boston: Houghton Mifflin Harcourt, 2018).

30 "How Advanced Is AI Today?" *CBS News.* https://www.cbsnews.com/video/60-minu tes-ai-facial-and-emotional-recognition-how-one-man-is-advancing-artificial-intelligen ce-tried-to-block-60-minutes/. Accessed July 12, 2019.

31 Dhruv Khullar. "AI Could Worsen Health Disparities." *New York Times.* https://www.nytimes.com/2019/01/31/opinion/ai-bias-healthcare.html. Accessed July 12, 2019.

32 Karen Harris, Austin Kimson, and Andrew Schwedel. "Labor 2030: The Collision of Demographics, Automation and Inequality." *Bain and Company.* https://www.bain.com/insights/labor-2030-the-collision-of-demographics-automation-and-inequality/. Accessed July 12, 2019.

33 "Zeynep Tufekci." *TED.* https://www.ted.com/speakers/zeynep_tufekci. Accessed July 12, 2019.

34 "Can A.I. Remove Human Bias from the Hiring Process?" *Big Think.* https://bigthink.com/amway/can-ai-take-human-unconscious-biases-out-the-hiring-process. Accessed July 12, 2019.

35 Bill Hanvey. "Your Car Knows when You Gain Weight." *New York Times.* https://www.nytimes.com/2019/05/20/opinion/car-repair-data-privacy.html. Accessed July 12, 2019.

36 Alon Halevy, Peter Norvig, and Fernando Pereira. "The Unreasonable Effectiveness of Data." *Computer.org.* https://static.googleusercontent.com/media/research.google.com/en//pubs/archive/35179.pdf. Accessed July 12, 2019.

37 Louis Columbus. "Using Machine Learning To Find Employees Who Can Scale With Your Business." https://www.forbes.com/sites/louiscolumbus/2018/11/30/using-ma chine-learning-to-find-employees-who-can-scale-with-your-business/#4adbd36b1ae7. Accessed July 12, 2019.

38 Cathy O'Neil. *Weapons of Math Destruction: How Big Data Increases Inequality and Threatens Democracy* (New York: Crown, 2016).

39 For more information on a civil case that challenged a New York police department's stop and frisk policy, see "Floyd, et al. v. City of New York, et al." *Center for Constitutional Rights.* https://ccrjustice.org/home/what-we-do/our-cases/floyd-et-al-v-city-ne w-york-et-al. Accessed July 12, 2019.

40 https://www.propublica.org/article/machine-bias-risk-assessments-in-crimina l-sentencing

41 Cathy O'Neil. *Weapons of Math Destruction.*

42 Julia Angwin, Jeff Larson, Surya Mattu, and Lauren Kirchner. "Machine Bias." *ProPublica.* https://harvardlawreview.org/2017/03/state-v-loomis/. Accessed July 12, 2019.

43 Julia Angwin and Jeff Larson. "Bias in Criminal Risk Scores Is Mathematically Inevitable, Researchers Say." *ProPublica.* https://www.propublica.org/article/bias-in-crimina l-risk-scores-is-mathematically-inevitable-researchers-say. Accessed July 12, 2019.

44  Ibid.
45  Currently 11 states use COMPASS either at arraignment, at sentencing, or in parole assessment. Other AI tools are also used by many other states. To see if your state is one that uses an AI tool in the criminal justice system see "Algorithms in the Criminal Justice System." *Epic.org.* https://epic.org/algorithmic-transparency/crim-justice/. Accessed July 12, 2019.
46  Sima Sahar Zerehi. "Michael Brown's Shooting in Ferguson Lost on Social Media." *CBC.* https://www.cbc.ca/news/technology/michael-brown-s-shooting-in-ferguson-lost-on-social-media-1.2740014. Accessed July 12, 2019.
47  Shoshana Zuboff. *The Age of Surveillance Capitalism: The Fight for a Human Future at the Frontier of Power.* (New York: Hatchett, 2019).
48  Jennifer Szalai. "O.K., Google, How Much Money Have I Made for You Today?" *New York Times.* https://www.nytimes.com/2019/01/16/books/review-age-of-surveillance-capitalism-shoshana-zuboff.html. Accessed July 12, 2019.
49  Paul Rowan Brian. "Meet Surveillance Capitalism, Our Terrifying New Economic Order." *The Federalist.* https://thefederalist.com/2019/04/12/meet-surveillance-capitalism-our-terrifying-new-economic-order/. Accessed July 12, 2019.
50  Noah Kulwin. "Shoshana Zuboff on Surveillance Capitalism's Threat to Democracy." *New York Magazine.* http://nymag.com/intelligencer/2019/02/shoshana-zuboff-q-and-a-the-age-of-surveillance-capital.html. Accessed July 12, 2019.
51  Jordan Valinsky. "Amazon Listens to your Alexa Conversations." *CNN.* https://www.cnn.com/2019/04/11/tech/amazon-alexa-listening/index.html. Accessed July 12, 2019.
52  "CEO of Facebook, Mark Zuckerberg Testified on April 10, 2018 before the US Congress." https://www.nytimes.com/2018/04/10/us/politics/mark-zuckerberg-testimony.html. Accessed July 12, 2019.
53  Carl Campanile. "B'klyn Turnaround Teachers Face Ax." *New York Post.* https://nypost.com/2011/02/07/bklyn-turnaround-teachers-face-ax/. Accessed July 12, 2019.
54  Samantha Cooney. "A Timeline of Sexual Harassment Allegations at Fox News." *Time.* https://time.com/4757734/timeline-sexual-harassment-allegations-fox-news/. Accessed July 12, 2019.
55  Dhruv Khullar. "AI Could Worsen Health Disparities." *New York Times.* https://www.nytimes.com/2019/01/31/opinion/ai-bias-healthcare.html. Accessed July 12, 2019.

# 6

# RESTORATIVE JUSTICE

We believe that any community committed to social justice must include restorative justice as part of its framework. Restorative justice derives its perspective on peacemaking from a variety of religious and philosophical teachings that range from Quakerism to Zen Buddhism. While there is no universal definition of restorative justice, many scholars and supporters of the concept argue that the current justice system, grounded in notions of retribution and "pay back," actually encourages crime because, not unlike the violent acts of individuals, the state engages in and distributes violent and punitive sanctions against members of its community. Once the criminal has "served" his or her crime, it becomes that much more difficult for the offender to integrate back into mainstream society.

Not only are mostly young black men stigmatized and consequently have difficulty finding a job in the United States, the criminal label profoundly hurts them and their families. Children become fatherless, family poverty is often the result, and despite best efforts, retributive justice reinforces racial and ethnic stereotypes that continue the cycle of shame and stigmatization.

The retribution model, sometimes called the "just desserts" model, is a very old system of justice: it even predates the Bible and enacts the biblical notion of an "eye for an eye, tooth for a tooth" from the Old Testament. The term in Latin is *lex talionis*; it comes from a code first developed from Hammurabi, the king of Babylon (1792–1750 BCE), who concerned himself with keeping order and writing laws that ruled the city of Babylon and its extended territories. As King Hammurabi's power among city-states grew, he saw the need to unify various peoples with one universal set of laws. Hammurabi, whose design was to support the weak, the poor, orphans and widows, was nonetheless often seen as brutal rather than just. One phrase, "an eye for an eye," became synonymous for revenge rather than justice. While Hammurabi can be lauded for his desire for a consistent and uniform set of laws, and "to make justice visible in the land" with legal codes written on tablets for all to see, some of the Code of Hammurabi was extremely harsh. Of the almost 300 written laws etched into a tablet or pillar, here are a few worth noting, particularly based on social class status and gender:

- Anyone caught committing a robbery shall be put to death.
- If a son should strike his father, his hands will be cut off.
- If a man knocks out the teeth of his equal, then his teeth shall be knocked out.
- If a man strikes a free-born woman so that she loses her unborn child, he shall pay ten shekels for her loss.
- If a son of a lover or a prostitute states that his adoptive father or mother is not his mother or father, his tongue shall be cut off.[1]

Although we could rightly argue that the current era's system of justice has changed drastically, designed to promote a more harmonious and less brutal society with equality and without prejudice, lengthy incarcerations and the stigma of felonies rule many communities, particularly communities of color. How much of the guiding principles have actually changed?

Professor Elijah Anderson, professor of sociology at Yale University, wrote a compelling comparison analysis, "How Racial Prejudice in America Has Changed in the Last Sixty Years," in which he compared two deaths of well-known, but tragic young boys: Emmett Till and Trayvon Martin.[2] Separated by 1,000 miles and only 60 years, the 1955 victim of racial violence, Emmett Till, was killed prior to the Civil Rights Act of 1964. Emmett was only 14 years old when he visited relatives in Money, Mississippi, and was brutally murdered by white men who were acquitted by an all-white jury. The defendants claimed that Emmett had stepped out of his place by flirting with a young white woman, the wife of a store owner.

The second boy, Trayvon Martin, was 17 when he was killed. In 2013, he walked into a Seven-Eleven convenience store near a gated community in Sanford, Florida, bought a snack, and was later shot to death at close range by George Zimmerman, a man who identifies as Hispanic, and who claimed that Martin had behaved suspiciously and seemed out of place in the white, gated community. Zimmerman was later acquitted of second-degree murder, under Florida's Stand Your Ground Law.

According to sociologist Elijah Anderson, "In the aftermath of Martin's death, a few reporters and columnists, and many members of the general public, made the obvious comparison: Trayvon Martin, it seemed, was the Emmett Till of our times."[3] How has the culture changed? What has changed between one murder and the other?

Anderson points out some obvious differences. The racial tension that led to Emmett Till's death was during the Jim Crow era, guided by an ideology of white racial supremacy during the early part of the twentieth century.[4] Trayvon Martin was murdered almost 50 years after the Civil Rights Movement's successes in the 1950s and 1960s that put to rest the racially-motivated Jim Crow laws and ordinances. However, racism hinges on the idea that blacks are an inherently inferior race, or a morally null group of people who deserve indifference and control. So while technically slavery had been abolished, Jim Crow laws dead and gone, the

Civil Rights Movement in full swing, along with the Voting Rights Act of 1965, it would still appear that some members of society think that just maybe people of color, particularly black and "ghetto," must get their "just desserts." This pervasive cultural association, Anderson argues, is that black skin equals ghetto and comes from historic, political, and economic roots of injustice. Persistent housing discrimination coupled with the loss of manufacturing and unskilled labor in urban communities throughout the 1980s to the present day means that people living with job loss, economic insecurity, and in urban isolation have little to no credibility, nor opportunities for upward mobility, and may even represent a dangerous class of potential criminals who are candidates for "stop and frisk," particularly for ghetto-looking young men who cannot visually pass inspection and must suffer the indignity of police hyper-surveillance and interaction.[5]

The racial prejudice that led to Trayvon Martin's death in 2013 is more nuanced than Emmett Till's, but it is also born of the same painful legacy of slavery and segregation, and guided by old concepts of racial order—that blacks have "their place" in society, and that is that you, Trayvon, do not belong in a white neighborhood. Why would Trayvon Martin head into a gated community while munching a bag of Skittles? He could not possibly belong there. After all, Emmett Till never would have accessed a similar community or lived during a time of professional opportunities and open spaces that Trayvon Martin lived in, with today's laws and supposedly more opportunities to live in inclusive, heterogeneous neighborhoods. As Professor Anderson (2013) writes,

> The pervasive cultural association—black skin equals the ghetto does not come out of the blue. ... Today, with persistent housing discrimination and the disappearance of manufacturing jobs, America's ghettos face structural poverty. In addition, crime and homicide rates within those communities are high, young black men are typically the ones killing one another, and ghetto culture made iconic by artists like Tupac Shakur, 50 Cent, and the Notorious B.I.G., is inextricably intertwined with blackness.[6]

As a result, the pervasive cultural association leaves little to the imagination: Hoodlums live in ghettos and the streets are dangerous. The misguided logic continues: while it may be true that everyone who lives in a certain ghetto is black, it is certainly not true that everyone who is black lives in a ghetto. Black people of all socioeconomic classes and individuals born and raised from the inner cities to those families and individuals who have never been to a ghetto, are by virtue of their color stigmatized. It is a powerful and ugly stereotype.

On July 16, 2009, Harvard University professor Henry Louis Gates Jr. was arrested at his Cambridge, Massachusetts home after a 911 call claimed that there was a potential burglary in progress, although when the recording of the call was released to the public, the caller said, "I do not know if they live there and maybe they are just having a hard time with their key."[7,8] The daytime call was initiated because the front door of Gates' home was jammed, so he and his driver, who had just picked him up from the airport after a trip to China, had to force it open.

Officer Jim Crowley from the Cambridge Police Department responded to the call. When Gates finally got his door open and entered his house, the officer appeared on the front porch. Crowley demanded that he step outside and show him some identification. A confrontation ensued. The officer insisted on an acceptable I.D., but Gates initially only produced his Harvard identification that did not list an address. Gates also refused to step outside and said, "Why? Because I'm a black man in America?" Once he proved that he was in his own home, he also accused the sergeant of being a racist. Gates demanded to know what the officer was doing on his porch and demanded to see identification and know his badge number, which he said Crowley refused to give him, although this "fact" is in dispute. The confrontation was heated and disrespectful on both sides, and in the end, Sgt. Crowley arrested Gates for disorderly conduct. Five days later the charges were dropped.

The arrest brought international attention, claiming that Sgt. Crowley, who is white, engaged in racial profiling. President Obama also commented on the incident, saying that Crowley "stupidly" arrested a prominent black Harvard professor. In an interview with ABC on *Nightline*, Mr. Obama said "(I was) surprised by the controversy surrounding my statement because I think it was pretty straightforward commentary that you probably do not need to handcuff a guy, a middle-aged man who uses a cane, who is in his own home."[9] Law enforcement groups of all kinds strongly disagreed and supported Crowley's arrest.

The backstory is that professor Skip Gates has an extensive career as an historian, journalist, filmmaker, author, and American literary and cultural critic, who serves as the director of the Hutchins Center for African and African American research at Harvard and has authored or co-authored 21 books and created 15 documentaries on African and African American genealogy and culture, with his most recent film a four-hour documentary series for PBS entitled, *And Still I Rise: Black America since MLK* (2016). After the arrest, Gates' lawyer said that he was not ruling out a lawsuit against the Cambridge Police Department, but more importantly, Gates' desire was to keep the American public across the country talking about issues of race, racial profiling, and law enforcement.[10]

The notorious arrest sparked an independent panel of experts to produce a report, published in the *Harvard Magazine* (2010) that admonished both Gates and Crowley:[11]

> Sergeant Crowley and Professor Gates each missed opportunities to "ratchet down" the situation and end it peacefully and share responsibility for the controversial July 16 arrest. Crowley could have better explained how uncertain and potentially dangerous it is to respond to a serious crime-in-progress call and why this can result in a seemingly rude tone. Gates could have tried to understand Crowley's view of the situation and could have spoken respectfully to Crowley.

Because of the high-profile incident, various news outlets all over the country asked for interviews. Even President Obama invited Gates and Crowley to the

White House for a "beer summit" in the hopes that, in the larger picture, the event would help reduce racial tensions between the police and persons of color. After the summit, Gates told the National Press Club that he had a great deal of empathy toward Crowley when Crowley told him, "Professor, all I wanted was to go home to my wife at the end of the day."[12] Crowley also told him that he was aware than another black man had been upstairs and did not know his status. He feared that at any moment he could come down and kill him. Gates told the National Press Club audience that this brought tears to his eyes as he began to understand Crowley's fear. According to Gates, he and Crowley have become good friends ever since they had an opportunity to sit down and talk and share their feelings with each other.

The iconic image of a ghetto may weave together the racism that led to Till's murder as it led to Martin's and possibly Gates' arrest. Emmett's place, after all, was in a field or the maid's quarters, or perhaps, as history tells us, at the back of a bus. If he is found out of place, like on a golf course or in an upscale gated community like Martin, or breaking into a home like Gates, he can be treated with suspicion, harassed, frisked, and even arrested, or in two out the three histories mentioned here, killed, for being "out of place." What is the difference between the set of circumstances among Martin, Till, and Gates?

The damaged social relations under racism and discrimination move easily from hurt to depression, and in many cases anger. In Michelle Alexander's book, *The New Jim Crow* (2010), one black minister explains the outrage at how easily decent men and women are picked up and charged with minor crimes: "Felony is the new N-word. They don't have to call you a nigger anymore. They just say you're a felon."[13] In fact, one study by the University of Georgia shows that 8 percent of all adults and 33 percent of black and African American adults, who represent only 13.4 percent of the total population in the United States, have a felony conviction.[14,15]

Why does our criminal justice system produce such racial disparity? Our current "just desserts" format certainly promotes the rule of law but without the capacity to restore damaged social relations. In fact, more evidence is published on the destabilizing impact incarceration has on families, children, and communities, particularly communities of color, as a result of the alarming number of mostly young men who are locked up and put behind bars. Once you are convicted of a felony, your hope for employment, or any kind of integration into society, starts to fade. "Today's lynching is a felony charge," Michelle Alexander (2010) writes:

> Tough politicians always focus on being "tough on crime" to keep families and communities safe. Beginning in the 1980s, a philosophy like this yielded "three strikes" laws across most states. Once you had a third felony, whether it was violent or not, you were locked up for life or given a mandatory minimum of 25 years. The idea behind this policy was rational choice theory, that is, once you realized that you were at risk for lifetime incarceration, you would evaluate and assess that it was time to cease your criminal activities.[16]

The US federal government now admits that this type of deterrence does not work.[17] In California, for example, the Three Strikes law imposed longer prison sentences for repeat offenders, based on the rationale that the offenders were unresponsive to the previous two sentences. Even a second offense, or "second strikers," earned an enhancement to their prison term, twice the amount of time otherwise required by law for a first conviction. On a third felony conviction, individuals can be jailed for 25 years up to life sentences, even if the third offense was non-violent.[18] Over the decades the incarceration data have demonstrated that the time spent in prison starts to desensitize the inmate, and the threat of a future incarceration is not taken as seriously as the first time spent behind bars, and so on. The American Civil Liberties Union studied the data and concluded that increasing severe punishments does not reduce criminal behavior; in fact, it may exacerbate repeat offending.[19] As one inmate, serving a four-year sentence, said, "I learned to be a good criminal in here!"[20]

Law professors argue that the biggest crime of all is the race-based system in which we delude the public into believing that we have a legal system that protects but does not target some groups, specifically Latino/Hispanic, blacks and African Americans, any more than it targets whites. It is this illusion of justice that continues to marginalize and control millions of people based on race and/or social class.[21] Mandatory minimum sentencing did little to nothing to alleviate the blatant discrepancies.[22]

The data indicate that police stop blacks and Latinos at much higher rates than whites, and in New York City, the most diverse city in the world where people of color make up half the population, nearly 80 percent of all suspects and over 75 percent of those arrested by the New York Police Department are black and Latino.[23] Once arrested, 80 percent of those individuals get processed through the courts, often represented by an overworked public defender, where they hope to work a plea deal to reduce their sentence. A plea bargaining agreement means you agree to admit to a lesser charge, but you must plead guilty to something, even when innocent, and often this can happen without understanding the full legal implications of your decision. The legal agreement between you, the prosecutor and judge means you now have a criminal record. Plea bargaining is common, and trials are rare. In fact, only 2 percent of federal criminal cases ever go to trial and those defendants who do are found guilty.[24] When the overwhelming majority plea bargain, that is not justice, plain and simple. It may be difficult to comprehend why someone who is innocent might accept a guilty verdict. One young black man explains this unscrupulous and amoral bargaining system in this way: "Who wouldn't rather do three years for a crime they didn't commit rather than risk 25 years for a crime they didn't do?"[25]

While we claim to be a nation of laws not ruled by prejudice or outright racism, society perpetuates punitive responses to certain types of crime. While "truth in sentencing" punishments were designed to mete out uniform, unbiased sanctions, prison sentences are not equal for all people. Our criminal system disproportionately impacts people of color and those who are in the low income bracket. The Pew Research Center, known for its rigorous and empirical methods and analyses, presents data that indicate some decline in incarceration rates, and while this is good news, the disparity between the number of whites, blacks, and

Hispanics/Latinos serving prison time remains statistically deplorable. The 2017 federal and state prison data that Pew experts analyzed show that blacks comprise 475,900 inmates, despite representing only 12 percent of the US population; whites make up 436,500 federal and state inmates and are 64 percent of the population; and the remaining inmates are 336,500 Hispanics/Latinos, who comprise 23 percent of the US population. [26] These broad racial and ethnic categories show that blacks and Hispanics make up larger shares of the prison population than they should: whites should represent a much greater total given their population density but make up only 30 percent of those sentenced nationwide. To put these statistics in another context, the Pew analysis also examined the imprisonment rate, which tallies the number of inmates per 100,000 people. In 2017 the rate of black inmates was 1,549 prisoners per every 100,000 black adults, a rate that is six times the imprisonment rate for whites. By comparison, the imprisonment of the white population was only 272 per 100,000 adults. For Hispanics, their rate was more than double what whites averaged, or 823 incarcerated individuals per 100,000 in the general adult population.[27]

From these data we know that our current criminal justice system is not focused on fairness, equity, neutrality, or egalitarianism, and by many measures is indeed racist. The United States incarcerates more people than any other nation in the world but the long prison sentences and harsh punishments have done little to nothing to deter crime.[28] To support this point, there is no clearer case study than a short examination of capital punishment.

Capital punishment is based on deterrence theory, a retribution model that requires the punishment to fit the crime: the punishment must be harsh if the crime was severe, and similar crime will be deterred because no one, knowing the severity of the risk, would ever want to get caught, not once, not twice, etc. Yet states that have the death penalty for first degree murder actually have more violent deaths than those states that do not have a death penalty.[29] According to the Death Penalty Information Center, an examination of murder rates between 1990 and 2016 showed that murder among states that use the death penalty are consistently higher than those states that do not have the death penalty.[30] Federal Bureau of Investigation data show that 10 out of 12 states without capital punishment have homicide rates below the national average while states that carry the death penalty have homicide rates 48 percent to 101 percent higher, Texas the most egregious of them all.[31] According to the NAACP, use of the death penalty is inherently racist; 42 percent of those awaiting execution are black and they had significantly fewer opportunities to plead for a life sentence when compared with white defendants with the same or similar charges.[32]

The National Institute of Justice reports unequivocally that "there is no proof that the death penalty deters criminals."[33] The National Academy of Sciences makes a similar claim: "Research on the deterrent effect of capital punishment is uninformative about whether capital punishment increases, decreases, or has no effect on homicide rates."[34] More and more evidence continues to surface, although surely we have plenty, that our current criminal justice system is criminogenic: policing, courts, corrections and mandatory sentences structure—and even cause—criminal behavior that dis-proportionally punishes and sentences to death individuals of minority status.

If lengthy incarcerations and the threat of death do not work, what does? One alternative method is restorative justice. The restorative justice approach means radically changing the way we think about our response to crime because it is a system that focuses on the rehabilitation of the offender in which he or she must take accountability for their criminal actions and work toward making amends to the victim(s), the victim's family, and the community. A plan to correct the harms, emotional and material losses that the offender has caused is a victim-centered response to a crime. Together with professional support, the offender and victim or victim's family establish an individualized program developed with conflict resolution, problem-solving, and therapeutic interventions to engage in a process that integrates the offender through community-building and supports public safety.[35] Punishments are not part of a restorative program; rather the goal is to restore, or to seek transformation of the offender such that he or she can effectively and pro-socially reintegrate into the community. This method of justice requires that the offenders and victims, or the victim's family, along with professional supports, construct a plan that satisfies the victim, the court, the community, and the offender. A common type of restorative justice is "drug court," discussed later in this chapter. This format requires no victims or their families to participate, and instead the offender's plan to make amends for his or her actions is determined and assessed by the court, a social worker, and other professionals.

Since we know that our current criminal justice system is not working, this philosophical approach to restoring justice seeks to create a more humane society that looks for justice without retaliation or revenge. The philosophical path forward is to shift the lens from a violation of a law to a violation against people and relationships: the offender is obliged to repair the harm done, and with intensive supports in place, the restorative justice process can work with individuals and families together, from crimes as minor as shoplifting to sexual assault survivors and families of murdered victims.[36] Under the restorative justice method, the offender is motivated to participate so that he or she may restore and reinstate himself or herself as "a good person" in society. The current criminal justice system generates no incentive for such an approach, nor does it encourage the defendant to admit wrongdoing. What the research shows is that our traditional, retribution model actually increases the likelihood of repeat offending.[37]

Victims and their families are largely left out of our current criminal justice system. There are never any personal consequences or personal contact for offenders to understand what they did to harm another human being, admit guilt, or come to terms with the damage they have caused to the people or the opportunity to make amends. They also do not have the opportunity to reflect and understand the hurt that they have caused for themselves and their families. According to restorative justice advocates and practitioners, people affected by any type of violence or non-violent crime can seek resolution more effectively with this model than our current criminal justice system permits. If the offender and victim are *both* willing, restoration of social relations between individuals and groups can take place in the community where the conflict originated. If that is not possible, victims, their families, and therapists meet inside prison walls and have conflict resolution sessions with the offender, among other options. These kinds of meetings are critical for social integration to take place, integral to fostering empathy, understanding, and peaceful community relations. The victim has the chance to voice his or her story, and the offender is given the opportunity to make restitution by understanding and admitting what he or she did was wrong. After the admission of guilt, the next step forward is to develop a specific plan that lays out a conflict-resolution strategy such that both the victim and the offender feel heard and understood. Often the offender might be required to attend drug treatment programs and receive psychological counseling. The goal is for both sides to come to terms with the crime, successfully reintegrate into the community, and return to a way of life with significantly less trauma.

On the victim's side, the survivor(s) or the family of the survivor always decides whether they wish to use the restorative approach, and their participation can vary widely. Referrals from a community-based justice worker, the criminal court judge or prosecutor indicate the offender is able and willing to proceed with a restorative justice process. Next, the justice worker asks the victim, or the victim's family if they wish to participate. If yes, the community justice worker prepares them for the process, and outlines their role, and the options they can consider. The community justice worker listens to their story, asks them to think about how the criminal event has impacted their lives, and what they hope to get from using this alternative method of punishment. Decisions about their participation are often based on the level of trauma and fear they experienced; how they felt about the offender; and even a willingness to see the offender helped in some way. Engagement in this method is voluntary, and at any moment the victim or the family can decline to continue.

The three primary components of restorative justice are inclusion, accountability, and responsibility. While there is no single universal definition of restorative justice, the mindset of how we respond to crime is of critical import, and the methods vary depending on the needs of the victim, the victim's family, and the offender. Inclusion means that all parties involved actively participate in determining the sanctions. Accountability means that the offender must own up to his or her actions: he or she must acknowledge that their behavior was harmful to others and agree to right a wrong. Responsibility means that the state is accountable for supporting and financing a plan that supports the offender, the victim, and the community. The process is designed to be transformational by taking into consideration the breadth and value of each participant. Such a holistic approach includes the appreciation of the physical, psychological, mental, emotional, spiritual, and social context surrounding each person in the conflict and the environment in which they live. Sociologist John Braithwaite writes,

> Restorative justice is conceived as a horizontal process of democratic deliberation that is integrated into external processes of accountability to courts and the rule of law. This integration of direct democracy and the rule of a

representative democracy's laws is an opportunity to enrich thinking about the relationship between responsibility and accountability in a democracy.[38]

Braithwaite argues that the restorative justice model deepens our democracy. The autonomy that all participant citizens have on both sides shifts the focus from the authoritarian state's requirements of "just desserts" to a supportive, democratic dialogue and plan of restitution between the offender and the victim. This process can mean direct, participatory democracy in the resolution of a criminal act. The stakeholders' voices are the loudest; the professionals only guide the process. Outcomes that plan to return individuals to a relatively stable, holistic sense of self, family, and community are based on the participants' satisfaction, not necessarily the courts'.

The principles and values of a restorative justice program have several components:[39]

1.  Harmful and criminal behavior is not just about breaking the law, but rather the focus is on repairing the physical and mental damage done to the individual(s), their relationships, and to the community in which the crime took place. The offender must admit to the harm he or she caused and work to make amends.

2.  All persons affected by the crime, including the victim(s), their friends and family, other support people, and the community, are included in the restorative process. This approach involves elevating the roles of those traditionally excluded in a court of law, and instead the focus is on the victim and the community. Inclusion mean implementing mechanisms of support, empowering voices, and ownership of the process.

3.  Offenders must take responsibility for their actions. Importantly, the offender must admit guilt and actively participate in understanding his or her role in committing the crime. Discussions with a social worker or therapist are common, as the participant seeks to understand the rationale behind his or her actions. Accountability means accepting responsibility.

4.  Safety is of primary importance and can take two paths. First, safety means restoration of security for those impacted by the crime. Second, safety refers to the need to create processes for restorative justice that are physically, emotionally, psychologically safe to pursue for those participating. Creating support structures within and around the intervention are critical. Safety involves ensuring the rights of participants, and this is imperative when the dynamics involve power imbalances among the individuals involved.

5.  Potential outcomes must be "forward-looking" for interventions that include healing, personal growth, reparation of harm, restoration of positive relationships, and creation, or re-creation of enhanced personal and communal situations. These goals apply equally to all parties, although they are not always possible within the scope and circumstances of the crime.

6.  Participants need choices in designing their programs and specific timeframes for each. This means developing a range of possibilities to meet the needs,

wants, and desires, for the best possible outcome to repair the damage caused by the conflict in its entirety.

7.   Most critical in this process is the need for respectful interactions. A humanistic, multicultural approach with empathy, compassion, dignity, openness, honesty, and equity is essential.

8.   Communication, direct or indirect, between those impacted, is typically, but not always, required. Depending on the crime, communication between the parties can be facilitated and supported in lieu of face-to-face meetings. Written correspondence, on line discussions, and video exchanges are also possible, particularly for multi-party representation.

9.   Whatever approaches are used, which could include victim–offender mediation, sentencing circles, circle-conferencing, family group conferencing, peace-making circles, video interactions, or face-to-face meetings, the process must be holistic: each participant must feel honored and respected.

Restorative justice programs vary widely, and some countries are more successful in implementing them than others. Mediation and conflict-resolution programs are common across Europe and Canada, but not so much in the US criminal court system, with the exception of drug courts. One promising area, however, is the use of conflict resolution techniques between students, students and teachers in a variety of school settings and among business colleagues who also have disagreements. Many service agencies and private businesses recognize the need for dispute resolution that does not involve criminal behavior but provides an alternative to traditional rules and regulations that a school, service agency, or business may have followed in the past. We believe that the more that we can implement the philosophy of restorative justice principles in our work and home environments, the more likely it is that we will participate in a more humane and just world.

## Critical thinking, women and the war on drugs

Women and girls are the fastest growing populations under criminal supervision. The War on Drugs produces over-policed and under-protected women, particularly women of color in impoverished neighborhoods. Mass incarceration ensues. The War on Drugs policy racializes incarceration: black women are 6.9 times more likely than white women to be brought under the justice system, and Latinas are 2.5 times more likely than white women to be under constant surveillance in the name of crime control.[40]

If we think critically about the intersectionality of women, surveillance, punishment, and mass incarceration of women of color, we find politicians largely silent about the hyper-presence of women in our criminal justice system. The failure to be sensitive to overlapping vulnerabilities of race and gender is a failure to fully investigate the structural and institutional intersections that contribute to risk and the consequences of punishment for women of color.

In the War on Drugs, we convinced politicians in regions like Eastern Europe and South America to adopt draconian policies on drug trafficking and drug use in order to prevent the flow of narcotics into the United States. If you are caught with cocaine, for example, you may spend up to 10 years behind bars. Abused and exploited, women caught in the drug war as "mules" are desperate for income and enter the drug-trafficking business mostly out of abject hopelessness. From Eastern Europe to Southeast Asia and Latin America, female drug mules are coerced into using their bodies to transport the illegal cargo. The women are relatively easy to catch, and in many cases are set up as the targets for drug interdiction while the big dealers of heroin and other drugs escape. Women are seen as easy money, and they know little to nothing about the inner operations of a cartel. As a result, women are expendable, having little information to reveal, which certainly limits their plea bargaining ability at trial. According to the American Congress on Latin America, the number of women serving time in prison for drug-related crimes in Argentina surged by 271 percent through the 1990s and 2000s, which is almost three times the rate of increase for men. In Chile, 68 percent of women in prison are there for drugs compared to 26 percent of men, and "almost without exception these women represent the lowest rung of the labor in the drug trade."[41] The patterns are worldwide, ranging from taking orders from a narco-trafficker to bringing a package from one point to another. They are low-level traffickers, or "mules," born out of pure necessity.

Unfair and biased punishment has trapped women in the criminal justice system. Women earn longer sentences largely because they have no information to exchange with the prosecutors to help them plead a lighter sentence. Accomplished author and lawyer Michelle Alexander likens this type of punishment to another era of "Jim Crow" laws in which there is only an illusion of fairness. The question is why the criminal justice system has not figured out the obvious gender inequality. Only some women in the UK are arrested and granted "victim status," according to Alexander, but the burden of proof is difficult and rarely used. While allowing victim status is better than incarcerating women, the point is to consider the conditions under which women are put in this criminally risky situation in the first place. As long as women are more vulnerable, women will continue to work as mules and get sent to prison. The irony is that mandatory minimum sentencing with the War on Drugs claims color-blindness while the exploitation continues. Victims of physical violence and rape in the drug war are not always recognized, nor do women mules feel that they can report the sexual violence to law enforcement. Similarly with drug trafficking, women continue to be exploited under the illusion of "equal justice." As long as there is money to be made, the most desperate and impoverished will sell drugs, or at least attempt to sell drugs, and go to prison as a result. The failed drug war has done irreparable harm to women and their children because while the women remain behind bars, children remain motherless and at risk for abuse and neglect.

Feminists advocate for equal justice under mandatory minimum sentencing, although to ensure that justice is meted out equally to impoverished women and women of color who are desperate to support themselves and their children does not appear to be a priority in our criminal justice system. Focusing on "equal justice under the law" ignores police strategies that capture the most vulnerable. These over-policing strategies often deployed in poor neighborhoods have produced dynamics of violence and inequality in both feminist and antiracist discourses. National mandatory sentencing guidelines disparately affect women who tend to play marginal roles in drug trafficking crimes, yet by tying sanctions to the quantity of drugs involved in the transaction and limiting judicial discretion in considering prior criminal history and family responsibilities, lengthy, unjust sentences for both women (and men) is the result.

## Critical thinking question

Is mandatory minimum sentencing fair to women? Should equal treatment or special treatment be allowed? In assessing the effectiveness of mandatory minimum sentencing and the role of gender in a structured sentencing system, what is just? How would you define it? For women, former Supreme Court judge Anthony McLeod Kennedy opposed mandatory minimum sentencing, saying, "I accept neither the wisdom, the justice, nor the necessity of mandatory minimums. In all too many cases they are unjust."[42]

The feminist dilemma: Should we have equal treatment versus special treatment of female offenders? How do we achieve fairness and integrity in the criminal justice system? While feminist legal theorists have argued for equal treatment at sentencing, other scholars have argued that women entail different risks, including child custody and other gender-based classifications that should allow differential treatment at the time of sentencing.

Consider the following case. Did this college student get special treatment? Was her sentence just in your view?

According to researcher and scholar Shimica Gaskins, drug conspiracy laws have been only minimally discussed in legal scholarship, and gender has not been given significant attention.[43] One woman, Kemba Smith, received a 24.5 year sentence for conspiracy to distribute cocaine.[44] She was 24 years old and a college student with no prior criminal record. As a student at Hampton University, she met Peter Hall, a man eight years her senior and the ringleader of a cocaine enterprise. By the time Kemba realized that he was a drug dealer, she feared for her life and was a victim of physical abuse. According to the prosecution, Kemba never actually handled or used any of the drugs, although her involvement with Peter Hall legally required the prosecution to ask for the same harsh penalties of mandatory minimum sentencing required in her case. Thankfully, Kemba was pardoned after serving six years of her incarceration due to a massive media campaign that highlighted her case as an example of a failed unjust "war on drugs."

In a similar case, Brenda Valencia gave her aunt a ride that resulted in her drug arrest.[45] The aunt, who did not have a driver's license, asked Brenda to drive to a house where, unbeknown to Brenda, the aunt sold seven kilos of cocaine. The sale of the cocaine implicated Brenda as an accomplice to her aunt's crime, and this was based on the dealer's testimony to the prosecution. Hoping for a plea-bargained sentence, he claimed that Brenda knew exactly what was going on, and on his testimony alone, she received a 10-year mandatory sentence, plus two years because her aunt had carried a concealed weapon.[46]

Is this type of sentence an insult to justice? In both Brenda's and Kemba's cases, mandatory minimum sentencing requires the courts to determine sentences by the quantity of drugs seized in the arrest and the size of the conspiracy, rather than the role an individual plays in the conspiracy. If a young woman with no prior criminal history is arrested for delivering to an undercover officer 48 bags of cocaine base totaling 6.854 grams, the sentencing guidelines for imprisonment rage from 4.25 years to 5.25 years. However, mandatory minimum sentences for drug trafficking are different and subject a woman to a minimum term of five years because the weight of the drugs must be used as the basis for computing the sentence.[47]

Some feminists and even pro-mandatory minimum sentencing advocates argue that unjust sentencing practices are too common, although at the same time, they see the benefits of professional and standardized mandatory minimum sentencing as fair. Mandatory minimums remove personal bias and are straightforward. Furthermore, the sentences, they argue, are a product of good intentions. If, for example, legislators who make the laws allow judges to affix certain penalties for a crime based on gender and age, only some women who could endear themselves to the court would receive special treatment. In 2017, US Attorney General Jeff Sessions argued in favor of mandatory minimum sentencing, largely, he said, due to race bias. Whites do not face the same consequences as African Americans, and for this reason, mandatory minimums are important to maintain. For too long, many minorities received and continue to receive unfair and disproportionately longer sentences that accentuate injustice. Mandatory minimum sentencing has done little to correct this egregious and prejudicial problem. Which side of this debate do you favor and why?

As mentioned earlier, one of the most widely used examples of restorative justice in action in the United States is drug courts, and approximately 3,000 are currently operating across the country.[48] Drug courts are a type of diversion program that keeps first-time offenders out of prison when faced with a drug or alcohol violation, or other drug dependency-related problems that require court involvement. First-time, nonviolent offenders are eligible. The most common engagement is with drug use charges and individuals arrested for Driving While Intoxicated (DWI).

The drug court model is comprehensive, including (1) offender screening and risk assessment, needs assessment, and importantly, their responsivity to making a change in their lives; (2) judicial involvement; (3) drug testing and weekly monitoring; (4) graduated sanctions and incentives; and (5) traditional and non-traditional treatment options and rehabilitation services.[49] The professionals who serve on the drug court will include a judge, a defense attorney, a social worker, and community corrections and police representatives, among others.

How effective are drug courts? The National Drug Court Resource Center has analyzed a variety of state data and found that drug courts have saved states and local municipalities a substantial amount of money when compared with an offender's alternative of incarceration.[50] Drug courts have also significantly lowered the rate of recidivism, or repeat offending.[51] In one study supported by the National Institute of Justice, an Oregon county drug court examined over 11,000 of its cases over a ten-year period and found that drug court participants were significantly less likely to reoffend and shaved a combined 14 years of incarceration off their records.[52] The researchers found in looking at post-release data within a two-year period, the most likely window for reoffending, the felony re-arrest rate fell from 40 percent before drug court to just 12 percent after drug court was implemented. In another county, felony re-arrest rates fell from 50 percent to 35 percent. After analyses were completed, part of their conclusion was that not only does the drug court humanize the offense, the offender, and the victim, it significantly lowers recidivism and saves taxpayers money. On average, per drug court participant, cities and towns saved $1,392 per person when compared with traditional incarceration costs. According to data analyzed by the National Institute of Justice, longer-term restorative justice programs produced even more savings, on average $6,744 per drug court participant, and if costs related to victim services are included, the public saves $12,218 per person when drug court is used over traditional incarceration.[53]

What makes this type of restorative justice approach successful? Would-be inmates have individualized programs, are rigorously assessed, and proper treatment is mandated from beginning to end and followed by the court. Ability to follow through on their program is essential, and steadfast support by others, including the participants' family and friends for things like transportation to group therapy sessions, help the participant succeed. Another factor in a successful drug case is the role the judge plays. The judge routinely interacts with the participant, often informally, in order to make sure that the program is being followed per the agreement. A judge and the drug court participant may see each other several times, especially if the individual does not comply with what he or she is court-ordered to do, such as attend a therapy session, or if he or she fails a clean urine test. During an appearance in court, the judge may have to threaten the participant with incarceration for non-compliance but is equally likely to offer encouragement and support.

As alluded to earlier in this chapter, conflict resolution techniques used in schools and businesses are also part of the restorative justice philosophy and practice. Conflicts are a normal part of everyday life for everyone, so it is how we resolve them that matters most. Conflict management means that we limit the negative aspects of an event, disagreement, or argument by focusing on a win-win approach that is balanced, empathic and respectful. The negotiation that takes place is done with neutrality and emotional agility, which certainly involves critical thinking and cultural cognition. Conflict management can be informal or formal, and in formal conflict management a professional mediator is hired to avoid self-serving biases, avoidance, or even escalation of the conflict. The goal is to get to "yes," to ensure that everyone is satisfied with the outcome of the mediation or arbitration, shakes hands, and moves onward.

Members of the Harvard Negotiation Project, Roger Fisher and William Ury, wrote a seminal beginner's book on conflict management that is still in print today, entitled *Getting to Yes: Negotiating Agreement without Giving In* (1981).[54] Fisher and Ury lay the groundwork for respectful interaction with one basic principle: Separate the people from the problem(s): This advice means notice yours and their perception of the problem, their emotional connection, and how everyone is trying to communicate their needs. We have values and feelings that come from our cultural backgrounds and personal histories that vary from person to person. It is important to be respectful of what each person brings to the negotiating table in order to build trust and understanding. When we have dug in and are stuck on our position, it is likely due to our values that underline the conflict or disagreement.[55] As practitioners in conflict, we may incorrectly deduce what the other side needs, but it will be a mistake if we do not take the time to understand what they value and what incorrect assumptions come from our own fears and values.

As we begin our journey into becoming successful conflict managers, three further tips from Fisher and Ury are extremely useful. The second one is to focus on interests, not positions. To focus on the interests the other side takes we need to think critically but empathically into their reasons for taking the opinion or action we disagree with. We all want our basic human needs and rights fulfilled, and their interests in the conflict may very well reflect the disagreement, even to the point of feeling stuck. In short, we must put ourselves in their shoes, which we can do only through critical awareness.

The third tip is to "invent options for mutual gain." This means that we need to think about how the resolution to the conflict can benefit all parties involved. We can brainstorm options that will impact each side of the conflict to reach agreeable, positive solutions. It may not be that everyone gets exactly what each side wants, but no one should feel that they have been manipulated or taken advantage of. In a "worst case" scenario, this strategy can turn out to be your best alternative to resolving the conflict.

In their final tip, Fisher and Ury urge the use of objective criteria. The goal is to always keep the conversation on topic and forward moving to a resolution. When we separate the individuals from the problem, we can keep an open mind and never be subjected to pressure, manipulation, or downright threats.

In conclusion, conflict management is a central component of restorative justice and one that we can use skillfully whenever the need arises. The principles of conflict management are the same as those deployed in larger restorative justice models: it is a perspective on peacemaking and empowerment that uses our skills of critical thinking, critical awareness, and cultural cognition to create win–win scenarios. We invite you to practice these skills with the conflict management scenario below.

## Conflict management scenario[56]

### Class activity/role play

While restorative justice and conflict management are used for legal remedies, the principles can be applied in everyday life, too, whether in a court of law, a boardroom, or school environment. Here we offer a roommate conflict to practice what you have learned from the material presented in this chapter.

The roommates, all graduate students, have come together for one of their regular monthly house meetings. Role-play a 20-minute house meeting with five students agreeing to role-play the characters in the scenario; stop for class discussion; finish the meeting within another 15 minutes. Use the problem-solving restorative justice framework and conflict resolution tips provided above. What is necessary for every roommate to get their needs met? While there are no criminals or crime victims here, there is unequal power, conflict, pain, strong feelings, and room for improvement. Finally, for further class discussion, how might solutions to the conflicts in this scenario apply to a restorative justice process involving criminal offenders and their victims?

## Roommate 1: Will

You are one of four graduate students sharing a five-bedroom, three-story house near Dupont Circle in Washington, DC. You have been living in the house for three years now, and in general you have been happy with the living arrangement. The rent is reasonable, which is hard to come by in this area of the city. The house is gorgeous, and while there has been a steady rotation of different housemates, in general roommate relations have been good. Because you have seniority in the house, this past year you also got to move into the choice upstairs bedroom of the house, which has a fantastic view of the city and more space than any of the other rooms in the house.

The house has monthly house meetings. They are usually dull and longer than you think they need be, but you figure it is a necessary evil in any group living situation. Unfortunately, you have a feeling that this month's meeting is going to be anything but dull.

Two months ago the house got a new resident, Grace. Grace is a grad student in religious studies and a strong believer in her faith. Unfortunately, there does not seem to be much room in Grace's religious convictions for your identity as a gay man.

It did not take long for you to realize that Grace was uncomfortable with your homosexuality. Her bedroom, like yours, is on the upper floor, and she did a rotten job of hiding her open shock when she ran into your boyfriend leaving your bedroom on the morning after she moved in.

Homophobia is not new to you, but thankfully up until now it was not something you have had to deal with from one of your own housemates. Now whenever your boyfriend of two years, or any male friend for that matter, comes to visit, you have to worry about Grace's reaction. While she avoids confrontation directly, she does not try to cover her negative judgment. She mutters to herself, snorts in disgust, and sometimes she acts like you and your friends are invisible, ignoring you entirely even when you try to be social with her. You have heard her talk on the phone with her friends and loudly complain about her "sinful roommate."

This kind of disrespect and hostility has to stop. This is your house too, and you and your guests deserve to feel welcome and respected here. You have a hunch you might be able to get her kicked out of the house. She has not signed the lease yet, and because you help out with minor repairs and improvements to the house, you have a good personal relationship with the landlord.

But trying to get Grace kicked out of the house is only a last resort. Despite your good relationship with the landlord, he did give Grace a verbal assurance that signing the lease was only a formality, and you doubt this is an issue in which he would want to get involved. Besides, Grace does seem like a bright and reasonable person in many regards, and hatred and homophobia is something you would rather try and confront and change head on, instead of just trying to get it to "move around the corner."

## Roommate 2: Grace

Two months ago you moved into a five-bedroom, three-story house near Dupont Circle in Washington, DC. At first, the living arrangement seemed perfect. Like you, your three roommates are all graduate students. The house is close to campus, rent is reasonable, and although your room on the upper floor is tiny, you immediately fell in love with its fantastic view of the city.

What you did not realize when you chose to move in was that one of your roommates, Will, was openly gay. You did not find that out until, after living in the house for a month, you were woken up in the middle of the night by Will having loud sexual relations with another man.

You have strong religious convictions and values, and you are proud of the significant place your faith has in your life. That includes beliefs and values that may not happen to be widely held or popular. That is OK. Your belief comes from your understanding of God's teaching, not any attempt to win a popularity contest.

You believe that your faith teaches you that homosexuality is wrong. It is an immoral and unnatural act, and not something to be endorsed or accepted. Up until now you have tried to just stay quiet about the issue. In the name of tolerance, you have refrained from confronting Will about his behavior, which you believe to be sinful. But you are growing more and more uncomfortable with this stance.

While you recognize the value of tolerance in a pluralistic society—you are a grad student in religious studies after all—your silence is beginning to feel like a form of endorsement of Will's behavior. You believe that his homosexual behavior is sinful, and not confronting that sin is beginning to feel like a disservice to yourself and your faith.

Things have to change. There is a regular monthly house meeting, and you think it is time to bring this up. Tolerance is one thing, but this is beginning to feel more like sheltering sin. You are not willing to move out of the house. Reasonably priced housing near campus like this is difficult to find, and you just paid moving expenses and cannot afford to do that again right now. What is more, why should you have to take on the inconvenience and cost of moving when Will's behavior—which you believe to be deviant—was not disclosed when you expressed an interest in moving in? Unfortunately, your negotiating power is a little weak here. Will has lived in the house for three years, longer than any of the other roommates, and although the landlord long ago gave his verbal agreement to your moving in, he has been out of the country for the past two months and so you still have not been able to sit down with him and formally sign the lease.

You are not quite sure what can be done. Will has male friends over all the time, and you are not sure how many of them he is sexually involved with—perhaps all of them. Since your room is upstairs next to his, every so often you even hear their "activities." You are not about to give up your view of the city, but maybe he could trade rooms with one of the downstairs roommates.

While having Will's behavior be less "in your face" would help, you would prefer if that kind of behavior just wasn't going on in the place you call home. Will could move rooms in the house or out of the house, but ideally you know the right thing would be for you to get him to stop acting on what you view as his 'homosexual urges'. You get along with the other housemates, who thankfully do not seem to engage in any deviant acts, drug use, or the like. Other than his behavior, Will seems like a reasonable, intelligent, and interesting person. This behavior which you view as sinful is something you would rather try and confront and change head on, instead of just trying to get it to "move around the corner."

## Roommate 3: Alex

You are one of four graduate students sharing a five-bedroom, three-story house near Dupont Circle in Washington, DC. You've been living in the house for two years now, and in general you have been happy with the living arrangement. The rent is reasonable, which is hard to come by in this area of the city. The house is gorgeous, and while there's been a steady rotation of different housemates, in general roommate relations have been good.

Every month the house has a house meeting, and you suspect that this month's meeting is going to be pretty exciting. Two months ago the house got a new roommate, Grace. At first it seemed like Grace would fit right in. She's bright and has a great sense of humor, and you've had some fantastic philosophical discussions with her. Unfortunately, you've noticed that her strong religious convictions, and in particular her view of homosexuality as a sin, are beginning to chafe with Will, the housemate who's lived in the house the longest, who is openly gay, and who, like Grace, has a room on the top floor of the house.

You are not sure how long tension has been building between Will and Grace, but from side remarks you've heard from both of them over the past week you know that things are reaching a breaking point. As a culture studies grad student, you're sensitive to the profound need for tolerance and empathy in a pluralistic society. But you also know that ideas like "tolerance" and "acceptance" are social constructs, and you don't want to see Grace's beliefs—no matter how much you happen to disagree with them—be mocked, marginalized, or punished simply because they aren't popular or your own. Maybe it would help if one of them moved downstairs. You would love to give up your downstairs room and get one of the upstairs rooms with the swank view of the city.

On a side note, at this month's house meeting you expect that your other roommate, Mallory, will probably bring up the issue of the downstairs study being messy. You're in the midst of writing your dissertation proposal, and for the past month you've been camped out in the study writing, researching, and taking breaks to unwind and think (play computer games and smoke some weed to take the edge off of some of your anxiety about the work). You know that ultimately this arrangement can't work forever, but you only have about one or two more months of work to go before you're done. And besides, as fellow grad students, you'd hope your roommates would understand the stress of the process and have some flexibility.

## Roommate 4: Mallory

You are one of four graduate students sharing a five-bedroom, three-story house near Dupont Circle in Washington, DC. You've been living in the house for two years now, and in general you have been happy with the living arrangement. The rent is reasonable, which is hard to come by in this area of the city. The house is gorgeous, and while there's been a steady rotation of different housemates, in general roommate relations have been good.

Every month the house has a house meeting, and you suspect that this month's meeting is going to involve working through some tough conflicts.

Two months ago the house got a new roommate, Grace. At first it seemed like Grace would fit right in. She's bright and has a good sense of humor. But you had a hunch things might get difficult when you began to learn more about her close-minded religious beliefs. Grace's opinions are clearly beginning to chafe with Will, the housemate who's lived in the house the longest, who is openly gay, and who, like Grace, has a room on the top floor of the house. You're not sure how long tension has been building between Will and Grace, but from side remarks you've heard from both of them over the past week you know that things are reaching a breaking point.

You imagine that Will probably just wants to kick Grace out of the house, and he might even have half a chance of pulling it off since he's close with the landlord and Grace has yet to officially sign the house lease.

But that option doesn't sit well with you. Grace was worried about not being able to sign the lease when she first moved in—the landlord was out of town, so it wasn't possible then—and you along with the rest of the roommates gave your word that it wouldn't be a problem.

But beyond that concession, you have a hard time sympathizing with Grace's plight. You are a fervent believer in tolerance and acceptance, and hate and homophobia aren't things you're prepared to put up with in a place you call home. You're not sure how much it would solve, but you would be willing to let Grace take your room on the second floor and you take her upstairs room next to Will—you've wanted one of the upstairs rooms with the great city view for a long time.

On another front, for the past month you have been growing increasingly frustrated at how Alex, your other roommate, has been treating the common study area on the first floor of the house. He's constantly camped out in the room, and although he claims to be working on his dissertation proposal, every time you walk into the room you find him just playing computer games and smoking pot. You are a sociology Ph.D. candidate yourself, and you remember the stresses of the proposal writing process. But this is a common space and you have work you need to get done there as well. You have tried gently bringing this up with him on several occasions, and although he keeps saying he will clean up and be better about sharing the space, nothing changes.

You think of Alex as a younger brother, and you want to push this issue not just so that you can use the space, but so that he can get on with the job of getting his proposal written and stop slacking off so much. Confronting him alone isn't getting the job done; you want to bring this up at the general house meeting so that the other roommates can get involved. They do not end up using the downstairs space as much as you, but it is a common area of the house and when issues like this come up it should be a shared responsibility for getting them resolved.

## Role 5 (optional): Jack

You are a next-door neighbor and friend of Alex's from grad school. You enjoy spending time over at the house goofing off. Alex is a good drinking buddy, and you've always like the vibe of the house. You have attended some house meetings in the past—mostly by accident, because you just happened to be around—and you've again found yourself unexpectedly in the midst of a house meeting.

Aside from being friends with Alex, over the past two months you've been getting close to Grace, though it is nothing serious or romantic. The two of you just hit it off, and you have been kind of fascinated by someone with such conservative Christian views (you were raised in a very conservative Christian home but have since strayed from the faith for a variety of reasons). Grace really seems to mean well, and you'd really like to see that she doesn't get too attacked or persecuted by the group just because her beliefs are different.

You are also hoping the meeting can get done with in a reasonably quick time period. You were hoping to do some drinking and play video games with Alex, which is why you came over in the first place.

If the group suggests you move in and swap places with Grace or anyone else, you have to decline. You just purchased the one bedroom condo you live in next door, and moving isn't an option for you. You want to help them get along and resolve this, but you cannot contribute any material resources to help.

## Notes

1 "Hammurabi's Code: An Eye for an Eye." *UShistory.org*. www.ushistory.org/civ/4c.asp/. Accessed July 21, 2019.
2 Elijah Anderson, "Emmett and Trayvon." *Washington Monthly*. https://washingtonmonthly.com/magazine/janfeb-2013/emmett-and-trayvon/. Accessed July 21, 2019.
3 Ibid.
4 "A Brief History of Jim Crow." *Constitutional Rights Foundation*. https://www.crf-usa.org/black-history-month/a-brief-history-of-jim-crow/. Accessed July 21, 2019.
5 "Floyd, et al. v. City of New York, et al." *Center for Constitutional Rights*. https://ccrjustice.org/home/what-we-do/our-cases/floyd-et-al-v-city-new-york-et-al/. Accessed July 21, 2019.
6 Elijah Anderson, "Emmett and Trayvon."
7 Cambridge is a wealthy community. According to the 2010 US census, the median owner occupied homes average $670,200. Only 10.8 percent of Cambridge's residents identify as black. Median household income is $89,435. 76.5 percent of its residents have bachelor degrees or higher. For more information see "Quick Facts," *United States Census Bureau*. https://www.census.gov/quickfacts/cambridgecitymassachusetts/. Accessed July 21, 2019.
8 "Henry Louis Gates Arrest Controversy," *Academic: enacademic.com*. https://enacademic.com/dic.nsf/enwiki/11842608/. Accessed July 21, 2019.
9 Abby Goodnough. "Sergeant Who Arrested Professor Defends Actions," *New York Times*. https://www.nytimes.com/2009/07/24/us/24gates.html/. Accessed July 21, 2019.
10 Ibid.
11 "Missed Opportunities." *Harvard Magazine*. https://harvardmagazine.com/2010/07/report-on-cambridge-police-sgt-crowley-professor-gates/. Accessed July 21, 2019.
12 "NPC Luncheon: Ken Burns and Henry Louis Gates Jr.," *The National Press Club*. https://www.press.org/news-multimedia/galleries/npc-luncheon-ken-burns-henry-louis-gates-jr/. Accessed July 21, 2019.
13 Michelle Alexander. *The New Jim Crow: Mass Incarceration in the Age of Colorblindess* (New York: New Press, 2010), p. 159.
14 "Quick Facts: The United States." *The United States Census Bureau*. https://www.census.gov/quickfacts/fact/table/US/PST040218/. Accessed July 21, 2019.

15  Alan Flurry. "Study Estimates U.S. Population with Felony Convictions," *UGA Today*. https://news.uga.edu/total-us-population-with-felony-convictions/. Accessed July 21, 2019.

16  Paul Street. "Felony Is the New 'N-Word': Michelle Alexander on Mass Incarceration as 'The New Jim Crow' in the Age of Obama." *Black Agenda Report*. https://blacka gendareport.com/content/%E2%80%9Cfelony-new-%E2%80%98n-word%E2%80% 9D-michelle-alexander-mass-incarceration-%E2%80%9C-new-jim-crow%E2%80%9D-a ge-obama/. Accessed July 21, 2019.

17  "Five Things about Deterrence." *National Institute of Justice*. https://nij.gov/five-thing s/pages/deterrence.aspx/. Accessed July 21, 2019.

18  The Three Strikes law in California was amended in 2017 such that only violent offenders could receive up to 25 years. For more information see "California's Three Strikes Sentencing Laws." *California Courts: The Judicial Branch of California*. https:// www.courts.ca.gov/20142.htm/. Accessed July 21, 2019.

19  "Ten Reasons to Oppose '3 Strikes, You're Out.'" *ACLU*. https://www.aclu.org/ other/10-reasons-oppose-3-strikes-youre-out/. Accessed July 21, 2019.

20  A comment made by an inmate participant from a meditation and stress reduction program for incarcerated male adults. 2011. Adult Correctional Institutions of Rhode Island.

21  Bill Quigley. "Fourteen Examples of Racism in the Criminal Justice System." *HuffPost*. https://www.huffingtonpost.com/bill-quigley/fourteen-examples-of-raci_b_658947. html/. Accessed July 21, 2019.

22  Marit M. Rahavi and Sonja B. Starr. "Racial Disparity in Federal Criminal Sentences." *Journal of Political Economy*, Vol. 122, No. 6 (2014): 1320–54. https://doi.org/10.1086/677255

23  James P. O'Neill. "Crime and Enforcement Activity in New York City." *NYPD*. http s://www1.nyc.gov/assets/nypd/downloads/pdf/analysis_and_planning/yea r-end-2018-enforcement-report.pdf/. Accessed July 21, 2019.

24  "Criminal Justice." *Pew Research Center*. https://www.pewresearch.org/topics/crimina l-justice/. Accessed July 21, 2019.

25  Bill Quigley. "Fourteen Examples of Racism in the Criminal Justice System."

26  John Gramlich. "The Gap between the Number of Blacks and Whites in Prison Is Shrinking." *Pew Research Center*. https://www.pewresearch.org/fact-tank/2019/04/30/ shrinking-gap-between-number-of-blacks-and-whites-in-prison/. Accessed July 21, 2019.

27  Ibid.

28  The *Pew Research Center* reports in 2018 that despite declining incarceration rates over the last twenty years, the US incarcerates more people than any other nation in the world. For more information see: John Gramlich. "America's Incarceration Rate Is at a Two-decade Low." *Pew Research Center*. https://www.pewresearch.org/fact-tank/2018/ 05/02/americas-incarceration-rate-is-at-a-two-decade-low/. Accessed July 21, 2019.

29  Raymond Bonner and Ford Fessenden. "States with No Death Penalty Share Lower Homicide Rates." *New York Times*. https://www.nytimes.com/2000/09/22/us/absen ce-executions-special-report-states-with-no-death-penalty-share-lower.html/. Accessed July 21, 2019.

30  Ibid.

31  Ibid.

32  "NAACP Death Penalty Fact Sheet." *NAACP*. https://www.naacp.org/latest/naacp -death-penalty-fact-sheet/. Accessed July 21, 2019.

33  "Five Things about Deterrence." *National Institute of Justice*.

34  "Publications." *National Criminal Justice Reference Service*. https://www.ncjrs.gov/App/ Publications/abstract.aspx?ID=269450/. Accessed July 21, 2019.

35  "Restorative Justice Law and Legal Definition." *USLegal.com*. https://definitions.uslegal. com/r/restorative-justice/. Accessed July 21, 2019.

36  M. S. Umbreit, W. Bradshaw, and R. B. Coates. "Victims of Severe Violence Meet the Offender: Restorative Justice Through Dialogue." *International Review of Victimology*, Vol. 6, No. 4 (1999): 321–43. https://doi.org/10.1177/026975809900600405.

37  Stewart J. D'Alessio and Lisa Stolzenberg. "Should Repeat Offenders Be Punished More Severely for Their Crimes?" *Criminal Justice Policy Review*, Vol. 30, No. 5 (2019): 731–47. 17pp. DOI: 10.1177/0887403417701974.

38  John Braithwaite. "Accountability and Responsibility Through Restorative Justice." http://johnbraithwaite.com/wp-content/uploads/2016/05/2006_Accountability-and-Responsibility-.pdf/. Accessed July 21, 2019.

39  "Restorative Justice." *Canadian Department of Justice*. https://www.justice.gc.ca/eng/cj-jp/rj-jr/index.html/. Accessed July 21, 2019.

40  "Public Health and International Drug Policy." *National Library of Medicine National Institutes of Health*. https://www.ncbi.nlm.nih.gov/pmc/articles/PMC5042332/. Accessed June 10, 2019.

41  Chris Roberts. "How the Drug War Unfairly Punishes Female Drug 'Mules.'" *High Times*. https://hightimes.com/news/world/drug-war-unfairly-punishes-female-drug-mules/. Accessed July 21, 2019.

42  "Wednesday's Your Views: Time to Repeal Mandatory Sentences." *The Daily Nonpareilonline.com*. https://www.nonpareilonline.com/opinion/wednesday-s-your-viewstime-to-repeal-iowa-s-mandatory-sentences/article_0a b3c8c9-3388-5ee9-b1b4-c38130b01bfc.html/. Accessed July 21, 2019.

43  Amanda E. Smallhorn. "Excusing 'Women of Circumstance': Redefining Conspiracy Law to Hold Culpable Offenders Accountable." https://www.quinnipiaclawjournals.com/content/dam/qu/documents/sol/law-journals1/law-review/volume-36/36-3/separated-pdfs/quinnipic-law-review-circumstance-smallhorn-volume-36-issue-3.pdf/. Accessed July 21, 2019.

44  For more, see "Kemba Smith." *The Sentencing Project*. https://www.sentencingproject.org/stories/kemba-smith/. Accessed July 21, 2019.

45  Mary-Jayne McKay. "More Than They Deserve: Judges Protest Mandatory Sentencing in Drug Cases." *CBS News*. https://www.cbsnews.com/news/more-than-they-deserve/. Accessed July 21, 2019.

46  Kyle O'Dowd. "Savage Sentences." *Washington Post*. https://www.washingtonpost.com/archive/opinions/1999/08/31/savage-sentences/5738f606-3fb3-49b0-aa5c-527f18b38947/?noredirect=on&utm_term=.66a3244e6490/. Accessed July 21, 2019.

47  "Mandatory Minimum Sentencing of Federal Drug Offenses." *EveryCRSReport.com*. https://www.everycrsreport.com/reports/R45074.html/. Accessed July 21, 2019.

48  "Drug Courts." *National Institute of Justice*. https://www.nij.gov/topics/courts/drug-courts/Pages/welcome.aspx/. Accessed July 21, 2019.

49  Ibid.

50  "Costs." *Justice Programs Office: School of Public Affairs* and *National Drug Court Resource Center*. https://ndcrc.org/resources/?fwp_search=costs/. Accessed July 21, 2019.

51  "Do Drug Courts Work? Findings from Drug Court Research." *National Institute of Justice*. https://www.nij.gov/topics/courts/drug-courts/Pages/work.aspx/. Accessed July 21, 2019.

52  Ibid.

53  Ibid.

54  Roger Fisher and William Ury. *Getting to Yes: Negotiating Agreement Without Giving-In* (New York: Houghton Mifflin, 1991), p. 221.

55  Carl Lyons. *I Win, You Win: The Essential Guide to Principled Negotiation* (London: A&C Black, 2007), p. 29.

56  John Windmueller created the multi-party roommate scenario. See John Windmueller. "Multi-party Roomate Conflict." *Conflict Management in Higher Education Report*, Vol. 5, No. 1 (2004): 1–9. www.creducation.net/resources/cmher_vol_5_1_windmueller.pdf/. Accessed July 21, 2019.

# CONCLUSION

## Developing the intellectual tools for social justice

### Working the problem

Engaged readers will have noticed that, while each of the preceding chapters represents achieving *critical awareness* as a step-by-step process, as if each stage of critical awareness was a discrete set of skills separate from the other skills in the other chapters, in fact the habits of mind we emphasize are equally at work simultaneously at every stage.

While intellectual competence is a prerequisite for critical thinking, they both arise together, simultaneously, because if we are to *think* about how we know what we know (and to learn how to do it better) we must question whether or not our reasoning is effective, and whether or not it is evidence-based, and logically sound; to seek growth and development is to practice self-reflection, a form of meta-cognition which helps us to take a step back from ourselves and ask, "How did things come to be the way they are?" How can we grow if we never realize the *need* to grow?

The whole of human consciousness is greater than the sum of its parts. Sometimes evidence and reason can get us only so far. Sometimes a flash of intuition, or a gut feeling, allows us to see into a problem and crack the code. A seemingly obvious solution presents itself to us, and indeed, when tested, works well. But none of this is possible without all the work that comes before and that prepares us to recognize flashes of insight when they come. In this mental space critical thinking and creative thinking meet, overlap, and give rise to one another. Human intelligence has the ability to make leaps, draw inferences, reason inductively, and invent persuasive causal arguments because once informed, we develop the ability to see beyond "just the facts." We "figure it out" as if by happy accident. The problems we currently face cannot be solved by the type of thinking that created them in the first place. For too long the world has been broken into "us versus them" conflicts, including humanity's devastating impact on the environment. The stakes have never been higher.

Had we more time and space we would address a host of other examples of the ways in which social injustices persist at the most basic levels of language and culture. From racist representations of First Nation peoples, to governmental policies hostile to the LGBTQ+ community, to the lack of support for the mentally ill, or for the homeless, or the elderly, or for special needs children, and for children in general who must live in the hands of the adult world, come what may. The ideal of universal human dignity establishes a moral magnetic north for our ethical compasses, guiding us to support causes that need our attention.

## Where to begin?

We offer this final chapter as a "how to" primer meant to help develop our intellectual competence, cultural awareness, and critical thinking skills. While the idea of critical awareness and restorative justice may seem like lofty, even impossible goals, the actual work involved is an assemblage of fundamental cognitive skills, all of which can be learned, improved upon, practiced, and mastered. The work should inspire all of us to further study. Meanwhile, we present information and exercises intended to introduce some of the fundamental skills associated with the contents of the previous chapters. In no way is what we present complete, and in no way does it attempt to replace the need for greater exposure to language, logic, and mathematics.

There is perhaps no better way to develop key skills associated with critical thinking than through writing. Today most of what we write has almost an unlimited shelf life as digital information, and represents how we think, and the quality of our thinking. We can be sure much of our written work will be read by people for whom it was not intended. If we work in human service settings, including health care, children's services, education, residential programs, and/or the criminal justice system, even case notes and emails can be incorporated into the permanent record, and subpoenaed and read in court proceedings.

## Writing as process

In our research about student writing, we have found that the number one obstacle to writing successful school products is giving the process sufficient time; thus we see students rushing to finish the first and final draft at the last minute. This may not be avoidable in some cases, but you should plan to give each assignment at least enough time to write three times before submitting. Why three times? Because we have also found that serious writing requires four stages: (1) organize thoughts and notes with the assignment as a guide; (2) draft a first narrative, making sure all your thinking is included in some logical order; (3) review the draft from the perspectives of social justice (Chapter 5) and the person who will read (and grade) it, reorganizing and re-writing as you do so. (4) In the fourth stage check for writing errors, including grammar, punctuation, syntax, word usage, sentence structure, and inadvertent plagiarism. At this final stage it is also helpful to have a proofreader before submission: we often fail to see some of our errors, but another set of eyes can catch them for us. We have found that basic writing errors occur less frequently when students have invested sufficient time and personal commitment to their products. If you have problems with any of these writing issues, obtain a helpful resource as a reference.

## Stage 1: Gathering and organizing information

Begin by making sure you understand what you are trying to accomplish as a writer: what is being asked of you? Whom are you writing to and for? Why? Are you writing for your boss? For your college professor? When taking on a high-stakes writing task you should begin right away by thinking about the task and making a plan. *The goal is to develop habits of mind that help to avoid the pitfall of procrastination.*

We suggest beginning by taking on simple, small tasks that pave the way for what comes next. Understand the assignment and its context. If it is a writing assignment, determine how the writing assignment reflects the content of the course, reading assignments, lectures, and so on. As professors, we design writing assignments to help accomplish course goals and objectives; as a student, you should try to understand how each writing assignment fits into the overall course. This understanding will help inform your writing. At this stage gather your notes. If you have no notes, you need to generate them now.

In order to avoid the overwhelming anxiety that often comes before procrastination, get started early by reading assigned material, or researching on your own for a few minutes (or more) every day. Always keep notes—some sort of record—of the books, articles, websites, and other sources of information you discover, read, and have thoughts about. Keep track of where you find it for citation purposes later.

Ask yourself: What kind of writing are we being asked to do? Is it descriptive, i.e., are we reporting information without interpretation or opinion of our own thoughts? Or are we required to offer interpretation and analysis about some issue, topic, question, or problem? What is the deadline? Be sure to plan ahead so that you can complete all four stages of the writing process.

As you make notes, or gather existing material, stay alert for possible connections among different types of information and try to group notes by categories based on its content, whether or not it is "popular" information of the sort that circulates on social networks, or it is scientific in nature, or comes from an academic sources, or is somewhere in between. At this stage you are merely making lists, groupings, preparing for an outline by looking for some kind of order to emerge from what you have been thinking and reading about. Some writers might do this with sticky notes, others with a spread sheet. The goal is to organize what you know, and by organizing your notes, you can review them and add new ideas along the way. Most papers begin with an introduction, move on to the main body, and end with a conclusion (perhaps with suggestions for further inquiry or research). You should take care to organize notes into and within the first three sections we mentioned earlier.

As patterns or connections emerge from your research, use consistent language to label how ideas, evidence, and insights are grouped together. Make notes of your personal thoughts or beliefs, if any, that may "inform" your approach to the material you have collected. This first stage of the writing process is the place; however, be sure not to inadvertently plagiarize from another writer. Always use quotation marks around phrases, sentences, and paragraphs directly copied from other sources. If there are no direct quotations but you use ideas, facts, and information borrowed from another source and rework them in your own words, you still must include the citation for that information. For high-stakes writing, include a list of sources cited, and keep track of bibliographic information from the very beginning.

## Stage 2: Writing it down rough

Once your notes are complete and in a provisional order, take it to the next stage by outlining your notes. What main and secondary point(s) are you trying to make? What should come first? Next? What information are you using to present and describe your points? What language are you using? These should be deliberate decisions.

It is important to write a very rough first draft. Here's a tip: It might make sense to write from the middle rather than from the beginning. Sometimes we discover the points we want to make after we have begun the writing process, so to demand a clear argument before we have actually written anything is unrealistic and liable to lead to anxiety and procrastination. Let it be rough. Whatever way we choose to organize our writing, our goal is to figure out what we know and then figure out what we think about it, in order to reason and communicate with clarity in writing. Once we figure it out, we can add or modify our introduction and conclusion. The point is to let the content lead you to a logical order after you review your points, figure out what information informs other information, and develop your logical progression of ideas.

Once we have something with a beginning, middle, and end, the next task is to attend to the organization and completeness of the narrative. An effective writer is an effective reader. We must read our own work. Does it make sense? Does the argument need elaboration or explanation? Are there missing connections that strengthen the links among our ideas? Similarly, are we including information that adds nothing to our point, or even distracts from it? If so, should we drop it or perhaps elaborate more clearly on its importance?

In other words, should we organize our thinking inductively or deductively? The logical inferences from one point to the next should flow based upon the evidence and information we present. Transitions between paragraphs help the reader follow along and indicate you have a clear sense of where you are going.

After the organization of the paper meets your satisfaction, read for accuracy. Use precise language that fits your topic. Informal writing might get away with a certain vagueness, but high-stakes, formal writing for school or work must be informed by precise language of the topic it purports to write about. Here's another tip: Precision requires clarity and exactness, so remove weak verbs, such as the verb "to be" and pack every sentence with as much specific detail as possible. Many professors abhor the passive voice (e.g., Relief was felt by everyone involved.): placing the verb ahead of the subject, or omitting the subject entirely (e.g., "Protesters arrested."), so it is unclear who takes the action (e.g., the police). By the end of this stage you should have arrived at a solid *working draft* of your writing.

## Stage 3: Figuring it out through revision

Ideally you may have time to set the working draft aside so that you might again return to it with fresh eyes, almost as a stranger might read it for the first time. Such an approach provides you with the opportunity to see gaps in logic or language that you had simply overlooked in the earlier stage of writing. The final draft refines the introduction based upon the conclusions proposed at the end. By the end of this stage you should be able to articulate in one or two sentences your main points and conclusion(s). Is the writing effectively organized? How clearly do you make your points? We suggest re-reading your work through the lens of the professor and what she or he is looking for in your paper. This will help identify the need for further elaboration, better organization, clearer language, and editing-out unnecessary and distracting discussions.

## Stage 4: Finished draft

English is one of the most complicated languages in the world. We have more words than almost any other language, and hundreds of words sound alike or are easily confused. English may also win a prize for being one of the least phonetic of languages, meaning we pronounce the same letters differently depending on the context. To check your final draft, certainly a computer spell-checker is helpful—but incomplete. The goal is to write without surface-level errors, for they distract the reader and damage our credibility as writers. We scan for homophones, words that sound the same but mean different things, like "to," "two" and "too" and "there," "their" and "they're." Be aware of unnecessarily complex sentences. Check punctuation, in particular the use of semicolons and apostrophes, and the placement of quotation marks (usually after commas and periods in US writing—but not in most other English-speaking countries). At this stage all of your citations should be clear and well-documented in a works-cited page, or as footnotes or endnotes. The type of formatting required for a high-stakes writing assignment might vary, so double-check the assignment and expectations to be sure the finished draft is properly formatted. Also make sure of the required citation format; this is usually based on the course's department and should be specified by the professor. If it is unclear, ask.

## On plagiarism

Plagiarism is claiming credit for others' intellectual products. In its most blatant form, a writer lifts entire sentences, paragraphs, and even longer works verbatim (as originally written) from another source, and pastes it into her or his paper without quotation marks. More frequently, plagiarism takes the form of taking credit for another person's ideas (without giving credit) by paraphrasing, or putting another author's work into one's own words. This usually involves rewriting the original ideas, perhaps substituting some synonyms or restructuring sentences or paragraphs, but still stealing intellectual property.

Without exception, plagiarism is a bad idea for a few reasons. First, it is theft. Original paintings, photographs, musical scores, films, recordings, and choreography are human creations, as are articles, books, oral statements, even tweets, blogs and so on. In short, if we present someone else's work as ours, we are stealing from that person or source.

If that is not convincing enough, plagiarism is risky, and the potential consequences are severe (up to dismissal from one's educational program or job, and damage to one's reputation). Anti-plagiarism software is getting progressively more sophisticated and can search a document for just this purpose. And as we said earlier in this book, artwork and written products, whether on paper or electronically, can live on forever.

Least pernicious plagiarism occurs by accident: a writer inadvertently uses previously-published language out of familiarity rather than from dishonesty. Occasionally we hear of an otherwise-respected and ethical author repeating language she or he read somewhere and internalized. This is still plagiarism, a form of theft, and always embarrassing when made public. Be sure to check your work out of respect for yourself and for others who are engaged in similar work.

We suggest taking stringent steps to avoid plagiarizing. First, when organizing notes for a paper, include the source and quote marks if you copy specific language. Second, when possible, rephrase a source's actual words (to be sure you understand the ideas and avoid unattributed quotes), but still note the source for citing in the final paper. Third, submit the papers to anti-plagiarism software (widely available) to catch any inadvertent errors.[1] But don't rely solely on anti-plagiarism software because even if the software doesn't flag it, professors and universities have access to licensed software that will catch most transgressions.

## Reason well: induction and deduction revisited

In Chapter 3 we discussed the differences between inductive and deductive reasoning. In both processes, we move from a premise to a conclusion. In inductive situations, we observe specific combinations of events or facts and try to build to generalized knowledge: every electric car I have seen is blue; I think all electric cars are blue. Deductive logic begins with generalized knowledge first and makes conclusions about specific cases: all dogs were once puppies; the new dog on my street must have been a puppy once.

In general, inductive reasoning leads to inconclusive results, meaning that it opens the door for further inquiry rather than proofs. Deductive reasoning, if done properly, can prove, or strongly support cause and effect. Both methods have potential problems, as we discussed in Chapter 3. Here, it is important to choose either approach consciously, and interpret the results appropriately.

An inference refers to a cognitive move we make when we "infer"—we see a connection—between something we think we know and something we think might happen as a result. We infer effects from causes. Yet in inductive logic what we believe are causes are often a mish mash of information and misinformation, and so the conclusions surmised are uncertain. But that said, inductive reasoning can be highly creative. Social and scientific advances have come through leaps of inductive logic and only later has evidence surfaced to confirm them. When we infer something as an effect of some cause, we are seeing a causal relationship—though the evidence is incomplete. What we conclude is *probably* true according to inductive logic, but not *absolutely*.

This is a lot like predicting the weather. While meteorology depends upon hard science, predicting the weather remains an inductive endeavor. Atmospheric conditions are the cause and the weather outside is the effect. Given that a particular set of atmospheric phenomena cause other atmospheric phenomena, a meteorologist might expect to predict weather more than two or three days ahead of time, although it is always an approximation from their analyses of the data. Because data must be interpreted, and the atmosphere is a dynamic environment, weather predictions are not guaranteed outcomes. Even so, predictions can be accurate when induction works well and used well. The cognitive moves we make—the inferences—often uncover causal patterns and a reason that produces a conclusion, which perhaps later proves deductively valid and reliable. But as in predicting the weather, there is always room for error. Many factors interfere with our ability to think clearly and effectively. The need for intellectual competency is paramount.

Deductive reasoning flips the equation in the opposite direction, such that causes for a phenomenon are looked at first, which then produce the effect. Premises connect to a conclusion. In a deductive argument a conclusion is *absolutely true* if the premises are true. Every argument aims to provide support for its conclusion, though sometimes our premises are more conclusive than at others times. Sometimes an argument leaves less room for objections than other arguments: The premise(s) must contain factual information accompanied by an inferential claim that supports something further. In deductive reasoning, inferential arguments must be linked to well researched facts that allow the writer to arrive at powerful insights by leaps of logic, sometimes unsupported by evidence, but inferred nonetheless. When we call inferential reasoning "deductively valid" we refer to the toughest standard of all for judging the authenticity of the premises in a deductive argument. Why? Because in a deductive argument a conclusion is *absolutely true* if the premises are true. If a premise's authority can in any way be undermined, the validity of a deductive conclusion is put in jeopardy. Can the premises be true and the conclusion false? According to deductive reasoning the answer is an absolute no.

Remember that deductive logic is an absolute, all-or-nothing relationship between elements in an argument. Inductive logic, on the other hand, should be organized according to degrees-of-strength, or what is most likely true, most probably accurate, and so on, all of which points to the conclusion, which is *probably* true. While deductive logic is the gold standard for scientific thinking, most of our day-to-day experiences with information comes as part of an argument, implied or not, but these kinds of arguments almost always employ inductive reasoning. The conclusion of an inductive argument is *likely*, given the circumstances, premises, examples, and so on. Given *this*, then probably *that*, or given this cause then probably this effect will result. As the accuracy of the premises increase, an inductive argument can achieve impressive validity, but if the premises are not *absolutely true*, the conclusions are only *probably* true, not *absolutely* true. We can only arrive at a probable likelihood that our conclusion is valid and reliable.

---

### DEDUCTIVE AND INDUCTIVE EXERCISE

- Outline an argument about the effects of DDT pesticide on the environment according to deductive reasoning. What kind of research must you do in order to establish true and valid premises? Organize your outline using the logical structure "if A then B, and if B then C, and if C then D, and in conclusion, if A then D." Each letter might represent a paragraph, or two, or even three. Your conclusion will be necessarily true if your premises are true.
- Now reverse the logic by outlining an argument about DDT pesticides according to inductive logic.
- Now use deductive reasoning to outline an argument about gun control. Use the same logical structure as above. Your conclusion will be necessarily true if your premises are true. But are they? Do some topics make deductive reasoning almost impossible?
- Now reverse the logic by outlining an argument on gun control according to inductive logic.

---

## Numbers

We have said that critical thinking involves words and numbers. In order to arrive at accurate understandings of the information we need and come into contact with every day, while avoiding being misled by false assertions, we require some basic knowledge about the properties of often-used operations that deal with numbers, including some basic statistics.

Terms like theory, variables, hypotheses, samples, averages, medians, coefficients, outliers, percentages, ranges, and sampling error often appear in media reports, research papers, and other public discourse. Here are brief descriptions of these oft-used terms' meanings (and misuses).

- A variable is the name given to a component in a data set that is measured and quantified for possible testing of cause and effect: if x then y. It can represent anything that has a quantity or quality that varies. Dependent variables are those elements that you want to explain (the effect), and independent variables are the symbols (words, phrases, numbers, etc.) that may cause the effect. In other words, the independent variable(s) try to predict the dependent variable.

- A theory is logical reasoning used to guide the researcher in constructing a testable *if...then* statement. A theory, and there are many from all social, economic, and political disciplines, attempts to scientifically explain or predict patterns and behavior.

- A hypothesis is an *if...then* statement, usually based on a theory, designed to predict an outcome using dependent and independent variable(s). Its goal is to test the relationship between the possible causes (independent variables) and the effect (dependent variable). In shorthand, $x$ is used to represent the independent variable and $y$ is used to represent the dependent variable. In social science research, the "educated guess" is established as a hypothesis and also as a null hypothesis, which means that no relationship exists between the variables selected for study. If the researcher does not find evidence to support the null hypothesis, then by default the original hypothesis may be true: the independent variables may predict the dependent variable. More conclusively, if empirical evidence disproves the null, the original theory is accepted as true. This is theoretically driven, deductive research.[2]

- Samples are smaller groups used to represent larger populations, and samples are the most common and efficient way to test a hypothesis. Precision in sampling is extremely important; the sample must be valid and reliable such that the researcher can reach conclusions premised in the hypothesis. The best type of sampling to ensure reliability and validity is called random sampling in which every single person or item in the study population has an equal chance of getting selected to participate in the research. In the US, for example, Gallup polls use random digit-dialing of cell phone and landline numbers to contact n=1,500 adults per week.[3] Depending on the information, achieving a random sample is difficult and time consuming, so other types of sampling methods are used. Most samples misrepresent their larger groups in some ways, typically by under-including minority group members, and researchers should not surmise that their results accurately reflect the larger population. In collecting evidence and examining the existing studies, notice the size of the sample and how they went about collecting the information for that sample. Many samples cannot be generalized to the entire population, so it is important to know the methodology that was used and how large their sample size was. A sample of convenience, for example, is a non-probability sample made up of people who are easily reached and agree to participate: it hardly, never, or almost never reflects trends of the general population and should be viewed with extreme skepticism.

- Sampling error refers to the unrepresentativeness of a sample the data come from. Sampling error occurs when a sample fails to accurately represent the group from which it is drawn. "Availability" or "convenience" samples include only those who are available and volunteer when pollsters, researchers or reporters ask them, e.g., the first 25 voters who show up at the polls on election day. It is highly unlikely that they accurately represent all voters that day, and the more or less variation there is from the population means more or less sampling error. Sampling error can also happen among random samples for a variety of reasons, e.g., if enough randomly-selected people refuse to participate, or the final sample is too small to capture variations within the larger group. Reporters should acknowledge and address these problems when they poll people for a news story.

- Margin of error is a statistic that expresses sampling error and reflects the validity of how well, or how poorly, a sample was drawn to represent the population. It is a mathematically calculated range that tells the researcher if the measurements are inaccurate. So, for example, when an opinion poll reports that Candidate A is leading Candidate B by 5 percent, with a 3 percent margin of error, that means Candidate A is ahead by anywhere from 2 percent (5 percent minus the sampling error) to 8 percent (5 percent plus the sampling error), assuming respondents answer honestly and accurately.

- Average (or mean) is a measure of "central tendency," or approximate midpoint of a group or population. The average is calculated by adding the scores or values (e.g., income) of everyone involved, and then dividing that sum by the total number of people in the group. The advantages are ease of calculation and comprehension: it is basic math and widely understood. The disadvantage is skewed populations, such as one or a few unusually high or low scores (outliers), which raises or lowers the average such that it loses its representativeness of the population or sample you are trying to describe.

- Standard deviation is a number that demonstrates variation, or how far apart or widely dispersed the data are from the mean, and is used in a variety of statistical calculations. When a standard deviation is low, this means the group in question has minimal variation from the average. When the standard deviation is high, this means the data being analyzed are spread out from the mean and further testing may be needed to have confidence in your results.

- Outliers are observations that are far removed from the rest of the group. Sometimes, unscrupulous reporters point to outliers as representations of a group. In extreme cases, politicians or news reporters will highlight a single case, like a person who voted illegally or an immigrant who committed a crime, to "prove" we need voter photo identification laws or restrictive immigration policies. Know the sample or population size and be wary of suspicious single-case reporting. Outliers also skew the mean and can result in higher than expected standard deviations.

- Median is the numerical midpoint of a group or population. It is calculated by arranging the group members' scores in numerical order, from lowest to highest, and selecting the score of the person or object in the exact middle. That score is the median. The advantage is minimizing the impact of outliers or skew, and the disadvantage is that it is more cumbersome during further calculations to arrive at some final conclusion. Also, medians lose the richness and nuances of participants' scores. Both averages and medians result in limited descriptions of a group, like unequal distributions. All we get is a midpoint.

- Mode is another "average" or central tendency measurement that represents the most frequently occurring value, or answer, in a dataset. The mode is the number that appears the most. It does not represent the distribution of the data, so it cannot be used in statistical calculations. For example, in a small dataset with participants' answers on a question represented by the output of 1, 6, 8, 6, 2, 8, 6, 8, 6, 5, 8, and 8, the mode is the number that appears most often, in this case, 8, with five participants answering "8" on the question, followed by a submodal value of 6, with 4 responses. If there was a tie between two answers, 6 and 8, then the term to describe them is "bimodal," and if it there were more than two with the same number of scores, the output is called "multimodal." While modes are not used in statistics, they are sometimes useful for understanding a group and subgroups, especially whether the midpoint statistic (average or median) may not represent a group.

- Percentages are numerical calculations, using 100 as any group's total. This is done by translating fractions to numbers, such as ¼ is 25 percent. The math is done by dividing the numerator (1) by the denominator (4): how many times 4 goes into 1. The answer is 0.25 times or 25 percent. Misleading reports cite percentages without letting the reader or listener know what the sample size is: If it is 25 percent of all the fish in the sea or stars in the sky, that may be interpreted quite differently from a report that says 25 percent of the population of Right Whales, the most endangered whale in the world, is now experiencing a certain $x$ effect.[4] It is important to know the size of the sample when reporting percentages so that the target audience is not deceived into accepting inaccurate conclusions.

- Ranges are reports of the highest and lowest scores. Ranges are easy to calculate but limited in their meaning. Averages, medians, etc. cannot be determined on the basis of ranges. All we know is the highest and lowest, although this information is often reported to express the breadth and depth of researchers' conclusions.

- Correlations are one of the most common statistics used in research and represent a connection or association between $x$ and $y$ variables. The correlation statistic describes the strength or weakness of the association between the dependent and independent variables and can be positive or negative. While a correlation provides evidence to support or reject a hypothesis, this statistic is weak and does not predict any causal relationship, merely an association, which could also be explained by another variable. The symbol $r$ is frequently used to represent the correlation statistic.

- Beta coefficients (b coefficients), or regression coefficients, are the most powerful statistical tool researchers have to "prove" their null hypothesis is false, and accept that their hypothesis (educated guess) is right. These kinds of coefficients, based on the mean of the variables established by the hypothesis, are products of a regression analysis, which is a set of statistical processes that assess the prediction likelihood of independent variables on a dependent variable. Coefficients from a regression model show causality between the independent variables and the dependent variable. If a coefficient is significant, the regression model demonstrates how strong or weak the causal relationship is in the form of a line. In other words, the coefficient demonstrates that as $x$ goes up (or down), $y$ goes up (or down). If the coefficient is positive the interpretation is that for every 1-unit increase in the predictor variable $x$, the outcome variable $y$ will increase by the coefficient value. While this may sound complicated for an introduction or review of regression analyses and the importance of b coefficients, it is an extremely useful tool to understand. When done correctly, coefficients give researchers the power of "proof" that the evidence they collected and the hypothesis they created is "real."

- Statistical significance is the measure used to assess how "real" a variable is related to, or able to predict, another variable. In other words, based on a calculated probability the researcher can reject the null hypothesis to reach a conclusion. Statistical significance is represented by the letter $p$ for probability, and typically accompanies correlations, coefficients, and other statistics to answer the question of whether to trust that relationship—is the outcome of the statistical test significant? In any research there is always room for error, so the p value identifies inaccuracies with sampling methodology and the way in which we measured the variables, among other possible errors. In research papers, this value is often expressed as p <.05 or p <.01, and sometimes with small samples, p <.10 appears with a disclaimer. Because this is a probability statistic that expresses the degree of confidence we have in our calculations, p <.05 means that the statistic it accompanies is at least 95 percent accurate in rejecting the null hypothesis, with 5 percent not able to reject. The p <.01 means that the statistic is at least 99 percent accurate, and so on. How confident can a researcher be in rejecting the null hypothesis? The p value for any statistic helps us to assess the data.

When we encounter numerical and statistical reports, it is important that we not shy away from them. By seeking to understand how information and reports are generated and how the data are presented and used, we acquire a skill set for interpreting a whole lot of things that affect our lives, including finances (personally, nationally, internationally), medical and health reports, food and water scarcities, news reporting, claims on social trends, conspiracy theories, and quite possibly how internet algorithms function to manipulate and aspire to direct our lives. Knowing the basics about data and how "facts" are presented to us is important because we live in a world that needs our intellectual competence and critical thinking skills to make sense of it all. We must work to avoid complacency.

In sum, the old saying that figures lie and liars figure is only partially true. Yes, liars often misuse numbers in order to deceive people into accepting misinformation, but figures do not necessarily lie. It depends on how rigorously statistical data are collected and measured, and how precisely they are reported. Given the pre-valence of misinformation available to us, the ultimate burden is on us, the con-sumers of information, to ask and understand what we consume.

## Practice exercises

- Assemble a group of people, preferably more than a dozen. Ask everyone to count all their pocket change—just the coins—and report both how many coins they have and the total value of their change. Zeros count. Make a list of each person's answers in two columns: one for total coins and one for total value. Add up both columns and divide by the number of group members. That will yield averages of both number and value of coins. Compare the average with each person's amount. To what extent does the group average accurately reflect each individual's contribution? What effect did outliers (no coins and a piggy bank's worth—if either occurred) have on the average? If there were no outliers, add first a make-believe person with zero coins and recalculate, then another make-believe person with $10 worth (a roll of quar-ters) and recalculate, to illustrate the power of outliers on averaging. Repeat the entire exercise with medians instead of averages, and compare the results. Consider that you could select something else, other than coins, like the number of apps people have on their cell phones.
- With the same or a different group, use a table of random numbers or pull names out of a hat to randomly select half the members. That is group A. Everyone else is in group B. Compare the two groups for similarities and dif-ferences, using age, gender, ethnicity, anything else you can think of. Repeat this process once or twice to notice the variation in the samples. This illustrates how random sampling is done, the fallacy that random sampling always results in representativeness, and this exercise also demonstrates the importance of multiple group members with minority characteristics. For example, if there are just one or even two group members over 70 years old, it is unlikely that both sub-samples will have that characteristic. As your group gets bigger, the two subgroups will become more similar or less dissimilar. If you have a group of more than 50, try random sampling (e.g., drawing names from a hat) until the sample comes relatively close to representing the whole group. How many tries does it take? The answer depends on the variability within the group, with respect to demographics and what other measures you may count. The more similar the full group members are to each other, the smaller your random sample needs to be.
- Obtain a few reports from opposing sources, like the Republican and Demo-cratic National Committees' positions on the same issue, the NRA and a gun control organization, an anti-abortion and pro-choice group, and/or an anti- and a pro-immigrant organization. Compare their uses of data: what they measure, how they measure, how much they disclose about their methods, what conclusions they draw, etc., as well as their use of inductive vs. deductive

logic, and highlighting of outliers. Critique their uses of numbers and charts and tables (next section). Think of questions you might ask them in order to get a clearer picture of the issues they address, including what you would need to know in order to accept or reject their conclusions.

## Graphs and charts

Charts and graphs come in a variety of styles. The line graph, the bar graph, the histogram, the pie chart, and the Cartesian graph are the most common.

*Bar graphs* (Figure 7.1) allow us to compare quantities across different categories. The question remains whether the quantities of each category are accurate and reliable:

*Pie charts* (Figure 7.2) display how the whole is divided into parts. Once again, a pie chart is only as reliable as the data it represents.

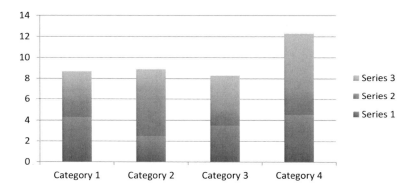

**FIGURE 7.1** Bar graph

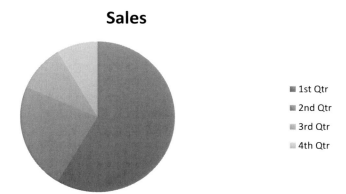

**FIGURE 7.2** Pie charts

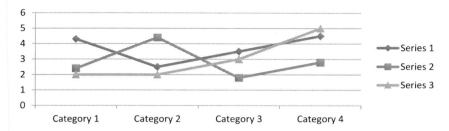

**FIGURE 7.3** Line graph

*Line graphs* (Figure 7.3) illustrate how numbers have changed over time. We use them when we have data that are connected and we want to see how they change over time—to track trends, small and abrupt changes, and otherwise organize information in ways that make it useful for analysis. The essential components of a line graph are the same as for other charts. The X-axis (horizontal) is the independent (suspected predictor) variable and generally shows time periods on the horizontal. The vertical Y-axis (vertical) graphs the dependent variable (consequence or result of changes in the predictor) and plots the change in data over time. Line graphs can easily mislead depending on the way in which the X- and Y-axis have been labeled. In the graph below, categories 1–4 (independent variable) are predicting amounts of something (dependent variable). For example, categories 1–4 may be different seasons, and the 0–6 vertical axis may be average visits to doctors' offices. The three "series" could be different age, education, religious, income or political groups.

*Cartesian graphs* have numbers on both axes which illustrates a fundamental causal relationship between x and y. It is the most common graph for mathematics and engineering. Cartesian graphs are the most common way of presenting data and are often referred to as X-Y graphs because the graph plots one variable against another. It is the origin of the line graph, itself a kind of Cartesian graph. The Cartesian coordinate system with four X-Y points plotted is shown in Figure 7.4:

In this graph, the midpoint (0,0) is the group's average education and income. Let's say the average education is 12 years and the average income is $24,000 per year. The four coordinates (0,0,; +2,+3; -1.5, -2.5; and -3,+1) represent four different individuals. The first number of the coordinates is the predictor variable's (cause) distance from the Y-axis (in this case, education above or below the average of 12 years); the second number in the coordinates is the result variable (effect) distance from the X-axis (in this case income above or below $12,000 per year). The 0,0 person would have the full sample's average income and education (12 years and $12,000 because she is zero distance from either number); the +2,+3 person would have 2 more years of education (14 years) and $3,000 a year more income than the group's average. The minus numbers mean less income or education than the group's average. The coordinates, -3, +1, mean that person has three fewer years than the group's education average (9 years), but still earns $1,000

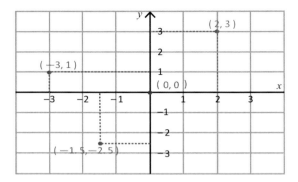

**FIGURE 7.4** Cartesian graph

above the full group's average, or $25,000. And the -1.5,-2.5 person is below the group's averages on both variables (1.5 fewer years of education, or 10.5 years; and $2,500 less income, or $22,500).

If the four data points (dots on the graph), align in a continuous upward pattern from left to right, we can conclude that education predicts income, based on inductive reasoning (four specific cases projected to larger populations). In this graph, however, we have two exceptions: the person with the least education has the highest income—the person with 9 years of education (-3,+1) has $3,500 more income than the person with 10.5 years education (-1.5,-2.5 on the graph); and the totally average person (0,0) has more education but less income than the person with the least education (-3,+1). Does that mean there is no evidence of a connection between education and income? Not completely, because if we consider the person with the least education (-3,+1) an exception or outlier, the other three present the continuous upward climb that supports the relationship between education and income. The next step would be to examine the outlier to see what factors may contribute to her/his higher income when compared with two people with fewer years of formal education. If we find that this person inherited wealth, and is receiving income from investments, or perhaps went to trade school and learned advanced electrical skills, we can propose a possible causal relationship between education and income, when those extenuating factors are not considered. Then we might test the correlation for causation (coefficients and degree of significance), using deduction-based methods.

We hope this very brief review, or perhaps introductory lesson, has been helpful. Knowing how to interpret data is an important part of critical thinking. It allows us to effectively conduct and evaluate research and make decisions about "credible evidence" and the veracity of an argument. These fundamental skills are the basis for logical thinking, and as we read information we need to discern fake news from scientific research, and equally important, assess how trustworthy the science is. Whether we use our statistical knowledge for educational pursuits, or in a professional field, interpretation of data helps us make sense of our data-rich world. For example, the government's consumer price index notifies consumers if the price of a major commodity changes. Large price fluctuations in food, energy, housing, clothing, transportation, medical care, recreation, and education can destroy a household budget.[5] Basic competency in statistics and math certainly allows us to more effectively plan how to handle financial responsibilities, whether they are our own day-to-day living expenses, or as part of our professional practice.

The next two exercises focus on helping us become aware of what we bring to any interaction with others. Emotional intelligence serves as the underpinning of critical awareness. Having emotional intelligence is as important as having any other skill discussed in this book. It helps us to more effectively understand ourselves as well as others.

## Emotional intelligence

Emotional intelligence (EQ) is an important component of cultural cognition and critical thinking. When we have emotional intelligence we have the capacity to be aware of and recognize our emotions and the emotions and feelings of others. Emotional intelligence allows us to understand our state of mind and body and communicate effectively with our partner, family, friends, colleagues, employers, and with complete strangers with empathy and compassion. Emotional intelligence plays a vital role in perspective taking, defusing conflicts, and relieving our own stress.

One way to develop empathy is to assess facial expressions that individuals communicate or emote. In this exercise you will need a few photographs from magazines and newspapers (although not the news stories or narratives that accompany them) that depict individuals who face a variety of challenges, conflicts, and struggles.

Next divide into small groups to discuss the emotions in each photograph you see, and speculate what might be happening with the person "caught on camera." What is their story? Be creative: you can invent a short description or narrative that might explain their facial expression. Try to identify the emotion(s) you see in each photograph. Is it anguish? Disgust? Surprise? Joy? Sadness? Anger? Trust?

Role play: Now, if you could meet with just one person from the photographs, what would you ask them and why? Select one photograph that generated the most discussion among the group and ask that one student volunteer role plays that person. Their role is to continue a credible scenario that helps explain the feelings and emotions in the photograph, perhaps based on a storyline that was previously started. The rest of the group asks many questions to understand this human being and what they are experiencing in that moment. Connect with the person's feelings and emotions. What questions might you ask that communicate empathy and compassion? (Hint: Be mindful of your tone of voice, eye contact, and the way you formulate each question or comment.) Where did the feelings in the photo come from? What are the cultural experiences this person might draw from that created or caused these feelings? What history underlies the emotions shown? Perhaps the group will arrive at some kind of solution for the role play, if there is one, or perhaps the role play will end with everyone having a more thorough understanding of a complete stranger's facial expressions and the importance of developing our own emotional intelligence.

## Exercise: applying the lesson

Read the following speech. It was given to a board of education in a small, conservative town in the northeast of the United States. The board of education was considering whether or not to change the high school's mascot. For more than 25 years they were known as the "Redmen," in reference to the Native American stereotype. At the high school, Native American iconography adorns the gym floor, sports uniforms, and so on. Should sports teams that use Native American cultural tropes, symbols, and stereotypes disavow such practices? Or is the issue a form of "political correctness" gone too far? Is it a threat to free speech? Read the speech that favors the mascot change and consider the questions that follow:

> From what I've heard most people don't want to change the mascot. People feel defensive and protective of their symbols and their history. Sometimes symbols are all we have left of years gone by. Change is scary and reminds us of how temporary everything really is. So we hold onto symbols of the past. In this way we feel a bit more anchored, a bit more permanent. Sometimes we have to change. We simply have no choice. But, sometimes we choose to change. This is one of those times. We have a choice. What is the choice? To exchange one symbol for another.
>
> It's not nothing. It bothers people. Consider that recently we have seen groups let go of flags associated with slavery and oppression. We see people letting go of statues that celebrate a past marked by profound, incalculable injustice. We see people letting go of using certain words to refer to people, to women, to others, because they demean and disrespect. And now we are debating whether or not to let go of a racist mascot for the same reason—just as others have done. Why have others done this? Because they recognize the power of symbols. What they stand for tells us who we are and how we relate to the world.
>
> Usually we don't have to think about such things. But now is the time for thinking and reflection. Who are we? Who do we want to be?
>
> If we remember our history we remember that it didn't go well for the indigenous peoples who were here before first contact with Europeans. They lost everything. And so while some say Native American mascots are a sign of our appreciation of the qualities of so called Indian tribes, such an assumption ignores the fact that the winners get to turn the losers into sports memorabilia. It should be noted again that the Mashantucket Pequots along with the Nipmucs have come out against mascots that caricature Native American culture. If we were wise we would listen to what they say about the way white culture fetishizes the "other" while denying it a true voice.

Some of the arguments for keeping the "Indian" mascot claims:
- It's flattering to them.
- It's inconsequential and it doesn't mean anything.
- It means everything. Changing it would change history.
- We will lose our past. We will have to throw away our memorabilia and so on.

If we educate ourselves about the history of indigenous peoples in this region we would set aside our old habits. We should change the mascot and keep hold of our past— but we must understand our past from a place of human compassion. I'm not hopeful. To change the mascot is only a symbolic act, but symbols matter. Giving up our racist symbols is a good thing. Learning how and why they are racist is also a good thing.

After the speech, and after other similar speeches were presented to the nine members of the board of education, the large, standing room only audience in the rear grew loudly hostile. Other towns had made this switch already, people replied, but this town, on this night, felt that they were losing something crucial to their collective identities, and they were angry about it, and they were the majority by far.

- What do you think about this issue? What deep down do you believe? What have you been taught growing up about this issue?
- How does the issue make you feel when you discuss it and try to figure it out?
- What is the nature of the problem in this scenario?
- Does this issue matter? Why? Why not?

## Conclusion

To practice critical awareness as social justice, and as a way to foster restorative justice and non-violence, means to accept that the truths we cling to are, at best, incomplete. John Keats, an English Romantic poet, suggested that the truth of a thing was somehow beyond the incomplete data, and that one must possess what he called a "negative capability" for solving problems. This means that we accept the idea that the "truth" of a thing is often a moving target, and to find the best possible solution to an issue, question, or problem—especially at the level of social practice—we have to accept a certain level of uncertainty. The truth, it turns out, lies in uncertainty and flux.

As a paradox, this points to truth by way of negation: the truth that we seek is beyond positive and negative assertions and requires a radical cognitive openness. The mind that can practice "negative capability" is a flexible mind, creative and insightful, open to information and possibilities. The opposite of this is a position of "fixed certainty." The unopened mind remains fixated on two-dimensional, black-and-white binaries, and has little facility for "thinking outside the box," or for metaphor, or analogy. Instead, charged by fear and ignorance, unopened minds see the world as a zero-sum game inhabited by winners and losers. Fixed certainty requires a belief in truth as a one-sided truth in which one side is right and the other wrong.

Those who seek to create a socially just society for all must ask: *how did things come to be the way they are?* Why? Because, as Einstein observed, the answer to any problem lies in understanding the nature of the problem. If we do not understand what the problem is, then we will not know how to solve it. In understanding the problem, however, one finds the answer.

And so we must be mindful of Keats' admonition that greatness of mind lies in one's facility for "negative capability," while on the other side of the coin, and no less true, lies rigorous empirical research, in the knowledge that facts produced via the scientific method can be believed. "To abandon facts," writes Timothy Snyder, "is to abandon freedom. If nothing is true, then no one can criticize power, because there is no basis upon which to do so. If nothing is true then all is spectacle. The biggest wallet pays for the most blinding lights."[6]

- Have we been blinded, trained to look away from social injustice?
- Would we know where to begin in answering the question: *how did things come to be the way they are?*

Remember that intellectual competence requires us to assume agency and responsibility over ourselves and what we think, and *how* we think. The first step is to take a bold step back and risk questioning everything.

- What do we know and how do we know it?
- Where does the "information" come from and how seriously should we take it?
- What are our standards for accepting or disagreeing with authorities' assertions and research findings?

Critical awareness depends upon our understanding of ourselves, our social and cultural context, our ability to reason to a conclusion based upon reliable evidence, all of which we temper in empathy, empathy for the humanity of others as if they were our own family.

Social justice requires that we take responsibility for our learning long after our formal education has ended. If we aspire to critical awareness, then this means we choose a life of curiosity, of questioning, and of practicing the habits of mind that demand evidence whenever possible, all in order to live out our individual agency in the world as defenders of human dignity.

## Notes

1  An internet search for free anti-plagiarism software produces several options. We will not recommend one specifically but encourage its use, especially if you struggle with writing and referencing your sources properly.
2  Not all scientific research uses a deductive approach that is theoretically driven. Exploratory research is inductive, whereby specific observations are made in the hopes of arriving at broader generalizations and theory development. Unlike the deductive approach, there is no formal theory that drives the research.

3  "How Does the Gallup U.S. Poll Work?" *Gallup.* https://www.gallup.com/224855/gallup-poll-work.aspx. Accessed July 12, 2019.
4  "North Atlantic Right Whale." *NOAA Fisheries.* https://www.fisheries.noaa.gov/species/north-atlantic-right-whale. Accessed July 12, 2019.
5  "The Value of Your Money." Bureau of Labor Statistics. https://www.bls.gov/audience/consumers.htm. Accessed July 22, 2019.
6  Timothy Snyder. *On Tyranny: Twenty Lessons from the 20th Century* (New York: Tim Duggan Books, 2017).

# INDEX

Note: Information in figures and tables is indicated by page numbers in *italics* and **bold.**

Made in United States
North Haven, CT
13 January 2023

31049149R00102